WHAT THE RUCK JUST HAPPENED

WHAT THE RUCK JUST HAPPENED

GARETH DE LA TORRE

What The Ruck Just Happened

First Edition
ISBN 9798852990389

For my gorgeous daughters
Grace & Daisy
Always my inspiration and motivation.
I have been on many adventures, but the greatest adventure of them all is the privilege of being your father.

RUCK-ING (VERB)// Walking with a weighted rucksack (aka backpack). It implies action, energy, and purpose. Rucking requires strength, endurance, and character......and builds it too.

TAB-BING (VERB)// Physical exercise unique to the military. Also known as loaded marching or speed marching.

Contents

Being friends with Gareth is analogous to watching a great TV series. You know there's always going to be something interesting happening next season and you look forward to seeing how creative the writers got.

When I met Gareth out in the Peak District climbing in the early noughties, he was relatively new to the climbing world but was already sporting his own climbing brand "Crimp" and pretty soon everyone I knew was wearing it (many of us still do!). After getting to know Gareth it came as no surprise when he revealed that in his younger life, he had played in a band, toured and released several records – mainly because I'd be more surprised if there's anything he hadn't done.

I've met very few people so brimming with ideas – that actually go out and do them. I always like people who are do-ers rather than talkers. Gareth is one of those rare people who is both a talker (the main entertainment on any escapade) and a do-er. So, it took a while to process what was happening when Gareth transformed from a hardworking livewire full of confidence to housebound, unemployed, and devoid of interest in anything after he was struck down by epilepsy.

It was shocking to see someone so full of life have his life ripped right out from under him. I watched for a long time as Gareth lingered in a deep hole, a whirlpool of epilepsy treatments and grim experiences. I wasn't sure he would ever emerge.

Then, suddenly, he met Emma, and somehow (I still don't know how) this catalysed a rebirth. Suddenly he was sparking with ideas again. The YouTube channel inspiring people to get outdoors. Drone flying, mountaineering, creating a brand, and of course running marathons in boots and military bergen.

The epilepsy is still there, but he's mastering it. I'm so grateful to have my old friend's million-volt energy back and looking forward to seeing how the next season pans out!"

Professor Michael Garton PhD
Canada Research Chair in Synthetic Biology
Institute of Biomedical Engineering, University of Toronto

It's hard to believe that it's been over 20 years since I first crossed paths with Gareth at work. From that very first day, we connected instantly. He's been a steadfast friend, a confidant and a source of inspiration throughout these two decades, and I want to take a moment to celebrate the incredible journey he's been on.

Over the years, we've discovered countless shared interests. Gareth has been the embodiment of dedication and excellence in all of them. But it's his deep-rooted love for wild camping that truly showcased his resilience and courage. Turning a childhood passion into a vehicle for overcoming the challenges epilepsy has thrown his way. Gareth's wild camping and rucking experiences, documented on his YouTube channel, have not only inspired me but countless others.

One of the toughest moments in our friendship was when I had to retire Gareth from my sales team due to his epilepsy. It was a decision I made with a heavy heart, knowing the implications it had for his career and future. But, Gareth's understanding, support and strength during that time only served to strengthen our friendship. The ability to find positivity in even the most challenging situations is a testament to his character.

This story written by my friend, is a tapestry of triumphs and trials, and through it all, unwavering determination and an unbreakable spirit. Gareth's drive to succeed in life, no matter the obstacles in his path, is truly remarkable.

So, here's to the past 20 years and to many more ahead, filled with adventures, shared passions, and the unbreakable bond of friendship.

Neil 'The Tash'

I first encountered Gareth in the 1980s when he and his family moved into the same street. As we struck up a conversation, I quickly discovered we shared common interests, such as fishing and camping, which laid the foundation for our friendship as adolescents and into adulthood.

I have witnessed first-hand Gareth having seizures during some of our adventures. Even as a qualified first aider, I was not prepared for the debilitating effect these have on him. In response, I have dedicated time to educating myself to better understand what my friend goes through and how I can offer more effective support.

I truly admire his resilience and determination, as he faces his condition head-on and continually challenges himself to surpass his limits.

Our adventures together have been a source of immense joy to me. Whether it's our wild camping excursions, trips to Scotland, or supporting Gareth as he takes on physically demanding challenges like the Special Forces Fan Dance and London Marathon. Each experience has added another layer to our forty-year friendship.

Paul 'Turtle'

Prologue

It's a strange feeling waking up in an ambulance, surreal and dreamlike. You lay there while strange people you don't know fuss over you, asking you lots of questions, usually very loudly, in a cacophony of confusion mixed with a sense of urgency. You're often travelling at speed, so you feel every bump and turn in the road, which then triggers that awful feeling of motion sickness. This wasn't my first journey to the hospital in the back of an ambulance. Since May of twenty-eighteen I'd gotten quite familiar with the routine. It was almost quite normal. The drive from my house to East Surrey Hospital is around forty-five minutes. The town of Horsham where I live had long since shut down its Accident and Emergency department, forcing all that live in the town to make this twenty-mile journey in the event of an accident. I lay in a half-conscious half-awake state as paramedics got on with a myriad of medical procedures, taking my blood pressure and inserting cannulas. On this occasion, the muffled chatter was about whether or not to insert one into a vein in my neck.

I had been lying unconscious for some time at the foot of my stairs before my mother and stepfather arrived. They had been alerted to my fall via my fall detection wrist strap. This was pretty routine for them. They were used to having to make the mad dash from their home, which was less than half a mile away, only to find me sprawled out on the floor unconscious. I'd blacked out on the stairs and crash-landed in the hallway, blocking the front door, so they had to come in through the back. How far I had fallen was anybody's guess, but I would estimate it was pretty much from near the top. This time, however, unlike previous falls, things took an unusual sinister turn. While waiting for the ambulance to arrive, I stopped breathing (or my parents thought I had stopped breathing) my eyes wide open and staring into space. My mother was convinced I had died. Panic then ensued. A vain attempt at chest compressions was employed by my stepfather, whilst my mother stayed on the phone with the ambulance people. I can't imagine the sheer scale of desperation they both must have felt. No parent wants to witness the death of their child.

The paramedics arrived to find me desperately cold, but breathing. My veins had sunk, and they were having trouble finding one to insert the cannula. I was loaded into the ambulance, where eventually, a very skilled operator of this procedure managed to tease one into my wrist. I didn't feel anything and I wasn't bothered. My body was being flooded with oxygen from the mask I was wearing, which inevitably took the edge off everything. Being strapped tightly into a bed limited the view to just staring at a blurred light overhead. This illuminated the area for the paramedics to be able to do their job efficiently. Closing my eyes made no difference. The light was so bright it shone through my eyelids. Sometimes (not all the time) the paramedic would switch it off once all the medical procedures and checks had been completed, offering some calm and tranquillity in what is normally a highly stressful situation. The journey continues in an awakening darkness, dark enough not to be able to see everything but light enough to prevent sleep.

Eventually, after some time the ambulance comes to a stop. The reversing alarm kicks in and the ambulance starts backing up until a sudden jerk signals the end of the journey. The back doors fly open, flooding the rear of the ambulance with the artificial light of a thousand strip lights, which line the perspex-covered drop-off area. Paramedics move around the gurney and start unclamping it from the floor, whereupon I am unceremoniously wheeled out into the cold air like a horizontal Hannibal Lecter strapped to a rolling bed.

Crashing through sets of double doors we enter the hospital itself, and I'm booked in. It wasn't busy and I wasn't knocking at death's door, so I was wheeled straight into a curtained cubical.

On busy occasions I have been left out in the hallway for several hours, just lying there, a living sculpture for all to stare at as they file past to get to the coffee machine. Luckily, this time, I was wheeled straight in. I usually try and get my head down for some sleep at that point. For the next few hours, things will move at an agonizingly slow pace. I was checked on once in a while and would have various procedures done. My blood pressure was taken, and bloods then extracted from the cannula which was inserted into my vein by the paramedics. Eventually, a doctor came in, had a quick chat and sent me off for a scan, just to make sure there was no bleed on my brain. Sometimes, like on this occasion, as I was just about to slide through the scanner, they would inject a fluid into my system via the cannula. I believe this is to help pinpoint any bleeds I may have. I don't know about that but it certainly leaves a very strange taste in the mouth, whilst making me feel like I was about to shit myself. Scan over, dignity still intact, I was then wheeled back to my cubical, to await my results.

Normally my wife would have travelled up in the ambulance with me. We'd chat and usually make a joke of it to lighten the mood. She'd keep the supply of tea flowing from the free tea and coffee machine in the hallway, and generally just keep me company. Not this time. This time I was on my own, with no tea caddy or fun conversation trying to guess what injuries those that were in the surrounding cubicles were in for. I found that this made the time go even slower than it usually did. I was on my own now, even a little scared.

The doctor poked his head in. All the tests came back clear, nothing sinister had shown up, so I was good to go, once I'd had a bag of fluids. A nurse entered and fixed up an intravenous drip, plugged it into the cannula and then gave the bag a good squeeze. All I then had to do was just lay there, doing nothing, contemplating life. It was in that moment, laying silent and still, just staring up at the ceiling all alone in a hospital bed, when the big unanswered questions started to surface. I watched the clock tick from second to second, thinking about all the mistakes, bad life choices, and the people I've hurt. I guess I shouldn't be surprised that my life had spiralled out of control and gone down the shitter. Where did it all go wrong? What the hell am I going to do now? These days all I have is time on my hands, lots of it, probably too much time, too much time to think. But I wasn't just thinking about my current predicament and challenges I now have with my health, I was now thinking about everything. I watched the clear bag of fluids slowly drain into my body. Alone on a hospital bed, I could do nothing else but think and reflect on my life, along with everything that has happened over the last couple of years. An epic 'car crash' of massive proportions. A fall from grace figuratively speaking. I had absolutely everything I could ever want. Now I had nothing.

What the ruck just happened?

Introduction

I am what most people would call a selfish man, I mean even my loved ones and closest friends would probably agree with me. It's a trait that has brought me both success and desperate unhappiness, all at the same time. But in some ways, it's been my greatest ally also. A personality flaw that mixed with stubbornness and determination has fuelled the part of me that refuses to quit, even when I am desperate to do so. That quiet voice inside my head that eggs me on, is both a blessing and a curse. Some days it pushes me through my limits and past what I think my body and mind are capable of. But on occasion it will turn me towards extreme stubbornness and selfishness, which leads to desperate unhappiness. It would appear (to me anyway) that one side cannot function without the other, the Yin and Yang in full effect.

In life, I am just a person, one of billions on the planet. I am in no way special, in fact, average would be a good description. I don't possess any unique skills nor am I particularly gifted in any way shape or form. I'm good at lots of things, but not great at anything. I have not achieved anything grand nor have I contributed anything meaningful to society. I am just like ninety-nine percent of the population. I laugh, I love, I hurt, and I cry. I feel all the same emotions as everyone else, emotions that I choose to hide, most of the time. I could be you figuratively speaking. We are maybe the same. I feel it's important that we start and finish this journey as equals, because believe it or not (and I have learned the hard way) we are all equal. We are all travelling on our own personal journey heading in the same direction, destination…death. You may or may not realise this or you may choose to ignore the fact, but it's an undeniable fact! Yet as we travel on our journey towards our own end of days, life will undoubtedly send us down some unexpected roads and pathways, usually when we become complacent in our attitudes and fat with gluttony. One minute you're a cliché family Christmas card, then a few bad decisions on the bounce, a couple of wrong turns, some bad luck and you're running through flaming hot lava in hell with your hair on fire. Don't be fooled into thinking "None of this could happen to me". In a blink of an eye, it can happen to anyone.

You may be forgiven for thinking that this is going to be a self-help or motivational book, a biography written as a cathartic way of healing, but it is not. I am in truth not sure what it is. It may be just a recollection of events, a record of my memories, a way of opening up and saying to the world "This is me". I've not always been a good person, so maybe this book is about purging myself in the hope that I and others can forgive. It would be easy to justify my bad behaviour on a tough upbringing or inconsistent presence of a father. I won't, I take full ownership of that myself. We've all done things we are immensely proud of and we've all done things we are not. I will shoulder all of the blame and responsibility for my bad behaviour and its consequences, but I shall also selfishly take all of the credit, for all that I have achieved.

All of us have some regrets (if you say you don't then I'm calling you out as a liar), things you wish you could take back. I certainly do. If I were Catholic, I would be on first-name terms with the priest and a weekly if not daily visitor to confession. These things from my past I have come to terms with long ago. To psychoanalyse myself now and question why I am the way I am, would not be conducive to my future personal development and growth. A journey to become selfless instead of selfish and to be a better version of me, Gareth de la Torre two point zero. What has gone before cannot be changed, so why dwell on what has been? Because right now, that space in our minds where we tend to relive our past and ponder the "what ifs" could be better used to start influencing our futures. Don't get me wrong. To move on we need to acknowledge our past mistakes so we can learn from them. But let's not spend our precious time thinking about what might have happened should we have done something differently, because we didn't. We all have a choice. We are all responsible for our actions good or bad. The good will always be overlooked and forgotten, and the bad? Well, nobody ever forgets that, and in the end, karma will usually sort it out.

So, what do I possess that makes me qualified to dish out any form of motivation or advice? Well, actually nothing. I have nothing. No money, I don't own my own home. I don't own a car and as of writing, I have no job. I'm also not comfortable giving advice or trying to inspire people, so I'm not going to try. I mean, who would want to take advice from me? I know I wouldn't.

All I have is a story.

Chapter 1

"I was enjoying life a little too much; I guess karma had to intervene at some point before I hurt more of those who cared for me."

The slow realisation that something was wrong starts to creep in. The high-pitched ringing was so loud I was sure that it would wake the house (I was yet to realise that I was the only person privy to this private orchestration of sound). I try to focus my eyes but I can't. My vision is stuck like the autofocus on a digital camera that can't quite grab onto its subject. I feel sick, like ten pints deep sick (but not a drop of alcohol has passed my lips). The room spins out of control like a cart on a fairground ride being spun by a dishevelled carnival worker. A wave of confusion washes over me along with another bout of nausea as I struggle to understand what is happening. I can feel the coarseness of the carpet on my cheek. All the while the high-pitched ringing between my ears gets louder. The dull ache in the back of my head turns into pain, excruciating pain that amplifies the nausea which is now a permanent fixture. Can I move? I raise one arm and, in the blackness, a hand finds the flat surface of the coffee table.

Panic starts to set in and I feel like I'm fading in and out of life. If I don't do something, am I going to die right here on the living room floor? I feel broken. My body is so heavy there must be something pinning me to the floor. I let go of the table and check, only to find I'm free of any falling debris. I try to call out in the hope that my fiancé will hear me upstairs and then at least I won't die alone in the dark, but I can barely let out a grunt. I reach out again. My right hand bangs the side of the coffee table and I grab it. If I can get to my feet, I may be okay. I roll slowly onto my side, my head so heavy it doesn't even move off the carpet. I brace myself pulling my knees to my chest. Now lying in the foetal position, one hand still resting on the table, I take a deep breath (trying not to empty the contents of my stomach onto the floor) and roll using my hand on the table as leverage. I've made it onto my knees.

"Good job Gareth. Now let's not be a pussy and get to your feet".

I need to pick my moment between the spinning room, the intense nausea, the screaming G above high C raging inside my head and the intense pain which now feels like the back of my brain is on fire. I kneel motionless, both hands now on the table.

"Get to your feet and into the hallway and we'll work out how to tackle the stairs when we get there".

I move my left leg up, my left foot now firmly on the floor, and simultaneously stand up on my left leg while using the coffee table to balance. Up, up, up! The room spins in the blackness as I fight off the nausea. I place my right leg down to steady myself. Where is my right leg? I can't feel my right leg, I'm falling! My head smashes against an immovable hard solid object. An intensely bright light flashes behind my eyes and the loudest chime like a hammer striking an anvil explodes inside my head. Nausea, pain, and a high-pitched whistle slowly ebb away, and the darkest blackness washes over me.

A low hum inside my head woke me from a deep sleep, and as I opened my eyes nausea and headache hit me at the same time, like they too had been sleeping and were now angered by the audacity of me waking up. I can't see. Is it still dark or am I blind? Where am I? I have all these questions but my brain can't figure out any of the answers, as a question doesn't remain in view long enough to get answered before it's pushed out by another. I try to turn and the softness of the mattress and the warmth of the duvet inform me I'm in bed. I made it! I lay silent, no recollection of how I got there, a little disconcerting but a welcome relief all the same. The world looks and feels different but I can't understand why, but for now, I am where I am supposed to be. I want to wake my fiancé and tell her I think I've had some kind of weird and strange accident, so we can laugh about how stupid I've been, and then everything would be okay. I then won't have to process the reality that I may have really hurt myself, but I refrain as she is sound asleep.

I lay motionless in bed letting the night creep on of its own free will, hoping that the headache and nausea will relent long enough for me to slip into unconsciousness. The body next to me stirs and we have a brief exchange of words which I cannot remember. Maybe I told her I'd had a fall or maybe she just asked me what the time was. Either way, we drifted into sleep.

And just like that the first domino fell.

Chapter 2

There are several phrases that universally transcend across borders and language. Quotes that are thrown out into the ether in times of dire hardship to inspire and motivate us into some form of action. An awakening to pull us from our darkness and metaphorically hold us as we slowly journey toward the light. Words that offer some form of comfort and hope. The kind of words you see written on driftwood hanging above upcycled doors that greet you as you enter. The owner may think that reading the black lettering on a sun-bleached rectangle of worm-ridden wood will brighten up what is usually a fucking shit day. I'll give you some examples!

"When you have hit rock bottom the only way is up."
Well, not exactly true. How do you know where the bottom is? How do you know when you have stopped freefalling, when you can look up and start to claw your way back into existence leaving the devastation behind, to be reborn into a world of rainbows and unicorns where everybody loves each other and the world smells of candy floss and toffee apples? I have been told on numerous occasions that "Now you've hit rock bottom the only way is up" and on numerous occasions I've managed to disprove the theory, and then with a swift kick to the bollocks, I sink to another level of shit and squalor.

"At least you have your health"
I agree with this, unless you don't have your health and then it's a stark reminder that no matter what you do, unless you have your health life is pointless.

"Kill them with kindness"
Now I've tried this on numerous occasions and the person I was trying to be kind to didn't die. They saw it as a sign of weakness, went for the jugular and before you know it, you're bleeding out your carotid artery and as you slowly slip into a metaphorical coma someone will say,

"Now you've hit rock bottom. The only way is up".
Oh, fuck off will you.

Before you all reach for the hankies and violins, I have to say that some of this (not all) is of my own making, so I'm not fishing here for any form of sympathy. This is only my perception of what I can only describe as some pretty tough years of my life, and how I managed to somehow navigate my way through the darkest times and stand again in the pale sunlight that shines between the rain clouds. I am not alone in this experience. We all go through tough times and each one of our experiences is as unique as we are.

There are, in most cases three sides to every story, mine, theirs, and somewhere in between lies the truth! I say this as I am the one fortunate enough to be recounting this tale, and whilst I will try to be as unbiased as I can, I am of course drawing from my own recollection, memories of events and those feelings that went along with them. I cannot speak for others whose memories and feelings may differ from mine, as perception is of course very subjective.

To understand the journey, we should start at the beginning, before the accident and way before my epilepsy diagnosis. This will hopefully put my life into some sort of context. Some of it may seem strange and off-topic, but its relevance to the story is important. The opening act, so to speak, as I travel from the good life I was leading, to the darkest of times I have experienced and had to endure, and everything in between.

Life was good. I was married, with two gorgeous daughters that I love with every cell in my body. I had a good job that was pretty well paid by today's standards which meant my wife didn't have to work, allowing her to be a stay-at-home mum. I worked in a highly driven and competitive sales market and my work took me all over the country, staying in the nicest hotels. I entertained my clients with long corporate lunches and nights out in the nicest of restaurants drinking expensive wines. I made full use of hospitality boxes at major events and I looked after my clients like family, in return, they rewarded me with their business and I nearly always hit my sales targets. A pretty good effort seeing as I was responsible at that time for delivering five million pounds worth of revenue. I would waft through the offices in sharp suits, the smell of expensive aftershave following behind. I thought I was important and I'm sure the rest of the staff thought I was a wanker, but I didn't care. I was earning good money and driving a nice new Mercedes Benz. Looking sharp, taking care of my clients, and having a good time was all that mattered. Of course, I would moan and complain about the stress and the hours I worked, but if I'm being honest this was just a façade so people didn't think I was having too much of a good time, which I was. I was living the good life.

We were not rich by any stretch of the imagination but we were buying a house and had two cars. We encapsulated the image of a happy middle-class family. I fucked that up, by my own admission I hold my hands up I'll take it all squarely on the chin. For the breakup of my marriage, I take full responsibility. I'm not proud of the husband I was in the end and if the truth be known I'm embarrassed and ashamed. I not only let myself down but my family as well and I do have certain regrets. Who wouldn't? I put my own happiness before that of my family, a decision that I deeply regret and have to live with every single day of my life. Like Jacob Marley, I have forged a long and heavy chain made from all my regret and guilt. Which I drag around with me to this very day.

What proceeded then I can only describe as a self-inflicted living hell. I had no idea that my long-suffering wife (who had been going through a living hell herself) had built up so much resentment towards me. She had buried this resentment deep down inside her soul, and was now ready to unleash it all. I didn't see any of this coming as I was too wrapped up in myself to notice, and by the time I did it was too late. She wanted a divorce and wanted me to move out of the marital home which, after several attempts by myself to save the marriage, I did. Having to leave my children broke my heart and that hurt has never gone away. My heart has never healed from that experience. There will be some that feel the punishment fitted the crime, and if the punishment is a lifetime of heartache, then I'm certainly doing the porridge. After a short spell living with my parents, I eventually moved into a rented three-bedroom maisonette having access to my daughters every other weekend; a standard absent father scenario.

Then came the divorce and two years of utter misery. My wife didn't want to negotiate a settlement or go through mediation. She even failed to turn up at the mandatory mediation session, which all couples should attend before going through the divorce procedure. She wanted her day in court and up until that court date she made everything as painstakingly difficult for me as she could. Even my divorce solicitor said she had never encountered such bitterness and vengefulness. In hindsight, I'm sure the whole experience was just as traumatic for the mother of my children as it was for me. The court date came and a settlement was eventually reached, and at last, I had my rock bottom moment. It was over. Time to look forward to a new life.

In the last six months before my divorce was finalised, I had started dating and had (I thought) fallen in love. Up until then, I had never bought into the bullshit of soulmates or unconditional love, which was the arena of pathetic verses written inside Valentine's Day cards, and those mushy couples who post romantic pictures of themselves on social media declaring their love for each other. My future wife came along at the right time, not just the right time for me but for her also. She "got" me, understood who I was, and that made me happy, so after a year of dating she and her daughter moved in. Things were great! All the kids got on and, on the weekends, when the girls came to stay the house was full of fun and laughter. It wasn't long after that we made it official and I popped the question. When she agreed to marry me, it was a dream come true, a second chance for both of us. However, as we started to plan our wedding, we were oblivious to the dark cloud that would shortly hit our family, (a big one full of wind, rain, thunder, and lightning which would unleash its full fury). To get through it, all you need is love, right? You are stronger together, and we were. I could write pages of all the mud that was thrown at us, but in all honesty, it's irrelevant now. Needless to say, moving on with your life and being happy will and did undoubtedly infuriate others. We didn't care. We consciously decided to ignore the games of the immature and continued to live life, a happy and fun life.

In the winter of twenty-seventeen, we booked our second family holiday together to visit friends in California the following August. We'd already been that year, flying into Las Vegas, and after spending one night amongst the neon-lit strip of Sin City, we then hired a car and drove through Death Valley and Yosemite National Park to California. It was an amazing adventure for us all and we couldn't wait to do it all over again.

As an absent father, it is (in the eyes of UK law) advisable to get written consent from the mother of your children before taking them out of the country. The previous year my ex-wife had been difficult regarding this. She did not sign the paperwork, or relinquish the passports until the night before. This as you can imagine was a big source of frustration all around. This holiday wasn't just about me and my children but it was my fiancé and her daughter's holiday as well. We were keen not to jump through the same hoops again. So, in anticipation of this, we gave plenty of notice and repeatedly asked again for the passports and the signature form. At this point I would just like to make it clear that I didn't need to have my ex-wife's signature, I'm allowed to take my children out of the country for up to thirty days without her consent (something she had done the previous year). I did however need their passports. We were trying to take the higher ground and do the right thing; we were as expected stone walled. Then at the final hour, I was told I needed to produce a letter from a doctor to say I was fit and healthy enough to be responsible for my children when in my care, or the girls would not be joining us on our holiday. Word had got back through my children to their mother that I had been experiencing some blackouts after my accident at home. We had played this down to the kids but in all honesty, blackouts were just the tip of the iceberg. I was not well and to make things worse I was completely ignoring the fact that I wasn't well.

I had fallen asleep on the sofa after an argument with my fiancé, and upon waking in the night I fell, hitting my head against a solid oak coffee table and knocking myself out cold. Once I came around, I struggled to stand, falling and knocking myself out again. A couple of days after my fall, I had a seizure in bed, waking up my fiancé and scaring the life out of her. Then a few days later, after a particularly heavy session in the gym, I started to feel very strange. I called my mother to come to pick me up, as I was having trouble focusing. Then in the car on the way home I had another seizure. As the days went on, I was having more and more until I was having several in a day. I still ignored the fact that I was not well and refused to go to the hospital, hoping that I would miraculously get better. I'm not one for being ill or going to the doctor. I often say jokingly that when I was young, I once died and my mother told me to walk it off! That was the environment I grew up in. As kids we never had days off school due to sickness. The only way you'd get a day off school in our house was if you couldn't physically walk.

Caught a cold? School.

Throwing up? School.

Diarrhoea? You went to school and hoped you didn't shit yourself on the way, you get the picture.

I was given less than a week's notice to produce the letter for my ex-wife from a doctor. I had yet to even visit a doctor regarding my little accident let alone produce a dossier stating my current medical condition. The whole scenario was highly stressful for all concerned. That's when Mum stepped in!

Mums are great. Well, mine is anyway. My mother, on a shoestring budget, pretty much brought up three boys single-handedly after my dad left when I was eight years old, back in eighty-three. My two brothers and I the indignity of queuing up every Monday morning at the school office to collect our free school meal vouchers. It was like wearing a sign around your neck saying your dad's fucked off and you're poor. Then, in nineteen ninety-three, my mother met my now stepfather, and a few years later we all moved into his large four-bed detached home. It felt like a mansion compared to our previous end-of-terrace council house. My mother was now financially secure, probably for the first time in her life. So, when I phoned my local doctor's surgery to enquire about a "fit to fly" letter and was pretty much told I had no hope of securing this through a local doctor, it was no surprise that Mum offered to pay for me to see a private consultant. A quick phone call to the local private hospital and I was given a choice of consultants to see. I picked the one recommended to me by the hospital and an appointment was set for a couple of days later.

The waiting room was spacious, clean, and very quiet. If you didn't know you were already in a hospital then you could be forgiven for thinking you were waiting in the reception of a big corporate office building. There was no hustle or bustle or the squeaking of nurses' shoes on linoleum floors, no loud bangs of double doors slamming, or the shouts of disgruntled patients who have been waiting for longer than they feel they deserved. A private hospital is a world away from your local NHS hospital. The receptionist checked me in with a smile and told me to take a seat and to help ourselves to tea and coffee. We grabbed a couple of hot drinks and sat down in large comfortable armchairs; we couldn't have sat for more than five minutes when my name was called.

Dr Chan was a tall and slender man and very well dressed. He looked like the kind of man who runs marathons, athletic and fit. He spoke very eloquently and was empathetic and polite and I wasn't at all made to feel like I was wasting his time, considering he was a consultant neurologist with impeccable credentials and I was a just bloke who had banged his head on a coffee table. After explaining my situation, he did an examination, after which he said I was fit to fly, and seeing as I wasn't travelling alone, he couldn't see any reason why my children would be at risk. He dictated a letter into his Dictaphone and said I would receive it in the next couple of days. The conversation then went from very positive to quite dark, (well in my mind anyway). Dr Chan stated that when I returned from holiday, he wanted to see me again so he could conduct some more tests. I was also started on anti-seizure or epilepsy medication. This was the first time epilepsy was ever mentioned. Up until then it hadn't even crossed my mind. We left the hospital somewhat triumphant. In the back of my mind, I think we were both deluding ourselves. We both knew at that point dark times were ahead, but we smiled, walked to the car and drove home. I'm sure we both thought that once we got away on holiday everything would be okay. How wrong could we have been?

It would be great to say that our trip to the USA was as enjoyable an experience as the one the previous year, and whilst it was great to get some sun and spend time with all the girls away from the stresses of home, it was marred by the obvious fact that I was not well and getting worse. I reacted badly to the anti-seizure medication and was vomiting after taking it, nearly choking to death in my sleep one night. I was also seizing (although we still didn't know if they were seizures or not) several times a day and it was getting worse. I would just lose consciousness and when I came around, I was confused, disorientated and for a while, I had no memory of who or where I was. It was terrifying and quite often left me in an emotional state. Even though I was surrounded by my family and friends I felt very much alone. Little did I know then lonelier times were ahead. We flew back to the UK; my daughters were delivered back to their mother in one piece and we then got to seeking some help and getting some answers.

The accident happened in the middle of May. It was now the middle of August and I was getting married at the end of September. I wasn't working due to the blackouts and everyone was feeling the strain. My soon-to-be stepdaughter was not getting much of her mother's attention as it was all focused on me. With all the chaos that was going on she got neglected, this is something that I now wish I had spotted and rectified. I often forget that those around me were suffering as well, mostly in silence so as to not add any more pressure to an already stressful situation, something I believe I still do to this day.

The blackouts continued at an alarming rate and I found myself on several occasions being ambulanced into Accident and Emergency. I was continually falling and banging my head, my forehead was now starting to take the shape of a Toblerone chocolate bar. To help with the nausea I was prescribed a different medication, whilst it didn't make me lose the contents of my stomach it didn't stop the blackouts completely either. It was around this time that I got an official diagnosis of epilepsy. I wasn't having blackouts. I was having epileptic seizures. It had been theorised that the meningitis that nearly killed me as a three-year-old could have left me with very mild epilepsy. So mild in fact that it may have just presented itself very occasionally as what we would call daydreaming, which is why it went undetected. The aggressive bang on the head that I recently suffered as a result of the fall at home, may have made an undetected existing condition much worse. It was the worst news. I was just about to start a new life and I was now suddenly hit with my own mortality. I found this very hard to deal with and combined with the medication I was on (one of the side effects was irritability) made for some dark times, not only for me but for those around me also.

So, I now have epilepsy. I was also suffering from severe anxiety which I now realise was some form of post-traumatic stress. I was also slipping into a deep depression which I was completely unaware of. I'm pretty sure I wasn't a barrel of laughs to be around. My fiancé was my rock and I clung to her like my life depended on it. She was at every hospital appointment and took care of me when I should have been taking care of her. I was in my own bubble, wallowing in self-pity, having between five and ten seizures a day. I was oblivious to the fact that others who love me were hurting too. I guess while all this was happening to me those that loved me felt powerless, they could not cure me or take away the pain I was feeling. All they could do was spectate, and they were just about to get a ringside seat to my own self-destruction.

It's very difficult to describe how I was feeling at the time. In the space of several months my life had become unrecognizable. In twelve weeks I'd gone from being a successful account manager, with a good career ahead of me, to somebody who couldn't and wouldn't get off the sofa. I was never very sympathetic to those who went on about their mental health. I fell into that bucket of people that would dismiss those as weak-minded and malingerers. "Get a grip on yourself and stop whining, playing the victim and looking for sympathy." Now, I didn't think I was suffering from mental health issues, I didn't think or feel that I was depressed but looking back the signs were there. I didn't want to leave the house, which should have been an early warning sign. In my mind, I reconciled this anxiety by believing it was just because I didn't want to have a seizure in public. That made perfect sense to me. I was withdrawn and was being a bit awkward and uncooperative. Again, I justified this by blaming the medication I was on. Slowly but surely, day by day I sank a little further into the darkness. Every seizure I had was tearing a little bit more of me away until I was numb. I had been successful. I had everything I could ever want. Now I felt like I was a piece of shit welded to the sofa incapable of taking care of myself, and worse, resenting those that were taking care of me.

I don't remember what day of the week it was, nor do I remember what happened before waking up in the bedroom. I remember a beam of sunlight shining through the blind on the bedroom window highlighting the dust in the room, like glitter floating in the breeze sparkling as it defies gravity. I remember lying on the bed motionless waiting to see if I'm to be struck with pain as my senses returned. It appeared this time I had escaped the lightning bolt of agony that usually succeeds a seizure, and a heavy fall. The house was empty. I was on my own and conscious of the fact that I was sobbing. I don't remember having a second seizure, but I do remember slowly becoming aware that I was upset, confused, and feeling very isolated. The feeling of tiredness that succeeds a seizure was present so I guess I did. I remember thinking this can't go on. My life cannot be a series of small moments bracketed between epileptic seizures, with ambulances to hospitals, worried loved ones frantically trying to sort out who's going to look after me, or who is picking whom up from the hospital. While I just lie there completely useless to anyone.

I slid off the bed and knelt facing the bedroom door, slowly leaning forward I rested my forehead against it. I don't know where the green canvas belt came from, whether I picked it up off the dresser or took it off my waist, but it was now in my hand. The sobbing had stopped but the tears had not. There wasn't a sound in the air except for the sound of me breathing. Who wants a sick husband or a sick son, a constant burden, a grown man that can't take care of himself? Sure, right now everyone was being sympathetic and wants nothing else but to help, how long before the resentment sets in? How long before you're seen as an inconvenience? The cancelled plans and frantic phone calls to say you're in the hospital…again? I immediately felt empowered and in control of my destiny, I was going to decide my fate. The universe will no longer dictate to me how my life was going to be. I and only I will control my destiny. It will not be left to fate or chance or even a roll of the dice. It was going to be me.

I threaded the belt through the metal buckle making a loop; placing it over my head and around my neck and pulling it tight. The other end I tied to the bedroom door handle in a reef knot taking in as much slack as I could and then, without hesitation, I violently slid my knees back straightening my legs, a sudden jerk and I felt the pinch tighten around my neck. Darkness moved into my peripheral vision before swallowing me up, then there was nothing.

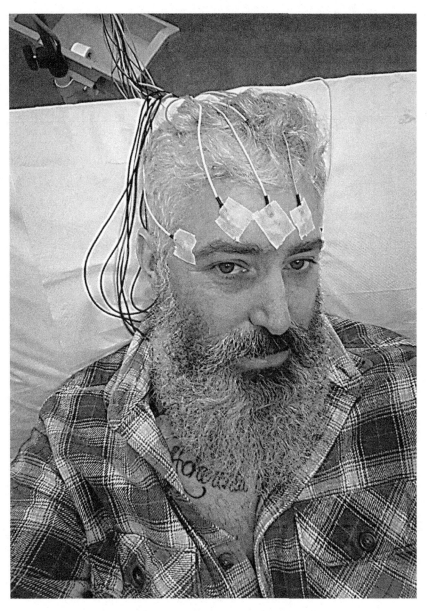

All geared up for an electroencephalogram (EEG)

Chapter 3

"I once sat in boardrooms convincing people to spend millions of pounds, now I'm sat in the back of an ambulance in handcuffs trying to convince people I'm sane".

Panic, I sensed panic. Someone was trying to move me but I couldn't work out who, as nobody was in the room. Shouting, I could hear shouting, several voices I think but I couldn't tell who it was. I felt my body jolt again as the shouting continued. I felt like I was being constantly kicked. It wasn't long before I realised that I was lying in front of the door and people were on the other side trying to force it all the way open. The door was already open a crack; a hand was reaching in pulling the belt off from around my neck. It was a relief to slip into another seizure.

The realisation that what I had done slowly came into focus as I regained consciousness. The presence of my fiancé, mother, and paramedics slammed reality into my face like the blast of heat you get from opening the oven door whilst checking the Sunday roast. The door was eventually forced open and the paramedics went to work, eventually lifting me onto my bed. As I lay on the bed, I could tell there had been some tears in the faces around me. What had I put my family through? The paramedics went about their business doing what they do, but I wasn't taking much notice. I remember trying to look through the gap in the blinds on the window to get a glimpse of the outside world, I guess trying to pretend that nobody was there. I refused to be taken to the hospital and signed the hospital refusal document. As time spanned forward people came and went, eventually, I was left alone in bed reflecting on my thoughts and actions.

I had nearly ended my life; I would have left my daughters without a father, a mother without a son, and taken away a brother. At that moment another link was forged and added to the chain of regret. What I thought would be an immense sense of relief turned into immense pain of guilt, something I was getting good at and getting used to feeling. The plan was almost foolproof, however as the noose tightened and I lost consciousness I started to convulse violently tugging at the belt, eventually pulling it off the door handle before I completely asphyxiated. I don't think I will ever be forgiven by some for my actions on that day, nor do I think I deserve to be.

"When you hit rock bottom the only way is up."

The days that proceeded blurred into each other and rolled into weeks; my mental health was declining but I only realise this now in retrospect. Looking back, I can't recall anything significant happening in that time frame but I know lots did, my memory chose to save it as a corrupted file with lots of data missing. It wasn't long before our wedding day loomed and everyone was getting excited, even me, that day however was almost ruined. We had friends flying in from America and people travelling from other parts of the country. We were all set for our big day. Then the day before I had a seizure at the top of the stairs. I fell down the entire flight and had to be blue-lighted into A&E with a suspected spinal injury. If I fell into a barrel of tits, I tell you I'd come out sucking my thumb. After several hours and several scans, I was told that no serious damage had been done. I downplayed the pain, told the staff I was feeling okay and we went home. The following day was a blur of excitement and joy. The pain I was in was numbed by some pretty strong painkillers that I was given by a friend who worked at a drug rehabilitation centre and plenty of alcohol, so I was flying and in no pain at all. Everyone looked fantastic and to see all the girls dressed up still brings a lump to my throat today thinking about it. That was a good day that shone like a speck of gold in a tin pan full of river water and dirt, just as it should be.

The months passed us by with more appointments with Dr Chan; I had a twenty-four-hour EEG (electroencephalogram) which is where they cover your head in electrodes to measure brain activity. The hope is that they can pinpoint the precise location of the seizure, which would then possibly open up the potential for more treatments. Mine however showed nothing, typical. There were also more changes in medication, however, nothing seemed to work as well as we had hoped for, even after several tweaks, my seizures were on average a couple every week. I was off the medication which had been making me irritable and was on a combination of drugs which left me tired and nauseous.

Christmas came and went without incident other than a seizure on Boxing Day, which ended up with me wiping out the Christmas Tree at my parents' house. I came around covered in tinsel and glitter, looking like a member of the chorus line from a children's pantomime. Then in January twenty-nineteen, I was called up to Glasgow where the Head Office of the company I worked for was situated. I sat in the boardroom opposite the sales director and next to him my boss Neil the Tash, who happened to be my best mate and had been my best man at the wedding back in September. It was then I received another swift kick to the bollocks, basically due to not being able to drive, as I was still having seizures, I was told my employment would be terminated. A major accounts manager that can't drive is like a welder with no arms. Of course, they went through the process of trying to find me an alternative role within the business which meant I didn't need to drive, but nothing seemed to come to fruition. Who wants an employee that could potentially be off sick every week? I was now unemployed. I felt sorry for Neil more than I did for myself. He was, and still is my closest friend. I could see he was visibly upset. The flight from Glasgow back to Gatwick felt longer than the hour it normally took. I sat in my seat trying to form some kind of plan that would save the day but nothing was coming. The only thing I could think of was to look into claiming some kind of sickness benefit. Never actually needing to claim benefits before I wasn't sure where to start. Up until then, I had been living off the profit from the sale of my marital home. I also couldn't claim any benefits until I had gone through my savings. It wasn't long before a company representative arrived at my house, I was then relieved of all my company possessions, laptop, mobile phone, and of course my new Mercedes Benz. My life was slowly unravelling and I was losing everything.

At least at home, I had all the support I needed and between my wife and mother, I couldn't have been better looked after. We struggled on and jumped through all the hoops necessary to claim Universal Credit, a process I wish nobody ever has to go through. I am unsure how an organisation set up to help the vulnerable can have so little sympathy or empathy. Here I was cap in hand struggling with my health and finances and was (in my opinion) made to feel like a freeloader or potential benefit thief. The face-to-face assessment wasn't much better and had my wife in tears. We had to describe in detail the previous eighteen months of our lives. After this we were sent on our way to await a decision, a decision I hasten to add made by a couple of people, none of them doctors or who had any experience in neurology. To add even more pressure my ex-wife had contacted the Child Maintenance Service because her child maintenance had stopped. Well of course it had stopped. I wasn't earning a salary or receiving any money! I just wanted to get better so I could make this all right and be able to support my wife and our children. I was feeling like a complete failure. I was depressed; I wasn't taking care of myself and I was relying on others too much. I needed to find something to do; something that would make me feel like I wasn't a patient but a person. Something that would give me a sense of identity and an escape from the house, which was starting to feel like a self-imposed prison sentence. But the motivation eluded me and we all ground our way through the months ahead pretending things were getting better, when the honest truth was, it was all slowly getting worse. I was oblivious to what was happening around me and adopted a confrontational attitude. How can anybody have the faintest idea what I was going through, how could they, this was happening to me not them. The irony was that whilst I was throwing this in the face of the people I loved, they were suffering too, only I wasn't letting them have a voice. I felt that I was the one who was sick not them. I was becoming distant and detached. Was this now my life?

The sofa in our front room was my best friend and as I lay there staring out the window the seasons slowly changed. In August we headed off with two of the girls for a short break in Vegas (we were very fortunate that my wife worked for an airline and got great concessions) and then in September, we celebrated our first wedding anniversary. How? I can't remember. Time meant nothing to me anymore. In a strange kind of way, I was time travelling from one moment to another with long gaps of empty space in between. On the outside, I was trying to portray a vision of positivity but on the inside, there was nothing, just a black space where my life should be. Then one night after a seizure, things got worse.

You see, as I was coming out of a seizure (a phase they call postictal) I sometimes went walkabout, a bit like sleepwalking. Well after a particularly bad seizure, I had managed somehow to elude my wife and exit the house. My mother (who had been called by my wife after she had noticed I was missing) found and followed me to make sure I didn't hurt myself or anybody else for that matter. On these occasions when I would go walkabout, I always headed for the same place, my nan's house. I had in my early twenties lived with my grandparents (who I was very close to and who had sadly passed away some years ago) for a couple of years. My guess would be my brain (which is in the recovery process of a seizure) was guiding me back to where it thought I lived. Although this behaviour has not been clinically proven it is in my opinion a fair theory which I happen to believe. My grandparents had lived in a semi-detached house next to a footpath which led to a river, which splits our local golf course in half. Before the course was built it was just fields where the local dairy herd would graze. As kids we would camp in the surrounding woods, fish, and swim in the deeper parts of the river. It was a significant place for me growing up. I wonder if that memory is so strong that as my brain reboots after a seizure it's where I want to go back to? That night I stumbled across the golf course like a drunk on his way home from a bar with my mother in tow, until entering a wooded area I lost her.

I instantly knew where I was as I slowly came around from the postictal stage of my seizure. I had no phone so I couldn't call to let anyone know I was safe. I remember thinking I better get home as I silently moved through the woods to pick up the footpath. It was dark but I wasn't scared as I knew these woods like the back of my hand. The street light at the end of the dark footpath shone like a lighthouse and signalled that I was almost at my nan's old house and therefore the road. A lighthouse is there to warn ships of the impending danger of the coastline; I wish I had viewed the dimly lit street light with the same caution.

One ambulance, two police cars, and a police van were parked adjacent to the footpath that I was slowly making my way along. I wonder what's happened here I thought to myself. I moved closer to the commotion, I then spotted my stepfather and then my wife. It took another couple of seconds to realise that this search party was for me. I stepped into the light knowing I was going to be spotted, which I was. I told everyone I was fine and I'm sorry to have wasted everyone's time and if they didn't mind, I'd be going home now as I was immensely tired. The problem was that it was my mother who was missing not me! She had got herself lost in the woods and the police were trying to guide her out over the phone. Officers were dispatched to a small road that ran parallel to the woods and were using thermal imaging to try and locate her. A dog unit was either on standby or had rolled up, I can't remember. There was even mention of a police helicopter being called in to help with the search!

All the while a strange elderly lady wafted between the vehicles with a lanyard around her neck trying to look important, I paid no real attention to her. When my mother finally showed up, she was ushered into the back of the ambulance, while my wife and I were ushered into the police van. I could see my mother was visibly upset as you would expect, but my main concern was that while the door of the police van was still open, it was starting to be encircled by several police officers. Conversations were going on between the officers and this mystery woman and it was making me uneasy. Who was she? My wife was taken out of the van and led away by a police officer and I was finally introduced to this grey-haired old lady. She told me her name (I don't remember what it was) and said she was a mental health nurse. She went on to ask how I was, to which I replied fine, I just wanted to go home and sleep. I tried to convey this to her as clearly and politely as I could, but she wasn't listening. She then exited the van to talk further with the police officers. My wife came back clearly agitated and told me that I had agreed to spend the night in a psychiatric hospital! No way. None of this had been mentioned to me. I was now starting to get angry. I stepped out of the van and informed everyone I was going home, knowing that I could not be kept unless I was arrested. The police officers panicked slightly as they knew I was right. We started to walk up the road towards home. There was a quick exchange between the police officers and I overheard one of them say that they were unable to detain me as technically, I had done nothing wrong. The old lady who was starting to remind me of nurse Ratched from One Flew Over the Cuckoo's Nest was on the phone. I later found out she was trying to find a bed at a hospital for me. I was ushered back to the police van under the pretence of some further questioning. This was getting out of hand now. I could hear Ratched who was sitting in the ambulance talking on the phone, I saw her hang up, she nodded to one of the police officers who then walked over to the van. I was informed that I was to be sectioned under the Mental Health Act, supposedly for my own safety.

I exploded out of my seat taking everyone by surprise and took off across the road and onto the adjacent football pitch. I was in my youth a winger for our town's rugby team and whilst I wasn't a great distance runner, I was able to call up explosive speed when needed. The police gave chase but they never stood a chance of catching me on foot. I had caught them off guard by playing the grey man, I was just too fast. If I could make it into the woods across from the football field, I knew for certain I would lose them in the maze of footpaths and tracks. This was my arena and my knowledge of the area with all its little hidey-holes was vast and detailed. That was until I hit the wet grass at Mach four. My body which had built up such momentum started moving faster than my legs could carry me on the soaking ground below. I went over but managed to roll back onto my feet, just as the faster of the four police officers loomed over me. I went low, grabbing him around the legs at knee height, like a prop forward in a rugby scrum slamming into its opposite number and lifted him clean of his feet. The kinetic energy of both of us travelling towards each other was like a head-on car crash that knocked the wind clean out of him. I slammed him to the ground landing on top of him with my forearm across his neck. He looked petrified. It was only a split second before the other officers piled on, which to him must have felt like a lifetime. I was unceremoniously removed from the police officer and was then pinned face down on the grass, a knee dug deep into the side of my thigh by one officer, another officer pinning my head to the ground by resting on my neck, while the others tried to handcuff me. At six feet, sixteen-stone, and being very broad I couldn't be handcuffed behind my back as my big arms just wouldn't bend that way, so I was handcuffed in the front and walked to the ambulance. Two officers joined me in the back and sat down. I ignored all of their questions remaining the silent grey man as we journeyed to God knows where, taking some satisfaction that they appeared to be more banged up than I.

It had gone midnight by the time we pulled up to the dimly lit hospital building which was situated behind the main hospital, unseen and out of the way, keeping the nutters locked away like the hospital's dirty secret. I was escorted in through a side door, still handcuffed, like a celebrity entering the Priory. I was then asked some questions, (which I don't remember) and booked in. It was dark and eerily quiet. A single small desk lamp illuminated the small office where I was sitting. The side door was shut and locked before the handcuffs were taken off. I was then escorted to my spacious room, lit by a single fluorescent strip light that reflected off the large glass observation window, which separated me from the nurse in the office. At one end was a mattress-sized blue crash pad, like a smaller version of the ones we had at school that we would practice back flips on. A smaller-sized one was placed on top. I can only assume this was supposed to be a pillow. The bars on the window to the outside world reinforced my incarceration as they too reinforced the window. The words "they lie" were carved into the concrete window sill by a previous occupant. The nurse entered and asked if I was hungry, to which I replied "yes", and whether I needed anything, again I replied "yes", as I had not taken my evening medication. I could see by her face that this was going to be a problem. She was now going to have to wake a doctor to write an emergency prescription and then get somebody to get the prescription filled. It was past one a.m. so no pharmacy was going to be open. She made some frantic phone calls hoping that I didn't have a seizure and then die in her care. Eventually, sometime later the medication turned up which I took with a drink of water and a pre-packaged sandwich that I had been given earlier. By now it was the middle of the night, but I knew I wasn't going to be able to sleep in this godforsaken place, no matter how tired I was.

I lay on the crash mat covered by a thin blanket staring up at the ceiling. Now and again the nurse rose from her chair and peered in through the large window to check I wasn't trying to hurt myself. The night slowly evaporated and the first sign of dawn whispered past the steel bars and onto the small window sill, leaving a small puddle of light over the graffiti. As the sun rose over the invisible horizon, then so did the occupants on the ward next to me which was separated from my room by a concrete wall. I can still hear those shouts and screams today. Human beings who were clearly not well housed in one ward feeding off each others' distress. I had to get out of here, I didn't think I was mad or mentally ill but a stretch in here and I'm sure it wouldn't be long before I was! I was detained under the Mental Health Act Section Two and had to be assessed by three doctors. This was supposed to be happening that morning. After that assessment, I could either be sent home or detained for up to twenty-eight-days! How could this be happening?

The morning dragged on for what seemed like hours. Where were these "experts" who were going to determine whether I was well enough to go home, or sick enough to warrant a twenty-eight-day holiday at Hotel Crazy Palace? All joking aside I'm sure the work done in hospitals like these is extremely difficult and requires a lot of patience and empathy, having to care for people who can't quite care for themselves or integrate themselves into society. I can't help but feel that if the way you are delivered into these places was less traumatic the course of treatment would be shorter and more effective. We all have dark days. Now try to imagine if those days never got any better, then maybe you can understand what these patients were going through.

Eventually, three suited gentlemen sat before me on foldaway chairs, all looking rather important, and all reading notes. The uncomfortable silence lasted an uncomfortably long time. Who was going to talk first…me? Was this some kind of test to see how long I could stand the silence. If I spoke first would that go against me? I thought fuck it! We can sit here in silence. I don't give a shit, I'm not talking first. Occasionally one of them would look up and stare at me as if trying to get a reaction. I would just stare back until they looked down again. I was starting to enjoy this game. The silence was deafening only ever broken by a quiet cough or the sound of someone turning a page. Eventually one of them was brave enough to ask a question, which then opened the floodgates. We had gone from complete silence to a full-on interrogation, each taking turns to fire questions. To this day I can't remember what was discussed, only that it seemed to go on forever. I gave as good an account of myself as I could bearing in mind, I had been up for over twenty-four-hours. After the questions stopped, they exited the room only to come back five minutes later. I was then deemed sane and safe and free to go home. A couple of hours later my wife arrived to collect me. We joked about the experience on the journey back, because that's what we did. It was our way of coping with the situation. Inside though I was thinking that I never, ever want to experience that again, as long as I live. I had to crawl out of this hole, for my health, for my sanity, and for my family.

"When you reach rock bottom, the only way is up."

Chapter 4

"It is said that to be totally free you have to lose everything, that is bullshit. To lose everything is an unbearable burden."

When you don't work the mornings seem to get later and later. I'd wait for everyone to leave for work and school, then routinely drag myself out of bed, into the lounge and onto the sofa somewhere around eleven a.m. Netflix had lost my interest long ago as I had pretty much seen everything, some of it twice, YouTube was now my poison. I opened up the app on my television and dived into the rabbit hole. I'd watch anything, from music videos to conspiracy theories. Who shot JFK? That sort of thing. I was intrigued by the quality of the production on some of these amateur channels. You would think you were watching The Discovery Channel if you didn't know. I lost hours immersed in the uncensored content of these media creators. It was during one of these tumbles down the rabbit hole that I stumbled onto an outdoor channel. A young lad who would head off into the woods and forests, wild camping. Sometimes he'd have all the best kit and sometimes he'd just be sleeping under the stars, just talking rubbish, chewing the fat.

It took me back to my youth. Friends and I would grab our BMX bikes, stuff a sleeping bag and a tin of beans into our paper round bags and cycle off into our local woods. The river which ran through our town had carved its way between the fields and woods situated at the south end known as The Common. The years of erosion had formed steep muddy banks along the river. large trees which stood on top of these banks had formed makeshift roofs, exposing their roots which hung over muddy caves, caves that were created as the river cut deep into the banks. These made excellent camps. Fires were lit and tins of beans cooked in the embers as we talked about the usual things teenage boys talk about. We'd stay awake late into the night before falling asleep, only to be woken by the dawn chorus. In the morning we'd fold up our sleeping bags and stuff them into our paper round bags, before cycling to the newsagent's shop stinking of smoke to collect our papers for our daily rounds. Upon reflection, it sounds idyllic, an eighties version of Huckleberry Finn I guess! The summers were always spent at the river either camping or fishing, long hot days spent with good friends. This was a very happy part of my life, which was in stark contrast to how I felt now.

As I headed deeper and deeper into the YouTube rabbit hole, I discovered this whole new world of wild camping, I couldn't watch enough of it. I uncovered more content creators and the whole culture of "leave no trace". The concept of camping somewhere and not being discovered, leaving no trace you were ever there…a subculture known as stealth camping. Could I do this? Could I take myself off into the woods and camp without anyone knowing, leaving no trace? What would happen if I had a seizure? All these questions went through my mind throwing up hurdles. Until the thought process turned into what would happen if I didn't have a seizure? Could this be the escape I was looking for, could this be something I could do that wasn't too far from home? Something that would give me some confidence and help me start to repair the damage my mental health had suffered. There was only one way to find out!

It was then that the world was turned upside down; There had been rumblings at the beginning of the year that a virus which originated from China was spreading across the world. If I'm being honest, we didn't pay it much attention. To me it was just another Ebola or bird flu, something that was happening elsewhere. We would all sit watching the TV saying to each other how terrible it was, but we didn't really care. Then the infection rate suddenly skyrocketed and here in the UK people were dying. It was hard not to take notice of it now. Covid 19 swept across the world and we were now in the middle of a pandemic.

Governments across the globe scrambled to try and slow down the spread, but it was like uncontrolled wildfire. Hospitals were inundated with patients. A shortage of ventilators and face masks fuelled unrest and our National Health Service started to buckle under the pressure, with too many casualties and not enough equipment or staff. Then in March, twenty-twenty (and to try and slow down the spread of this virus and ease the pressure on our hospitals) the country was plunged into lockdown and the government shut it down. There was no choice. The impact of this lockdown had far-reaching ramifications which we are all still feeling the effects of even today, but the immediate effect was dramatic. My wife who worked in the airline industry was working from home, then she was furloughed and eventually put on notice of redundancy, the second time within two years. Now everyone was stuck in my self-imposed prison, with no escape, "Stay Home, Save Lives, and Protect the NHS."

We all suffered during this time, the uncertainty of all our futures lay in the balance. My wife didn't know if she would have a job to go back to. My stepdaughter was supposed to be taking her exams and I couldn't see my own children. I now had two cellmates, and whilst we all tried to make the best of it, I'm sure all of us found it extremely difficult. We did our best and soldiered on as we always did. Then in mid-May we got some good news. My wife would keep her job and there was a planned end to lockdown. I was also going to be able to see my daughters who I had missed so much. Covid hadn't gone away but we were starting to win the war. A vaccine was imminent and we all started to breathe again, (maybe a bit prematurely with the luxury of hindsight). With things looking up, I turned my attention back to the Great Outdoors, and in my mind, I committed myself to being better, a better me, a better husband and a better father. I was going to use my childhood love of the Outdoors to fuel this positive change in my mental attitude.

I didn't have much in the way of kit, and neither did I want any. I wanted to be old school, just sleeping under the stars and staring up at the universe. I bought a cheap camouflage tarp, a sleeping bag, a small titanium twig stove and mug so I could boil water. I purchased an army-issue canteen and then splurged on a nice new backpack to put it all in. And so, at the end of May on the spur of the moment and on a slight whim, I loaded up my gear and got my wife (who I think thought I was completely mad bonkers, although we all knew I wasn't as I had a letter from three psychologists to prove it) to drop me off at the lessor known entrance to our local forest.

I shouldered my pack and headed down the small footpath which dissected two pine forests in half. The path dropped down into the heart of the forest to a small wooden bridge which crossed a medium-sized creek. Bearing right I followed the creek until it narrowed enough for me to cross and headed up through the long grass to a secluded wooded area. In between the thick pines, I found a small clearing big enough to set up my tarp, which I did in a plough point configuration. One corner was tied shoulder high to a tree with some para cord (multi-strand cord covered by a thicker nylon outer and quite often used in the military) then the opposite corner was staked into the ground with a peg, which I had cut and whittled myself from a small limb of a fallen branch. This left the two opposing corners which again were pegged into the ground with makeshift pegs made by myself. My shelter was up. How did I know how to do all this? Well, YouTube, of course. Everything I watched I soaked up like a sponge and was now putting it into practice. It was early May and although sunset wasn't till around eight thirty p.m. the sun had just dropped enough for the light to start to fade. I sat listening to the sound of the forest, the wind gently pushing its way between the leaves and the occasional crack of a twig made by some small animal, possibly a deer. As the light slowly dissipated, I sat staring at the sky through the small opening in the canopy, waiting for the universe to reveal its jewels. Slowly but surely one by one the stars started to appear like diamonds thrown across a jeweller's cloth, to be inspected by an old man wearing an eyeglass to ascertain their purity. It was hypnotic. I could have sat there for hours watching the universe's free light show. I realised then that the universe and nature were far bigger than my inconsequential problems will ever be, and for a brief moment, I could see the infinite enormity of the entire universe in a single frame in my limited vision. It felt like a wave smashing away my problems. My epilepsy and anxiety crashed against the rocks and exploded into a million water droplets thrown into the air before falling and disappearing into a limitless ocean. I felt free and not mentally confined to a body where at any moment my soul would leave, causing the empty shell to crash to the ground wherever it stood. It was intoxicating!

I reached into my pack and retrieved a small black nylon pouch in which the twig stove was stored. Four square sides, a base and two small cross braces for the top which the pot stands on. I clipped three sides together then slotted in the base followed by sliding in the final piece. There it stood a four-sided titanium cube that stood about six inches high, slightly lifted off the ground by four small legs, a perforated grill at the bottom to catch the embers and open on one side so twigs can be slid in. The open top allowed me to feed in fuel from above through the cross braces which acted as the pot stand. I stared at it in all its glory, as if it were the gold fertility idol in the opening scene of Raiders of the Lost Ark. I hastily gathered up several handfuls of finger-sized twigs and set them down next to the fertility statue. Reaching into my combat trouser side pocket, I produced a large piece of silver birch bark, which I had collected from a fallen tree on the way in. Unrolling the birch bark silver side up I lay it flat on the ground, I unsheathed my hunting knife. This was the only piece of kit I had left over from my childhood camping days. How my mother ever let me have a knife that size as a child I will never know. I began to scrape the top layer of bark into a powder. When I had scraped enough to form a pile the size of a fifty pence (fifty cents) piece I pulled from my pocket a ferrocerium (ferro) rod. A ferro rod is cylindrical in shape and is commonly the size of a short pen. It's made of ferrocerium or auermetall as it's sometimes called and contains cerium and iron. Its low ignition temperature makes it great for starting fires. I placed the rod tip just in front of the pile of silver birch bark shavings, took my knife and with the spine firmly placed at the top of the rod, pulled up hard. A million hot sparks showered across the birch bark illuminating the small area like a mini firework. It was however not enough to ignite the small mound of bark shavings, so I reset to try again. This time I pulled harder exerting more upward force, creating more hot sparks that showered perfectly onto the neat pile of shavings. As the light from the mini-explosion faded, it was replaced by the gentle flicker of a small flame atop the birch bark shavings. It wasn't much, but to me, it was a significant moment, I had created fire!

I piled on some small twigs and soon the small flame was a small fire. Once I was confident that it wasn't going to go out, I carefully transferred it to the twig stove. I fed in larger twigs and watched as the contained fire grew, and as it grew so did my confidence; I felt an overwhelming sense of achievement. I was only going to boil some water so I could eat the curried noodles I had brought with me, but it felt more than that. I had unlocked something inside me. A reawakening. I had spent so long locked not only inside but inside myself, it was liberating to re-engage emotions and feelings again. For too long had I been sitting in the darkness of a self-imposed prison. I was now free, free to think and feel. There were no walls out here and my mind could wander just as my body could. I now know that to really go deep and think, you have to do it outside in an open space, not shut in or physically incarcerated indoors. You have nowhere to go and neither does your mind. My motivation had all but left me. I had been welded to the sofa and my mind couldn't travel any further than the living room. Nor did I want it to, that would have required some effort on my part which I wasn't prepared at that time to put in. I had been rotting in self-pity and couldn't see any way of driving out the soulless blackness that was eating into me. But that small flame sitting on top of a small pile of bark shavings was inspirational. With that tiny flame, I could have destroyed the whole forest, burnt it all to the ground. That's the power it had. Instead, I contained it, fed it fuel and it burned so hot the titanium stove started to glow orange the heat was so intense. I was going to take this very moment and like that small flame, I was going to contain it, fuel it and turn it into something that would melt metal.

I've found that usually anything you cook and eat outdoors tastes amazing, and the curried noodles were no exception. I wolfed them down with a hot chocolate and then slid into my sleeping bag. I lay silent staring at the red embers of the last small pieces of wood burning in the stove, listening to the ambient sound of the forest. I fell into a natural slumber. I drifted in and out of sleep, but not the kind you get at home when your mind won't rest or you're worried. It felt like a natural pace, a rhythm maybe as if I was in sync with the world. When I finally did awake with the birds, I felt completely rested, all be it a little stiff from sleeping on the earth. I lay silent, soaking up every last moment as the morning rays broke through the canopy, casting beams of light that fell randomly between the pines. It was then time to leave.

As I started to break camp, I felt that cold darkness again looming in the corner of my mind. But this time I held onto the image of that tiny flame. The flame I had produced from nothing but my own learning and a couple of tools. It wasn't bright but it was enough. I had been just a person camping in the woods enjoying the outdoors, not a patient who was sick or a man reliant on others who had to be ferried between hospital and doctors' appointments. That night showed me I could be (in certain situations) reliant on myself, breaking life down into its basic rudiments of water, food, shelter and fire. It was just one night, but it showed me I could be content with just the basics. All the other bullshit we're led to believe will make us happy like nice salaries, fancy suits and flash cars is just that; bullshit. Epilepsy, unemployment and the other pressures in my life hadn't featured once in my thought process during the past twenty-four-hours, until I shouldered my pack and hiked the mile or so out.

After crossing the wooden bridge and heading up the steep track to meet the road, I stood, leaning up against a metal gate and waited for my wife to collect me. It was still early and only the sound of the awakening forest could be heard, until a black SUV appeared in the distance, it cruised to a stop. I opened the back threw in my pack and jumped in the passenger seat. My wife asked how I had got on. How could I possibly put into words everything that had happened the previous night. I'm not sure how I replied. I think I just recanted a story of a deer that ran through the camp in the night scaring me half to death, which did happen. We chatted as she drove us home, but all I could think about was when I could go again. It wasn't going to be long.

The following week I was already planning another night out into the forest, but this time I was going to try and capture it all on camera and then (like my favourite content creators) upload it to YouTube. I had in previous years filmed, edited and uploaded some motorcycle trips I'd been on with several friends. It was a great way to remember the trip and by uploading it to YouTube everyone that went could watch it. So, I was no stranger to editing software and the procedure of uploading the finished article. I looked at it like a work project, something to keep me occupied. At that time, I was sporting a very large bushy beard and a full head of unkempt lockdown hair. It was mentioned that I was starting to look like Grizzly Adams (a character from an American TV show from the seventies). So, at the end of May twenty-twenty the "Big Grizzly Outdoors" YouTube channel was born.

It was great to not only be out again but also doing something creative with my time. Over the next couple of months, I spent one night a week out in the woods making short little YouTube videos. They were mostly centred around camping kit and just being in the outdoors, and people were watching and subscribing. I would always get a few positive comments and this spurred me on to keep going. I eventually set up more social media and a website where occasionally I'd upload a blog. I was filling my time with something positive, instead of loafing about feeling sorry for myself. I did have seizures occasionally while I was out but it never worried me, I was on my own who would know? I was also not too far from home and in regular contact should I need to visit the hospital. I'd also found an old mate via my newly created social media page who fancied joining me on some of my wild camps. This made my family more comfortable knowing I wasn't out there on my own, should anything horrible happen.

I had grown up with Paul, nicknamed Turtle (I have no idea why he is called Turtle). He had been unfortunate in the fact that he had never grown any taller past his thirteenth birthday. His short stature emphasized a unique waddle when he walked. He was and still is frustratingly antagonistic in his personality, which even more annoyingly he is completely unaware of. He has however got a heart of pure gold (which isn't in the best of shape and requires a built-in defibrillator to ensure it continues to work). He would do anything for you without hesitation or expecting any form of gain or reward, a rare trait in people today. Growing up he lived five doors down. Being a little older he would look out for me as a kid. It was Turtle who gave me my first-ever tent when I was thirteen! He had got himself a new tent and gave me his old one, which I pitched in my garden and slept in all through the summer holidays that year. He still lives in the same house at the end of my old street with his father and was always keen to get out. He had been a Scout and then a Scout leader, so his love of the outdoors was as strong as mine. He's a great friend and if it wasn't for Turtle a lot of my later achievements would never have happened.

I was starting to feel much better mentally. My wife was now secure in her work and I was convinced that things were finally looking up. We were going to get over this and come out the other end much stronger for it. Even though I was still having seizures and still signed off work, I had started looking for full-time employment. We'd even talked about potentially moving. Where we lived was fine, but my wife had moved into my house and we both thought we should have somewhere which was our house. I was going to get it all back, the job, the car, the money and a new house. I had a plan, and was for the first time in a long time excited about the future.

Then on the afternoon of September tenth two weeks shy of our second wedding anniversary and on my mother's birthday, my wife sat down at the other end of our brown L-shaped sofa and told me she was leaving me. I wasn't sure that I believed her. She said I should have seen it coming however I didn't, maybe because I had been so wrapped up in my own self-pity for so long, or maybe because we had been through so much already, I never thought she ever would.

She took her time to explain why, I understood everything that she was saying. It had been difficult dealing with my epilepsy for both her and her daughter. My wife and my mother had started to bang heads regarding my care, with my mum insinuating on several occasions that my wife's efforts were not good enough. On top of that my ex-wife was continually criticising the behaviour of my sixteen-year-old stepdaughter, thinking she was a bad influence on my daughter Grace, which she wasn't. And me? Well, I was burying my head in the sand and ignoring everything that was going on, leaving it all for my wife to take care of. Not just the constant grief that seemed to be circulating between her, my mother and also my ex-wife, but the running and taking care of the house. This was all going on whilst I was wallowing in my own pity party.

Looking back, I'm not sure that I was capable of, or had the cognitive ability to understand what was happening around me. I was just trying to get better. I don't think my wife understood the everyday struggle I was going through just to make it through the day, which I'm sure made me oblivious to her cries for help. My world started to fall apart again, I begged her to stay but she didn't. Nothing I could say was going to change her mind. That night she slept in her daughter's bed as she was staying with a friend. The following morning, she started packing. I left the house as I couldn't bear to watch her leave. In my mind she was packing an overnight bag and going to stay with a friend for a couple of nights. In the meantime, we'd talk and between us, we'd sort it out. I came back a few hours later and everything was gone, the furniture she had bought (except the sofa) and all of her clothes and toiletries. Her daughter's room was empty; they had even taken the bed. Nothing in it, nada! All gone within two hours. The house looked empty.

She had been my source of strength, and I always said to myself no matter how bad it gets we'll always have each other. We both hung on for several months, being together but living apart in the hope that we could resolve our issues, which were more external than internal. But as time went on, I slowly realised that it wasn't going anywhere. I had become a dirty secret, she was hiding the fact that we were still together from her daughter and friends, which to me spoke volumes and I was starting to wonder, not only if I still loved her, but whether I had ever really loved her at all. Looking back, she went through so much and held on for as long as she could. Maybe, I was the anchor dragging her down to the seabed with me and to save herself from drowning she had to let go. In the end, it was all too much and she had to do what was best for her and her daughter.

The heartbreak came and went reasonably quickly and whilst I didn't fall to pieces as I expected to, I turned the hatred and self-loathing in on myself. I didn't blame my wife for leaving, I blamed me and I tortured myself relentlessly. It was a strange time, I felt relieved from the pressure of being in a relationship. I felt that I was emotionally better off on my own, but at the same time, I was back to hating myself for letting it fail. I wasn't good at dealing with failure; I looked at everything in life like a competitive sport and I hated to lose. Then one day she popped in to say 'hi'. We chatted for an hour before she decided to leave. She hugged me, said goodbye as she normally did and walked out the door! I closed it behind her and as of writing I have never seen or heard from her again. If it had just been her and me then maybe we'd have got through it. However, the external pressures of having a blended family and the politics that go with that had finally cracked the dam and she couldn't hold back the water any longer. It wasn't long before I started to remove the pictures of us together from the walls and shelves of my home. Things were going to be different now I was living on my own, but I saw that as a new beginning and not an end.

I now had nothing, no career, no wife and the split had also affected the relationship I had with my children, which for me was the hardest part. I had however learnt a very valuable lesson. The very thing she said she would never do…she did. We had some great times together when the living was good, but when it got bad and times got hard, she chose to run away. She loved me when I was at my best and left me when I was at my worst. The failure of my second marriage taught me a valuable lesson, I will never again trust a person on the words they say. Love is just a word, but I've since learnt that it's your actions and not your words that truly show who you are and your love for somebody. I will also never, as long as I have breath in my body beg anyone to stay in my life again. If you choose to leave then the door is right there, but it only swings one way. At the time I wasn't sure how I was going to get through another breakup. Now, I'm glad she left me, because I never would have left her.

"When you reach rock bottom, the only way is up"

Living on my own now presented some challenges. In the event of a seizure who would be there to make sure I didn't say swallow my tongue or fall against a hot radiator? To an epileptic the house is a death trap with danger everywhere! I hadn't even thought about what would happen if I had a seizure and left a frying pan on the stove, or left something in the oven. It felt like there were booby traps everywhere and every scenario ended in pain, hospital and potentially death. I had early on after my diagnosis solved the problem of handling a boiling kettle full of water (which if dropped during a seizure could potentially cover you in scalding hot water) by purchasing a static water heater. Just stick your cup under it, push a button and hey presto you have a cup of near-boiling water for a brew. I didn't have to use the cooker as a lot of stuff could be heated up in the microwave. However, I did what most men don't do and went through the instructions for the cooker and learnt how to set the timer. So, if I was to have a seizure while cooking a roast dinner, for instance, I wasn't going to have the additional health problem of smoke inhalation or burning myself alive in a house fire. But to be able to keep more of my independence I was going to have to come up with some kind of alarm system. I did some research online and found a company that manufactured fall-alert wristbands. The device is connected via Bluetooth to your phone and in the event of a fall sends an alert to your nominated contact or contacts, along with your location. If the alert is not cancelled, it then goes to a national desk that will then call your nominated contacts to say you've had a fall. If they can't raise any of your contacts then the emergency services are called and sent to the GPS location of the wristband. My parents only live a two-minute car journey from my house, so can be with me quite quickly if alerted. I discussed it with my mother who thought it was a no-brainer and we purchased one along with the monthly subscription. I believe that this gave my family enough peace of mind and alleviated some (not all) of the worry about me living by myself. That wristband has and continues to this day to alert someone when I've fallen due to a seizure. As dramatic as it sounds this has probably saved my life, possibly on more than one occasion. It wasn't long before it was put to the test. Another seizure on the stairs, another alert sent to my mother from my wristband, another mad dash to my house, to find I'd fallen down the stairs again. Another call to 999, another ambulance and another trip to Accident and Emergency, and here I was again.

It was now the early hours of the morning, although you wouldn't think it as the lights in Accident and Emergency are always on. The sounds of heart rate monitors and mumbled conversations leaked from the cubicles around me. The squeaking of nurses' footwear on the polished floors would give me false hope that I was going to be seen, but they would mostly pass by, leaving me wondering when will it be my turn, like a dog tied up outside a shop thinking that everyone that comes out will be their master. As I lay on the hospital bed waiting for the last of the fluids to drain into my arm, reflecting on where it had all gone wrong, I decided it was time to start taking responsibility for my actions and just start trying to be a better person. I had to try with all that I had to turn things around. You make your own luck, right? Every time I thought that things were starting to go in the right direction, when I was just starting to get somewhere, the universe would snatch the rug from underneath me and give me the middle finger. I was now living on my own, with nobody to rely on and the safety net was at best, flimsy. The situation didn't look good from where I was lying. I had two failed marriages and I was an absent father. My daughters no longer wanted to stay at the house, I had no job, no money and I had uncontrolled epilepsy.

As the bag of fluids plugged into my arm slowly drained empty I lay, wondering what life was going to look like from then on. I was determined not to sink into another depression or feel sorry for myself, but I wasn't completely sure how I could prevent this from happening. One thing I was sure of, I was going to continue with the journey and not look back. Although each step may have to be small, I was going to make sure I learnt something taking every one of them.

"When you hit rock bottom the only way is up."

A nurse appeared and went about removing all the apparatus and cannulas, I was then free to go. I staggered out into the hallway in my joggers and trainers, covered in plasters from the cannulas and sticky pads from the ECG machine. I opened the door into the waiting area and found my mother and my uncle Peter (who had driven my mother to the hospital) waiting to take me home. I was lucky to have such a good family around me, especially in those situations. We all exited the hospital via the main sliding doors and into the cold night air of the carpark. I climbed delicately into the car and we headed home. My uncle Peter kept me entertained with funny stories about growing up with my mother and grandparents. This wasn't the last time he was called into action to bail me out of hospital, but he never complained once, or at least not to me anyway. I guess that encapsulates what real families do. They look out for one another.

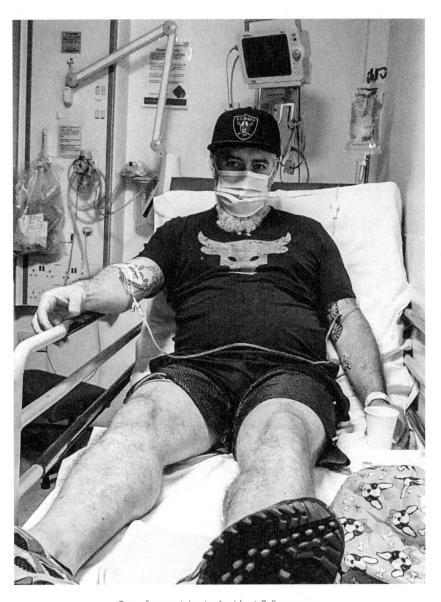

One of many trips to Accident & Emergency

Chapter 5

"If you can find adventure in everything you do, then every day is epic."

I never realised how hard the loneliness was going to be. We often think how nice it would be just to get some time on our own, but the reality is that we are as humans social animals, so spending a significant time on your lonesome can have a negative effect. Don't get me wrong. I'm very happy in my own company. Waking up in the morning after sleeping in a bed you're used to sharing and then spending the day on your own, waiting for the light to fade before you retire back to the same empty bed, is a dark existence. It wasn't that I was missing my estranged wife so much but more the company, the sounds in the house that other people make is comforting. You only ever realise this when you're the only person making any noise. Loneliness doesn't come from being alone, it comes from feeling that nobody cares. At least I had Lemmy, my fifty-kilo English bulldog. He was one of the only things that wasn't removed in the split when my wife left. Maybe it was because he moulted everywhere and could peel the paper off the walls with one of his farts. He also slobbered everywhere, but he was now my only companion. Whilst he can be very needy and a complete liability, I wouldn't be without him. He's my mate and would lay with me, protecting me whenever I was having a seizure. Mum would pop in most days to see how I was, but I was always conscious of what I said as to not worry her too much. Some days I saw nobody. Some days I sat in silence staring at a blank TV. I didn't feel depressed. I felt abandoned and I felt that was all I deserved, but I was (as strange as it sounds) okay with that.

I tried to keep myself busy most days and continued with my little adventures into the forest. The YouTube channel was slowly gaining subscribers and I enjoyed making these little films. The creative process of thinking up an idea, picking a location and then putting it all together and uploading it for the world to potentially see, was giving me a sense of purpose and fulfilment. I wanted to move on to bigger things, making videos of new bits of camping kit, or how to set up a poncho shelter was good but I wanted to make something real. I wanted to go to the mountains. I wanted to see the snow-capped peaks of the Scottish Highlands. The forest is great, full of nature and wildlife and I would lose myself in them at every opportunity. If my mind and body could be freed in a few acres of woodland, then what would the impact be of standing in hundreds of square miles of open space?

In my mid-twenties to mid-thirties, I had been a very keen rock climber and was lucky enough to travel all over the UK and Europe climbing. I climbed on the Gritstone crags of the Peak District to the Vajolet Towers in the Italian Dolomites, (made famous in the Stallone movie "Cliff Hanger"). I was also very lucky to climb with some great guys. We had a small clique of friends and were constantly planning trips away. We often found ourselves in the mountainous regions of Snowdonia in Wales or the Scottish Highlands, either hanging by our fingers on some famous route or just scaling the mountains like Ben Nevis or Snowdon. I was no stranger to the mountains. Mike, or Mad Mike as he was known, was the best climber in our group, a complete madman as the name suggests. I wasn't even sure whether he was a better climber than the rest of us, but he certainly had the biggest bollocks, ticking off some very impressive super-hard gritstone routes and putting up some first ascents. He always had some harebrained scheme in his head and a smile on his face. He was a bit of a joker with not a care or worry in the world, I liked that about him. Nothing was ever very serious to him, not even the climbing I don't think. After our return from a trip to Italy in two thousand and five, Mike announced he was going to try and be the first person to solo the Troll Wall in Norway, the biggest vertical rock face in Europe, a typical off-the-cuff Mikeism. So off he trotted on his tod to Norway. I had stayed in contact with him while he was away, however after a couple of days the text messages stopped. I had just assumed he was on the wall and was expecting to hear from him in a couple of days. I didn't speak to Mike again for quite a while.

During his ascent of the Troll Wall, a large piece of rock which Mike was standing on gave way and he fell, breaking his neck. He was eventually airlifted off the rock face by helicopter. The Norwegians were not wanting to leave what they thought was a dead body hanging off one of their tourist attractions. It was only after he was winched inside the helicopter that they realised he was still alive, barely. Mike would never walk again and was now paraplegic. He spent over a year recovering in hospitals in both Norway and then in the UK. During that recovery period, I and some friends pushed and pulled him up to the top of Mount Snowdon in his wheelchair raising money for charity. I never climbed hard again after that.

To this day Mike continues to be a big inspiration to me. He went back to university and completed his degree and then a PhD. Mad Mike is now Dr Mad Mike. Mike is at the forefront of protein development trying to find ways of using our proteins to heal ourselves of injuries and illness. Real futuristic stuff. He works out of his labs at the Institute of Biomaterials and Biomedical Engineering in Toronto, Canada. Whenever I think that I can't do anything, or I'm feeling sorry for myself or feel down about my epilepsy, I think about Mike and what he went through and what he has achieved. I always look forward to our monthly FaceTime calls and although he is now a responsible doctor, to me he's still a bit of an idiot! Over the last couple of years, we have grown closer as friends. Although my illness nowhere near compares to what Mike went through, I feel it has created a bond between us. Mike's adventurous streak continues to this day. A recent visit to the UK saw us catch up in the Peak District, where much to the annoyance of our partners we discussed the possibility of a paraplegic and an epileptic crossing of the Artic, reaching the North Pole on foot and sledge! That will either be another pipe dream or an epic adventure and material for another book.

So, with the spirit of adventure in my mind, I decided I was going to Scotland. I decided this all on my very own. Now I was single and living alone there was nobody to tell me what a stupid idea it was, which was then usually followed by the comment "In your condition". I wasn't however stupid. I was going to rope some poor unsuspecting person into this little jaunt North. My old gym buddy Paul (who was just starting to get into mountaineering) got the call, and he didn't take much persuading. Paul was a big lad, an ex-rugby player who had recently been competing in natural strong-man competitions, winning the world championship in twenty-nineteen. He cast a very intimidating shadow, with thighs made out of mahogany tree trunks and twenty-stone of pure muscle. He was and still is a good friend and I trusted him, which is key when heading out into the mountains, he was also extremely fit. We planned to hike up to the summit of Ben Nevis by the Carn Mor Dearg (or CMD as it more commonly known) arête route. A knife-edge ridge opposite the granite walls of the north face. From the summit, we would then drop down the south side of the mountain to a river called the Water of Nevis and camp by Steall Falls, a waterfall which was used as a location in one of the Harry Potter films. The next morning we would head east following the river until we reached a bothy (these are small stone buildings scattered throughout the region and used by hikers, climbers and mountaineers for shelter). After crossing a river, we'd head north, hike over a saddle between two Munros, finally stopping overnight at the Lairig Leacach bothy. The final day would be a hike into Spean Bridge finishing at the famous Commando Memorial. Paul was keen to get some training in, but I had climbed up Ben Nevis before by various routes including the CMD arête so I knew what to expect. However, what I didn't take into consideration was that I was now eighteen years older and two stone heavier! I couldn't wait to get up into the mountains and enjoyed the planning and prep for the trip. Then one evening in November twenty-twenty, we caught the train into London and boarded the coach for the overnight five-hundred-mile trip to Fort William, Scotland.

We rolled into Glasgow in the early hours of the morning to catch our connecting coach, which had been waiting for us to arrive. Our coach from London was a little late. Needless to say, the coach driver and passengers who had been waiting for over an hour were none too impressed, but we didn't care. It was all part of the adventure. As we travelled through Glen Coe towards Fort William, I stared through the coach window. The morning sun was cresting the snow-capped peaks. It was the first time in a long time since I had gazed upon the mountains. Light and mountains reflected into the lakes below as if a mirror had been laid out across the miles of moorland before these majestic monuments of stone. I refocused my eyes and stared at my reflection in the window. All that had happened, all the pain and hurt that I had suffered that I had kept locked away inside, I could now see in my own eyes. I was staring into my own soul. So much had changed that I hardly recognised myself; I wasn't the same person and maybe that was the point. Maybe that was the purpose of the journey. Not just this trip to Scotland, but the road I'd been walking and falling on for the last year and a half. I was getting better both mentally and physically, but I wanted to grow and learn how to be a better person. Maybe I was put on this path to get to where I needed to be, to learn what I needed to learn. But to get there I'd have to smash to pieces the person I had been before, only then could I start to rebuild and put myself back together again. I wondered if the physical and emotional pain I had suffered, was it all part of the process? The free-flowing thoughts in my brain sparked as the mountains slowly rolled past the window inviting me to wander in their space.

We pulled into Fort William station eager to get to our start point by the north face of Ben Nevis, not before we ate our own weight in burgers in the McDonald's opposite though! After our somewhat unhealthy lunch, we caught a taxi to the north face carpark. As the taxi left us, we shouldered our heavy packs and started on the slow climb upwards to the north side of Ben Nevis. Winding up through the thick pine forests we eventually crested the top of the path. Moving out of the forest, we joined the river Allt a' Mhuilinn. The world opened up before us and there in all her glory was Ben Nevis. On the right the steep rock walls of the north face, to the left the route upwards to the CMD arête.

The terrain was very undulating and we had to search for a while to find a flat spot to camp. After a time, we found a suitable area big enough. Before we knew it the tents were up and we were brewing coffee and eating MREs (meals ready to eat) out of the bag. There is something unique about being in such a vast open space, the smell of the air and the deafening silence. The way the light reflects off the mountains painting them in the soft glow of the afternoon sun, watching the light fade into dusk as the colours then change to a harder pallet, draining the saturation out of the landscape, mountains casting dark shadows across the glens. I was overwhelmed with the feeling of both wonder and amazement, but also feeling slightly wary at the same time. A good thing really as the weather can change quickly in the mountains. One minute you can be bathed in glorious sunshine the next shrouded in thick fog and rain with very limited vision. That's when it can go horribly wrong. I wanted to get some great film for the YouTube channel, so earlier on I spent an hour getting some fantastic aerial shots with the drone. I was having the best time in the most amazing arena with a good friend…perfect. As we slowly moved into night the first spots of rain appeared. We retired to our tents and I listened to the hypnotic rhythm of the rain bouncing on the nylon into the night, lulling me to sleep like a child's nursery rhyme.

The alarm on my phone woke me around five a.m. and I could still hear the light patter of rain on the tent. Without getting out of my sleeping bag, I unzipped the door and stuck my head out into the damp crisp morning air. It looked grim and not the sort of weather you wanted to hike a mountain in. I shouted across to Paul who I knew was already awake, as I could hear the clinking of metal pots and the rattling of a stove emanating from his tent. After a brief exchange, we decided to wait a couple of hours to see if the weather improved. I lit the Jet Boil stove in the vestibule area of my tent and boiled some water for a brew and breakfast, which was chocolate porridge. This was a homemade concoction of my own which consisted of porridge oats, powdered milk and a big scoop of chocolate protein powder all mixed in a silver Mylar bag. I have to say in all honesty it was like eating chocolate-flavoured wallpaper paste. The recipe needed some work. After breakfast I started packing up my kit, ready for the off and the start of our adventure. The rain had stopped and as I exited my two-man tent I looked up to the summit of Ben Nevis, it was now beautifully snow-capped. Whilst lower down in the valley it had rained in the night, up high that rain had turned to snow. It was epic! I hastily packed away the tent and stuffed it into my pack. Paul had packed away his gear, and as we hoisted on our packs we gazed up at the snow-covered cliffs of the north face to our right. To the left the CMD arête, which was hiding from us behind a damp mist, and so our journey upwards began.

We started to climb slowly, the packs were heavy and the thought did cross my mind that I was carrying too much. The terrain was easy to navigate and to walk on, but it was steep and after an hour I was struggling and needed to take regular breaks. Paul was moving well and I was conscious of the fact that I was holding him up. We all walk at a certain pace and we all know how frustrating it is when walking with someone slower. I thought my slowness would start to infuriate Paul, but he kept calm and was very supportive offering kind words of encouragement. The views were amazing and I wanted to capture as much of it as I could. It was a welcome break to get the drone out and do some filming, however, we couldn't spend too much time messing about. Time was ticking on. We carried on upward and soon hit the snow line. I was now suffering badly. It was clear that I was in no way fit enough. I had ignored all of Paul's advice about getting in some training and I was now suffering for it. The wind started to pick up blowing sleet in every direction. I was now taking two or three steps and then having to rest, anyone would have thought I was on Everest.

I kept trying to push on following Paul's footprints in the snow. Then all of a sudden everything went black. I came around and fortunately I was still standing but I was struggling to focus. I could just make out the bright colours of Pauls's jacket as he continued to make his way up to the arête. I was having a cluster of absent seizures and trying desperately to get control of it. I'm guessing Paul had turned around, seen I was in trouble and come down. As we both sat in silence a couple of lads who had passed us earlier in the day came back down off the arête. They told us the conditions were terrible and they had abandoned their attempt to summit. That was all the information Paul needed. He then made the decision that we should head back down. To my knowledge Paul has never once told anyone we backed out due to my lack of fitness or the absent seizures. He has only ever blamed the weather. A true friend. I wasn't disappointed that we turned back, but I'm sure Paul was, however, he hid it well and has never mentioned it. We would have to revert to our contingency plan.

We headed down the long descent back to the north face car park, both confirming that descending was just as hard as ascending, our knees groaning in protest. Moving through the snow and the mist it wasn't long before we could see the valley and the end of the snow line. We didn't rest at all. We just kept descending. We followed a mountain stream back down towards our original campsite, it was then that I had a little fall, Splash! Right into the stream. Paul helped me up and we had a bit of a laugh. I was lucky that I was wearing my waterproof kit. My boots although old still managed to repel most of the water, for now. We didn't hang about and kept descending passing a few weirs and a dam, after which we crossed a small bridge and entered the forest. The steep path that winds its way back to the carpark seemed to take longer than when we ascended the day before. We arrived at the carpark around dusk. I was completely spent. The plan now was to get a taxi to the carpark near to Steall Falls, where we would camp the night and carry on the rest of our route the following morning.

Faint lights of a car speared through the darkness; with no light pollution, the night was black. The taxi came to a halt and Paul jumped in the back leaving me to ride shotgun. We pulled away down the dark track, heading off to another carpark several miles away on the other side of the Ben. The taxi driver was very chatty with the topic of conversation centred on Scotland's handling of the pandemic. Our driver was very vocal about his thoughts, which were not very complimentary about his country's leadership. We swapped one dark road for another and began to work our way to the end of the track. We decamped, grabbed our kit, paid the driver and started to walk. It was pitch dark when we left the carpark. The beams of our head torches cut through the blackness exposing a narrow footpath. We ambled through the darkness crossing small springs that trickled over the path. In some places the ground dropped away sharply to the right and into the abyss. Eventually, we emerged into the valley on the south side of the Ben. From here we would start to look for some flat ground to pitch up. We headed east, head torches searching for a suitable campsite, like a cop slowly driving down a dimly lit street looking for a burglar on the run with his spotlight. Then, in the distance, we could hear the faint noise of water crashing to the ground. As we walked closer, we came to the realisation that it was the waterfall we were using as a marker for our second camp, although we were yet to see it through the blackness. We managed to find some flat ground, set up the tents, ate, then crashed. I then fell into the deepest of sleep. It had been an epic day. Although we didn't make the summit via the CMD arête, we still covered a fair few miles. We had adapted to our surroundings and situation and we had stayed safe.

The following morning was damp but clear; it had rained in the night but had stopped by morning. As we emerged from our nylon dwellings we were treated with great views of Steall Falls. To the north, we looked up to the south face of Ben Nevis, but our journey now lay to the east. We packed away our sodden tents and headed off. The ground was very damp underfoot and boggy. We had several miles to cover before our route turned south, so we squelched on as best we could. We soldiered on through the bog for a few miles keeping tabs on the map and of where we were, we didn't want to miss the right turn. It was however pretty obvious, the River of Nevis bore round to the right, like an arrow pointing us in the right direction.

Paul and I didn't speak much as we picked our way through the less boggy areas of our route. I guess we were both happy to listen to our own thoughts for a while. It felt like a slog and I was tired, tired of feeling tired. We crossed the river at the narrowest and shallowest part that we could find, then turned south looking for the saddle between the two Munros to the east. We eventually found the narrow footpath, which headed upwards between the mountains. We had a quick break, refuelled and then started to proceed up the slope. I was dreading this part! Any form of elevation was tiring and was no fun at all, but surprisingly it wasn't long before we reached the top, cresting the top of the saddle. The path descended into another valley, taking us towards the bothy. I had stayed in this bothy before, so through experience, I knew that it wouldn't come into view for a while. The sun had now dipped behind the mountains. We still had the evening light, but it now gave the valley a more sinister look. It was as if we were looking at the landscape as a black-and-white picture. I was keen to get to the bothy, get some hot food into me, sit and chat to my mate about the day, then retire to bed.

The track continued. As the light faded even more, there was no sign of the bothy. Had we got this wrong? Were we in the right place? Had we crossed the Munros at the right point? All these questions passed through my mind. I knew our navigation was good, so I shouldn't question it I thought to myself. Then in the distance just visible with the naked eye, at around half a mile away, a small brown square appeared at the edge of our vision. This had to be it, the bothy. As we got closer the small stone building with a slate roof and brick chimney came into focus. The area around the bothy was sodden, due to the proximity of the river. We squelched up to the large wooden door of the small stone dwelling, lifted the catch and went to open the door…it was locked! You are joking I thought. Just as I was thinking about using the twenty stone of muscle I had brought with me (namely Paul) to take it off its hinges, a voice from inside the bothy drifted out, "Hold on".

The door was unbolted from the inside and a small gentleman probably in his late fifties let us in. The dank smell of wet clothes seeped out. The clear starlit night was the only thing that illuminated the small square room. At one end against the entire far wall was a set of large homemade wooden bunks, the upper and lower just about large enough for two people to sleep on. Opposite the door against the back wall was a shelf, which had some old tinned food on it, on the wall itself a map of the area hung. To the right of the door was an old stone fireplace blackened by years of abuse, which on this occasion was not lit. The guy had taken the entire bottom bunk for himself, his kit and his dog. We asked if it was okay to stay and he was cool with it.

There was no light or electricity in the bothy, so we were reliant on our head torches to sort our kit out and square away our bedding. Paul and myself were going to have to sleep top and tail on the upper bunk. We got busy getting out of our wet clothes and into our dry ones, which gave us a sense of warmth and comfort. There was idle conversation between the three of us, but it couldn't have been that interesting as I can't remember any of it! I was tired, hungry and probably a little irritable. I decided to venture outside to get some water from the river, which I then filtered into a two-litre bladder bag. I then poured a quarter of this into my stove mug and lit the stove. As the sound of my Jetboil blasted away, I hung my wet underwear and wool socks on the makeshift washing line that was strewn across the empty fireplace. My feet had gotten wet earlier on in the day at the river crossing. I didn't much fancy the rest of the trip with wet socks and feet, that would be miserable. Water boiled over the cosied pot which sat on top of my stove, making a loud hiss informing me my water was now boiling, a bit like a whistling kettle perched on top of an Aga. I turned down the stove and placed a ready-meal bag into the simmering water to heat it up. I sat watching the dull flame light up the small area of shelf upon which it sat in a faint glow of burnt orange. I tried to tune into the conversation that Paul and the stranger were having, but I was too tired to make any significant contribution. I sat quietly on a rickety wooden chair eating my hot meal and drinking hot chocolate, my eyes feeling heavy and tired. The dim light within the bothy was fuelling my sleepiness. It wasn't long before I dragged my tired body onto the top bunk into my sleeping bag and then onto my inflated mat, I immediately fell asleep.

"STOP SNORING!"

I awoke rapidly, I had been in a deep comfortable sleep but was now thrust sharply into reality. It took a second or two to remember where I was, then a few more seconds to work out what was going on. Paul had no tolerance for people who disturbed his sleep, especially those who disturbed it by snoring. Now I know that I only snore if I sleep on my back or if I'm blind drunk and I was neither, so it had to be the old man. Paul fidgeted in his sleeping bag letting out a loud huff every now and again. The bothy slowly returned to a quiet peacefulness, just as you would expect sat in the empty valley of the Nevis range. Then in the darkness, the stranger again let out an unholy snore, as if the devil himself was in the bunk below.

"STOP SNORING" screamed Paul. If the old man was awake I'm sure he'd be shitting himself and shaking with fear now, the thought of the Hulk in the bunk above him spitting with anger wanting to rip his head off.

"What's the time?" I whispered to Paul. The phantom snorer below beat Paul to the answer

"It's twenty-five to five lads." Paul sat up in his bag and after a very brief conversation, we decided we would get a good start to the day and head off. We bolted into action, boiling water for a brew and stuffing sleeping bags into our rucksacks. We couldn't get out of there fast enough, swigging tea from tin mugs while getting out of our dry night clothes and back into our damp base layers. We knew it would be cold this early in the morning because of the clear sky the night before. With no cloud cover the cold air would sink into the valley making it even colder. We took our time layering up making sure that our clothing was all done up. Socks pulled up tight to avoid them rucking up in our boots, laces tied firmly with double knots so they didn't come undone, before putting on our gaiters which cover the tops of the boots and lower leg. We were packed and ready to go. Once again we shouldered our rucksacks and opened the large wooden door, exposing ourselves to the cold morning air. Just as we were about to step out the door a voice from the bottom bunk said "Errr sorry lads, it wasn't twenty-five to five, it must have been twenty-five to two. I misread my watch as I didn't have my glasses on." I checked my watch and it was two fifteen a.m.! I was standing behind Paul who was in the doorway, so I gave him a little nudge out the door just to make sure he didn't about turn and rip this guy's arms out of his sockets, which I am sure he was perfectly capable of doing. We were both seething!

"Fucking two fifteen, TWO FUCKING FIFTEEN" I kept repeating it out loud. The more I said it the more wound up I was getting; well at least we got a good start on the day!

The sky was still clear with bright stars guiding us up the road. After a while we both laughed about the old fart in the bothy with his dog and his brand new fluorescent Hoka hiking trainers. We both knew that they would be covered in shit by the end of the day, as he was heading the way we had come the previous night. The moment between night and dawn was now upon us as we continued our way up the wide track towards Spean Bridge. There was no sunrise as yet as it was still early, but the stars now sat on a dark navy-blue blanket rather than a jet black one. The mountains loomed above like they were painted in oil on canvas in blacks and greys. We moved through the valley, laughing and joking loudly about the morning's events, two solitary figures isolated in an arena of rock and stone. I didn't want to be anywhere else but exactly where I was at that time.

We rolled into Spean Bridge just as the sun was coming up. This small village didn't have much, just a small shop, a hotel and a train station. Paul went into the shop and purchased some drinks. I sat on the wall opposite feeling kind of sad that the trek was nearly over. We sipped on sugary energy drinks and then headed up the main road toward the commando memorial, which was about one kilometre away. The memorial was built to remember those commandos who sacrificed their lives, for King, Queen and country. The mountain ranges of Scotland were their training ground, so it was fitting that this fantastic memorial was here. I walked on ahead leaving Paul to take some pictures of the sunrise over the mountains. As the statue of the three giant commandos in full kit, which stood on top of a stone plinth came into view, I felt a surge of emotion and a few tears rolled down my grubby face. I'd made it. It may not have been an expedition to the far reaches of the world, but it had felt like it to me. As I stood in front of this amazing tribute to some of the bravest people who have walked the earth, I felt the warmth of the sun brush my face as it pierced through the cloud, casting a golden beam of light from the sky, as if to acknowledge my presence.

The journey back home was inconsequential compared to the last three days. It had not just been a geographical journey, but also (without sounding like a hippy) a spiritual one as well. We had used a map and compass to find our way between the mountains, guiding me along that dark path between negativity and hopelessness. Whilst not every part of this little adventure was enjoyable, it showed me that persistence and perseverance are rewarded with an overwhelming sense of achievement and success, which in itself is enlightening and highly addictive. I was going to come back to Scotland, I was going to be fitter, stronger, both physically, mentally and emotionally. It was time to let go of what has been before and of who I was, because I couldn't move forward holding onto the past hoping things would change. I left a part of myself in those valleys, the part of me that says "You can't."

Chapter 6

"I had over three hundred friends on social media, but I can now count on one hand the friends that call or sit on my sofa drinking my coffee, making me laugh."

I turned the key in the lock and pushed open the door, squeezing myself and my huge rucksack through the frame and into the hallway of my home. I dumped the huge pack on the floor, stepped out of my boots and headed up the stairs to the bathroom and turned on the shower. I sat down on the toilet seat waiting for the water to heat up. I felt overwhelmed with tiredness due to the overnight coach journey back from Scotland, but I was very lucid in my mind. They say alcoholics before getting sober, experience a moment of clarity. Maybe this was what I was experiencing. I decided there and then that I was going to start to take better care of myself. I had started the journey but I was only playing at it and not giving it my full attention. I was going to get back in shape and I was most definitely going to plan a return journey to the highlands. I wanted to create a clear path of focused effort with no distractions. I was going to try and let go of the past and only focus on the future. I was still somewhat tied down with some emotional baggage due to the split from my wife, but a line in the sand needed to be drawn. As the warm mist from the shower filled the room, I made a mental note in my mind. I was going to give myself twelve weeks to purge myself of all the shit I would feel from a break-up, then not give it another thought and move on. I thought back to that evening in the forest where I produced a small flame from a spark, which I turned into a small fire, which I contained and fed into a small twig stove until the titanium glowed a cherry red. It reminded me that from nothing you can create something. A controlled energy that, as long as you keep feeding it would burn indefinitely.

I undressed, stepped over the bath into the shower and washed the dirt, sweat and grime of Scotland away, along with my old life.

As the calendar days ticked by, we rolled into winter, and it wasn't long before the decorated Christmas trees started to appear in the windows of houses in the streets around my home. As I ran past the empty streets, the warm air I exhaled merged with the cold crisp air of the night and formed faint clouds of smoke, keeping rhythm with my pace. The twinkling of Christmas lights emanated from living rooms, splashing the pavements with a multi-coloured glow which guided me in the dark, like the landing lights on an airport runway. The whole town looked like a Dickensian scene. I ran only at night (and in secret) as the streets were empty and my anxiety was kept under control. If I had a seizure while I was running, I wouldn't have the embarrassment of a crowd of people filled with do-gooders reliving their favourite episodes of E.R. The training programme was going okay and I was highly motivated and committed, although I was at the time having quite a few bad seizures, which erased days out of the week. I was also suffering from the side effects of the anti-seizure drugs I was on and often felt tired and lethargic, but as my neurologist kept saying, we have to keep evolving the combination of drugs to try and hit that magic formula. It felt like a Chinese puzzle, a continuing twisting and rotating of pieces and secret movements to finally unlock the box. Motivating myself to get out and run, was much easier than motivating myself to take a handful of pills twice a day, knowing they would make me feel like shit. Shamefully I have to admit there were days where I just couldn't face either, the running or the pills.

But it was nearly Christmas and I love Christmas, especially the years when I have my two daughters for Christmas Day. During my divorce we had agreed that we would have them on alternate years. One year they would spend the day with their mother, and the year after with my family and me, and so on. Mum would always go overboard with the food and my brother Phillip who lived with my parents would help Mum cook the Christmas dinner. My brother Michael and his husband David would usually spend Christmas day with us on the years I had the girls. There was lots of banter, food and gifts and it was always a great day, probably my favourite family day of the year.

Whilst my attitude and outlook on life was slowly changing it would appear that my luck was not. Karma hadn't finished with me yet. Several days before Christmas I had a massive seizure, it was a full-on crash to the ground, out for hours, piss my pants kind of seizure. My mother had been alerted via the fall-alert wristband I was wearing and had rushed over, probably crashing through my front door like S.W.A.T knowing her! As I slowly regained consciousness I ran through my mental checklist. Am I alive, check? Am I in pain, check? Can I move, check? Everything seemed to be in order, other than some paralysis down my right side and a pair of pissy pants. My Mum asked if I was okay, I went to respond and…nothing. I could hear the words forming in my head but they wouldn't vocalise and exit out of my mouth, I couldn't even get my mouth to form the words. No matter how hard I tried I couldn't talk. Epilepsy had now robbed me of my speech. I tried for hours but the frustration was starting to make me angry, so I stopped trying. I didn't want the stress to bring on another seizure. I opened the app store on my smartphone and downloaded a text-to-speech app. I could at least now communicate, although I now sounded like the late physicist Stephen Hawking, which was a source of entertainment and made light of the situation.

It was the eve of Christmas Eve and my speech was slowly starting to come back, but every word was an extreme physical effort. A sentence would leave me physically tired and very frustrated. Even worse my mother was finishing my sentences for me which was so infuriating. Why would I bother arranging a sentence in my head, planning and forming the words in my mouth only to have someone then finish it? I've never wanted to, nor have

I ever felt the urge to punch my own mother in the face, but in those instances, I think I came close. I texted my daughters who were at the time eleven and fourteen, just to let them know what had happened so they wouldn't be too shocked when they arrived Christmas morning. In the end, a FaceTime conversation took place and they could see the difficulty I was having with my speech. As always, they were both very supportive and sympathetic.

Christmas that year was still the festival of food, drink and banter albeit just a little quieter than usual, which didn't detract from the occasion at all. As I sat at the festive table adorned with decorations and Christmas crackers with my daughters, brothers and parents enjoying our roasted turkey, another piece of the puzzle fell into place. Growing up in a one-parent family we had learnt to support each other, whilst we were not the type of family to openly display our affection towards one another, we shared a bond that was born out of hardship and tough times. As one moves out, marries and starts a family of one's own, you can sometimes forget where you came from. Many, many people drifted away and out of my life when my circumstances changed. People who I never thought would, did. That is when you see the integrity and fortitude in the people you surround yourself with. The ones, who portray themselves as selfless are usually the selfish I have learned. I often wonder if I had been that person, have I distanced myself from a friend or acquaintance at a time when they needed support, help and hope? I think I probably have. Now life was showing me exactly what that feels like. I realised at that moment all the support I would ever need in my life was sitting around that table. The ones that loved me unconditionally and would never leave.

I carried on training getting fitter and losing a little bit of weight and continued to get outdoors as much as I could, but I still didn't feel like I had a plan. I had an idea of where I wanted to get to, but how to get there was eluding me. I needed something to focus on, a goal that I could work towards. The actual solution was obvious when I thought about it. I was longing to get back to Scotland, but didn't necessarily want to head back to the Nevis range as I wanted to see other areas. As a kid I had a fascination with Loch Ness and the Loch Ness Monster. My grandmother had a book in her home which was about strange mysteries and featured stories on UFOs and ghosts, along with the fabled monster of Loch Ness. I pored over this book, fascinated that there could be a prehistoric monster living in this large body of fresh water. It was a no-brainer; I was going to Loch Ness!

Some research on the internet threw up some great ideas, but the one that stood out was a hike called the South Loch Ness Trail. The official route was around thirty-seven miles long and followed the east side of the loch from Fort Augustus to Inverness. This seemed perfect, not too strenuous, with great scenery, along with the added bonus of a bit of Nessie hunting as well. Again, I wouldn't be able to tackle this on my own for obvious reasons. This hike had some very remote parts, if anything were to happen, well the consequences didn't bear thinking about. A quick text to Turtle and much to my surprise he was in! A week later we had tickets booked on the overnight sleeper train from London to Inverness for the following October, a much more sedate way to travel than thirteen hours on a coach. This time I was going to be prepared; I was not going to be an unfit lump dragging himself around the Scottish countryside breathing out of his eyeballs. I was slowly getting fitter and healthier, but training was sporadic and not very consistent. It was mid-March, so I had around seven months to get out there and get some miles under my belt.

Mid-March also meant that my twelve weeks were up. The diary alert on my phone flashed up with the words "time to move on." In those twelve weeks, I had on occasion thought about the failure of my second marriage. The actual implications that it had on my life were negligible, the reality was I'd moved past it, almost without thinking about it. I didn't have any feelings other than some resentment of the whole situation in general. I did however harbour a deep-rooted hatred towards myself for another failed marriage. There was no sense of loss or ill feeling towards my estranged wife, in fact, most days it felt like the marriage never happened. It was easy to move on alone and I didn't have anywhere near the outpouring of emotion like I did when my first marriage collapsed. For some reason though all the hate that I had for myself was still there, buried within me. I was the reason my first marriage ended, but I was made to feel that the second was also my fault. When you're told you're no good for long enough you believe it. It's a hard road when the only company you have is yourself, and you don't particularly like who you are. I was however still pushing forward never giving in, I also didn't have any ties to a relationship that were going to stop me from doing what I wanted to do. I did feel lonely at times, I did feel sorry for myself. I apportioned some of that blame onto my ex-wife, maybe a bit unfairly. I wasn't completely alone, I had family around me and a few friends that stuck about, so in reality it wasn't all that bad. I had accepted and resigned that part of my life to history and wasn't going to let it affect my destiny.

During March of that year, I had a stroke of luck, my brother Phillip had been given a gym-grade treadmill! It was old but in perfect working order. He had put it in the garage at my parents' house and only used it a couple of times. There seemed to be an issue with the electrics in the garage, every time the treadmill was switched on it tripped the fuses for the house, so it sat idly doing nothing, gathering dust. This piece of equipment would be fantastic for me, it meant I could train harder but a lot safer. I was grateful for his generosity. So, one morning we threw it in my mate's van and drove it around the corner to my place, brought it in through the back door and set it up in the living room. That treadmill was a godsend. I set up a training programme and stuck to it, battering myself to near exhaustion on that thing daily. I was starting to feel fitter and healthier, both physically and mentally and people were starting to comment. I'd often bump into someone who I hadn't seen for a while and they would say how great I looked. Granted I had lost some weight and the lockdown beard and hair had been trimmed and cut. Bloody hell had I looked that bad the last time I had seen them…maybe I had! Maybe the way you look on the outside is a reflection of how you feel on the inside. Now I was feeling a lot better in myself, maybe I was looking better?

It wasn't long before the suggestion of dating was mentioned, however, I wasn't ready to start dating again; I didn't need the love of another in my life, it would only be another person that would potentially leave. Anyway, in all honesty, I wasn't such a great prospect for anyone. I had nothing. Who in their right mind would want to date a severe epileptic with no money, no job and no prospects? I dismissed the idea and carried on with the job at hand, which was getting in shape for The South Loch Ness Trail. I was sticking to my training programme on the treadmill, but was it enough? Then in the early hours of the morning when sleep was eluding me, I got up and thought to myself. "Could I hike ten miles with kit?" This was going to be the daily average mileage that we would need to do on the trail. I'd been training consistently and feeling like my fitness although not athletic was enough to tackle the task. I packed a daysack with some water, a first aid kit and a set of waterproofs and headed out the door. I would be able to track my progress via my smartphone and this would give me a benchmark to work from. That morning before the sun rose, I headed to my local forest, like Frodo on his way to Mordor.

The path leading to the forest was around a mile and a half from my home and I had to cross town to get there. This however wasn't so bad as it was still early in the morning and there was nobody about, so my anxiety was kept in check. It was cold and wet, although I wouldn't be cold for long, but it did mean that some of the forest paths were going to be mud baths. I slipped passed the dark terraced streets unnoticed. The world is different and exciting when you're the only one in it. I reached the end of town and picked up the path that would take me into the heart of the forest. I left the street lights behind and headed down into the blackness. The avenue of trees stopped any of the early morning light from penetrating the thin canopy. I wasn't at all worried about the darkness, or being alone in the woods. I'd been wild camping in these woods and making YouTube videos for well over a year now, so I wasn't intimidated at all by the solitude of the darkened forest. I had a rough plan of the route that I was going to take. I worked out that it was around two miles to the heart of the forest from home, that would equate to four miles, two there, and two back. All I had to do was walk a six-mile loop of the forest and then head home. It felt good wandering in the woods alone, especially in the twilight hours of the morning. I thought about stuff and worked through some things that were rattling about in my head. I found it very therapeutic, like I was taking all the darkest things hiding in my consciousness, then leaving them there in the blackness of the forest. It was gardening for the soul, pulling out the weeds, turning the earth and then planting flowers which I would water and feed in the hope that they would blossom. My mind was roaming, left free to wander down any path it chose.

It was about the six-mile mark when I noticed that my feet were becoming a bit sore, not painful, but sore enough to catch my attention. I wiggled my feet in my boots hoping that some blood flow would cure the problem, but as the miles ticked by the problem got worse. This was now turning from what was a fantastic moment of enjoyment and liberation to a test of endurance. I continued on with the pain slowly getting worse. Was I going to be able to make it home? With the six-mile loop completed, I headed out of the forest. With only two miles left to go, my feet were now very painful. I wasn't sure what was happening exactly but I was sure I had blisters. But I'm so stubborn I didn't give up, which can sometimes be my downfall. What I should've done is to stop, take off my boots and socks and act accordingly, like applying some first aid. I however did not. I chose to hobble the last two miles home in agony. I slumped on the doorstep of my house. I'd covered ten miles in four hours and five minutes, a terrible effort. Up until mile six, I was making good time, then it all went to pot. I took off my boots and then the socks. My feet were in shreds. Broken blisters had covered not only the backs of my heels but also the outside of both heels where the heel meets the sole. I sat in the living room feeling extremely sorry for myself, feet in a bowl of hot salty water gritting my teeth, eyes watering with pain.

This wasn't the greatest of starts, if I couldn't comfortably get around an easy ten-mile loop of my local forest carrying a small daysack, then what chance had I of hiking the entire length of Loch Ness carrying all my kit, tent, sleeping bag, spare clothes, camp stove etc. The negative thoughts and darkness started to slowly creep back, forcing out all of my confidence. I sat bare footed looking at but not watching the TV, hoping the air would dry out the leaking open blisters on my feet. The feeling of failure which was all too familiar to me was now consuming my every thought. I was starting to feel angry. Angry for being such a pussy. Angry for doubting myself and angry for being angry. I shouldn't be feeling like this, I needed to spin the whole situation on its head and learn from it. I finally concluded that as people in everyday life we don't always walk ten continuous miles over different types of terrain. Concrete paths, muddy tracks, steep hills and steep descents, all place pressure on different parts of the feet. Our bodies are generally not used to that level of impact. I limped over to my day sack which I had abandoned in the hallway, opened the top flap and removed my first aid kit. I unzipped the olive-green pouch and removed a roll of athletic tape and some lint-free gauze. I cut the gauze to the same size as the open blisters, rubbed a small amount of antiseptic cream on and then taped up my feet. I wasn't giving up; I was going to keep going, blisters or no blisters.

The following morning after breakfast I slung on a pair of shorts, pulled a pair of wool socks over my heavily taped feet and stepped into my US Marine Wellco boots. I made sure they were done up tight, tight enough not to allow my feet to move around in them too much, but not so tight that it would restrict blood flow to my throbbing feet. I grabbed a towel which was hanging off the bannister and proceeded into the living room and stepped onto the treadmill, which I had now nicknamed the "dreadmill". It represented, to me, hard work and sweat, which I never enjoy doing until the hard work and sweat was over. I wanted to see how my feet felt after a day's rest, and whether my taping effort would stand up to the rigours of sustained uphill walking. I set the incline of the dreadmill at five per cent and the timer for an hour. I felt certain that would be long enough to give me a clear indication of whether or not my feet were protected enough. After an hour the dreadmill ground to a halt. Taping my feet had seemed to work and more importantly hadn't made my feet any worse. I triumphantly stepped down of the dreadmill, took off my pack and sat on the coffee table sweating onto my imitation Chinese rug. Tomorrow I was going back out to redeem myself on the ten-miler.

It was still dark when I arrived back at my front door. The motion sensor light at the bottom of the stairwell had turned on illuminating the line of properties in the apartment block on the ground floor. I pushed the stop button on my watch and in the dim light read the time, three hours, nine minutes and twenty-four seconds. I'd knocked nearly an hour off the time from my previous effort, which I had labelled a complete failure. Even though I was exhausted, covered in mud and tired from the three-thirty a.m. start, I was ecstatically happy with my performance. Yes, my body was aching and my feet a little sore, but nowhere near the same state as they were two days ago. I opened the front door and was greeted by Lemmy. We sat on the step together, watching the world wake up, Lemmy licking the sweat from behind my ear. Eventually, we retreated indoors; I fed the mutt, had a long hot shower, took my medication and went back to bed feeling like I had achieved something.

I was treating my body as a machine, as long as I looked after it, maintained and fuelled it correctly it should perform at the level which I asked it. Pushing my body past what we conceive are the limits had never been a problem for me, but as I've got older, I have come to realise that my body needs more looking after and taking care of. I played a lot of sports at school and also played rugby for my town. After finishing and leaving school I then entered the world of rock climbing. I spent ten years pushing the physical limits of what my body was capable of before hanging up my harness and ropes. I had kept in reasonable shape throughout the years and a couple of years prior to my accident I had started bodybuilding, stacking on weight and muscle. All this had taken its toll on an already tired body. With the addition of all the knocks and bangs from the seizures I was having, I was now pretty banged up. I had started to get pain in my shoulders on cold damp mornings and my knees (although still pretty good) creaked and groaned as I got in and out of chairs. I now wake up sore most mornings until I get going; it seems that I always have a couple of ailments that are niggling at me. I used to be a super-fast, lightweight sports car, capable of extreme acceleration and speed. Now I'm like an old diesel locomotive, needing to be maintained daily, requiring a bit of love before it can be brought back to life, slowly building up to a head of speed. However, once it's going it's almost impossible to stop.

I continued on with the ten-milers over the forest, completing at least one a week. I was mixing it up with dreadmill work, this pattern of training seemed to work for me. I was also trying to be careful with what I ate, trying to fuel my body with good quality protein and carbs. It felt good to feel that tiredness you get when you're in training mode. My mental health was also improving along with my physical health. I'd committed to get in shape and in doing so had unlocked another door to a sense of fulfilment. I was spending time in the forest making YouTube videos, as well as out there training. I felt busy, and keeping myself busy was doing me the world of good.

The evenings, however, were still a lonely time for me. I'd try and stay motivated and positive but the lack of social interaction was making it hard. I didn't have anyone to share my day's news with. I was missing that "How was your day" moment, the interaction as you went back and forth sharing the highlights and conversing on the key moments. Idle chat that reinforced thoughts and feelings which you shared with a friend or loved one. I didn't need another relationship or girlfriend. I was not going to put myself out there to be rejected or open myself up to more hurt, but I desperately missed that text you would get as you sat down with your meal for one that read:

"Did you have a good day?"

It had been suggested that I try online dating, but I'd never done anything like that before and was, if I'm being honest very sceptical. I certainly didn't want to be part of the swipe left, swipe right brigade. I wasn't looking for an intimate relationship; I guess I just needed to increase my social circle. Inevitably when you split from a partner, you lose a certain number of mutual friends. This isn't always because people take sides. It's just the way it is. But the reality of this meant trying to meet new people is much harder, especially in your forties. I guess I had nothing to lose, if I made a friend maybe it would be worth it. So, one evening I looked at some online dating sites. I decided to pick a site that was maybe not so popular or well-known; a site that was specific to people that loved the outdoors. That way there was always an ice breaker and a topic of conversation, a common interest. I settled on a site, set up a profile, paid for a month's subscription and threw a Hail Mary into the end zone hoping a wide receiver would catch it.

I continued with my training and prep for the trip to Scotland, spending hours hiking around my local forest or slogging my guts out on the dreadmill. Turtle however was making excuses to not get out and train. It was always next week with him. He started work very early in the mornings and was understandably very tired in the evenings. We did however manage to get out some weekends for a bit of a hike and wild camp in the forest. Turtle would always take far too much kit, it was comical to see his two little legs poking out from below his giant bergen, then watching him slowly waddle along the footpaths. He looked more like a tortoise than a turtle. It didn't matter how heavy that pack was though he always made it. Not always in the greatest of conditions, but he always got there. I enjoyed wild camping with him. It was never boring and he always made me laugh, most of the time unintentionally, which made it even funnier. It was great to share that time with him, we'd either head deep into the local forest or head over to my friend's farm where we could have a proper campfire. We would grill fat steaks and cook baked potatoes in the embers. We'd eat till our bellies were fit to burst. After which we'd retire into our sleeping bags, coiled up like giant anacondas slowly digesting a meal. I was never sure what else Turtle ate, because whilst my belly was full of the fare we had eaten that evening; Turtle's was usually full of gas, which he would slowly release throughout the night in between his snoring. He maintains to this day he never sleeps well when we're out wild camping, but I would have to disagree as he's always fast asleep well before me, farting and snoring until the morning chorus of birds wakes him from his gentle slumber. He then moans like hell that he hasn't slept well and his back hurts, usually because he slept on a tree root! He then takes a piss and lights up the first of many cigarettes of the day.

It was around this time I banned him from cooking breakfast. I awoke one morning looking forward to a full English breakfast of eggs, sausages, bacon and black pudding. Even better that I wasn't having to cook it as Turtle had offered. I got the fire going by using the last of the glowing embers from the night before, unfolded the metal grate and placed it over the fire. Turtle emerged from his tent with a bag of food in one hand and a giant skillet in the other to cook it all in. It was shaping up to be the breakfasts of all breakfasts. Turtle placed the skillet on top of the grate and poured some oil into the pan to heat up, he then turned to carry on the conversation we were having. All of a sudden WOOF! The oil in the pan ignited, the resulting flame I'm sure would have been visible from the International Space Station. It was so intense I felt the heat from where I was standing approximately ten meters away. Turtle however was still carrying on his conversation. How could he not have noticed! It was like being in the path of a nuclear explosion! I interrupted him "Pan's on fire",

"Huh!" he replied

"PAN'S ON FIRE!" I shouted as the flames started to lick the overhanging branch of the ash tree we were camped nearby.

"FUCKING HELL!" he yelled, Turtle leapt into action, the fastest I've ever seen him move. He grabbed the skillet by the handle with both hands and carefully removed the towering inferno from the fire. He placed it on a clear patch of ground. As the heat died down so did the flames. Eventually, the fire extinguished itself. Turtle held aloft the blackened skillet. We bowed our heads in silence as we mourned the passing of the Teflon coating. "That was bloody brand new that skillet," mumbled Turtle before tossing it to the floor with as much contempt as if it was a bag full of dog shit. We both stared at each other before bursting into fits of uncontrollable laughter. I grilled some sausages and we sat eating them, backs against the ash tree, giggling about the morning's events, trying to decide whether we should give the skillet a proper burial.

Chapter 7

"The universe always amazes me, if you can believe it will happen it quite often does."

Online dating looked like it was going to be a slow burn. I guess this was because I wasn't giving it much attention and wasn't very hopeful of meeting anyone, if I was being honest. I would periodically check the mailbox on my profile. Whilst I did get several messages I didn't reply. I was starting to hate the fact that I was being judgmental and picky. I was looking for a friend not choosing a new pair of trainers on the internet. Some of these women may have been genuinely nice people, but I found I was dismissing them on looks and even on where they lived. This wasn't for me; I was tired of reading the same profiles over and over again, similar biography just different profile pictures. I'm not sure who these women were looking for, but the bar for most of them was set extremely high. If the perfect men they were searching for did exist, I'm sure they wouldn't be single. Some of the criteria and requirements that needed to be met or exceeded, were probably why some of these women were single in the first place. I gave up on the whole idea and decided that I was just going to let my subscription run out and not renew it. I was doing okay on my own.

The phone on top of the bedside drawer buzzed, alerting me to incoming email. It was still early and I was in that space between being awake and asleep. I picked up my phone and opened the email to see how full the inbox was with junk. Since being let go from my job the only email I now seemed to get was junk and bad news, that morning was no different. I sat in bed deleting the deluge of advertising material and spam, until I got to one that read "You have new matches". Ah, what the hell I thought. It was always entertaining to see how the dating algorithm had scanned the many profiles on the site and then picked my future spouse for me. This particular week (which happened to be one week before my subscription ran out) I had two matches, lucky me. The first one had no profile picture, which to me was a red flag, she either had two heads or was so bad with technology she didn't have the basic knowledge to upload a profile picture. Either way, it was a no! Yes, I know that's a bit harsh but come on. The second was a pretty lady called Emma; I clicked on her profile and read the blurb. It was pretty standard stuff as online dating bios go, however, it appeared she wasn't looking for a Mr Perfect like the many before her which was a good start. There was just a minimum height requirement, like a roller coaster I thought to myself. I assumed that maybe this was because she was quite tall herself. She was pretty and seemed interesting, however I exited the site, deleted the email and got on with the day, completely forgetting about the three minutes of amusement online dating had given me that morning. What I had failed to realise however was that when you click and read someone's profile, they are notified that their profile has been read and by whom. I knew this because Emma had been notified that I had read her profile and then she had read mine, of which I was then notified. This was now just prolonging the inevitable. In my mind I was thinking that now she's read my profile she wouldn't be interested, just as I hadn't been interested in those that had contacted me. This was the harsh reality of rejection that is online dating. I hadn't as yet messaged anyone or even replied to any messages that I had received. I thought sod it, I had nothing to lose. If I was going to get rejected by anyone it may as well be by someone tidy, like Emma. I had one week left on my subscription and then my profile would be deleted anyway, so who would ever know? I don't remember what I wrote to her, but it would have been very basic and uninspiring. I hit the send button, it felt like passing a note to a girl you liked in class.

The week dragged on. I was training very early in the mornings which allowed me to take my anti-seizure medication when I got back around eight a.m. I would then shower and go back to bed and sleep off the side effects, a combination of seasickness and overwhelming tiredness. I would doze in and out of sleep till around lunchtime, when I would get up, eat and wait for my mother to call in. She'd normally check up on me around two. It was a routine that was working, but as with all routines…well, it got routine. The monotony of training was broken up with appointments with the consultant Dr Chan and the odd visit to A&E after particularly strong seizures and falls. Even sliding in and out of the CAT scanner was now becoming very familiar and routine. I'd lost count of the number of times I had MRI's and CAT scans. Sometimes it was really hard to stay positive.

A welcome break from the monotony came one morning when I received a reply to the message I had sent Emma! Bloody hell she must be desperate if she's replying to me, I thought. Although she played it pretty cool, leaving it a few days before sending a reply. It was a short message that acknowledged my very bad effort at an icebreaker. The question now was do I reply? This may seem quite trivial to some, but when you've been through a horrendous divorce and then had someone just get up and leave you when you were at your lowest, you become very guarded and build huge emotional walls around you to protect yourself. Not just from new romantic relationships but from new friendships in general. But just having that communication lifted my spirits slightly so I replied. Over the next couple of days, a few messages went back and forth. We talked about the minefield that is online dating and generally just gossiped. It was great to have that moment of the day to share what we'd both been up to. All the correspondence had to be done through the dating site. I guess this was a safety feature and also kept you locked into your subscription. I however wasn't going to renew mine so I had a choice, just disappear into the ether or give her my number. That way it was up to Emma if she wanted to carry on communicating. I sent a message with my mobile number attached. She could then decide if she wanted to carry on communicating, if she did, and then turned out to be a psychopath, I could just block her. To my surprise at eight fifty-nine on a Sunday morning, I received a WhatsApp message from an unknown number "Hi it's Emma. Enjoy your day with your girls". Bloody hell a real live woman just gave me her number, I was genuinely surprised. It felt good to make a new friend, even if we were to never meet each other, just to have that little bit of contact was something extra in my day that wasn't there before.

Coincidentally, it turned out that Emma lived in the same town as me. I say coincidentally, this could have been one of the reasons why we were matched in the first place, that and the fact that I met the strict height requirement of course. Once we had both established this fact then what came next was unbelievable. Emma and I were the same age, although she was several months older than me. This then prompted the question about which secondary schools we both attended, as there were only three in the town at that time (and only one of those was co-ed). Amazingly, we went to the same school. Up until this point, neither of us knew each other's surname as it's not listed on the dating site. I asked Emma what her maiden name was. I couldn't believe it. After learning her surname, I realised that we were actually in the same form at secondary school together and had attended the same junior and infant schools together as well! Not only this, but she had worked in the baker's and the greengrocer's as a teenager right opposite the house I grew up in! It wasn't long before the school year photograph emerged and there we both were. Neither of us had recognised each other from our dating profile pictures. Out of all the potential people in the United Kingdom I could have met online, I was matched with a classmate from school, who also happened to live a ten-minute walk away from my house. The odds of that happening must be unimaginable. This was great, as we then delved into deep conversations about old classmates we still saw and teachers we liked and disliked. Over the next few weeks, we continued to talk via text and seemed to be getting on well, so I decided to go for broke and ask her if she wanted to meet. She said "yes".

Trying not to get too distracted I kept up my training schedule and slowly but surely my ten-miler times were creeping down, so were my five-kilometre dreadmill times. Everything was heading in the right direction with regard to my training. Although this kept me motivated and engaged, I was still finding life hard. Although this time it wasn't because I was depressed or miserable about my epilepsy or losing my job or even my wife leaving, living was just difficult. I am fortunate enough to live in a country where we have a reasonably good benefits system. I was on disability benefit, so yes, I was getting free money, but be under no illusion that it afforded me any kind of lifestyle other than survival. What I was receiving was still less than the government minimum wage for a forty-hour week. Inevitably as I headed toward the end of the month, I sweated the day my benefits got paid. I would walk the dog to my parents' house most mornings when I wasn't training, so I would get a free breakfast and lunch. As I got to the end of the month, it was sometimes a toss-up between paying the bills or the rent. My parents helped me out no end and Mum would often bring bags of shopping around and also leave money. It's a very unique feeling sitting at home wondering not when or what you're going to eat but if. My brother Michael let me piggyback his Netflix and Disney subscriptions so at least I could watch movies without the added cost. I classed that as a nice little luxury. It felt horrible having to accept charity from friends and family. It makes you feel like a complete failure, but if I didn't have that level of support, I'm not sure what I would have done or how I would have coped. During this time the YouTube channel hit one thousand subscribers. Outdoor companies would then on occasion send me kit to try and review. On particularly tight months I would sell these bits of kit on to Turtle, cheap. It worked well, he got some great kit for not much money and I would then have enough cash in the bank to be able to pay my direct debits. Every month felt like (and still does today) a hustle. I'd pretty much forgotten about the days of being able to afford whatever I wanted whenever I wanted and having nice holidays. I had taken it all for granted and now here I was living hand to mouth. I didn't and still don't feel like I am hard done by; I'm still a lot more fortunate than some. I look at it as another challenge, something that is helping to build and shape my character. If you are sitting reading this book then please know that I am very thankful to you for your purchase, I can now probably pay my water bill this month!

One thing about being skint is that your wardrobe reflects your financial position. I couldn't remember the last time I bought anything decent to wear. Most of my recent clothing purchases had been from online Army Surplus stores, cheap, recycled (good for the environment) and extremely hard-wearing kit for the outdoors, not what you would wear out on a date. It was a damp Sunday morning and I was due to meet Emma for our first (possibly last) date. I say first date, we were just meeting up in the forest so she could walk her dog. I didn't however want to go looking like an extra from Saving Private Ryan or Platoon. We were meeting around two o'clock. This was because she had been out drinking the night before with her sisters (of which there are three) and would probably be slightly hungover. I opted for jeans and a Fjallraven (high-end outdoor clothing brand) olive green sweater which I had got for free and a North Face body warmer. The right attire for a nice walk in the woods, whilst not looking like I was about to deploy to Afghanistan.

I walked the two miles to the forest carpark and waited for her to arrive. I was nervous and the thought did cross my mind of sacking it off and going home. But that would be quitting and I don't do that. Anyway, suffering a bit of rejection was nothing compared to what I had been through, so I waited patiently. It looked like she was running a bit behind schedule, which made me start to think that maybe she had sacked it off. She arrived fifteen minutes late. As she stepped out of her car, I recognised her instantly. All arms and legs, just as I remembered her from school. The years had been kind to her and it was obvious that she had taken good care of herself. I don't think she would have recognised me from school; I now had a head full of short grey hair and was sporting a rather large grey beard. I looked like a middle-aged Santa Claus before he got into mince pies and port. As she wandered over a tiny black dog came bounding up, I looked down at this little black fluffy thing sitting at my feet wagging its tail.

"What's your dog's name?" I asked

"Brian" she replied laughing slightly

"Brian", she had named her dog "Brian". The thought crossed my mind that if it was to get lost in the woods, we'd both be running around shouting "Brian, Brian!" and other people would assume we'd lost a child. We headed off up the path chatting like we had known each other for years, I guess technically we had. Emma was going through a tough divorce, I sympathised with her greatly as I could relate to some of the trauma that she was going through. We talked about growing up and what we had been up to since we both left school. She had two boys a couple of years on either side of my two girls. Emma had gone to the local sixth-form college and then to university. She had become a teacher and was now the Head of Primary at a special needs school. She had done very well for herself. Then we got onto the subject of what I did, which was part of the conversation I was dreading. Emma and her husband had done so well in life and both had fantastic careers, I seemed to be so far removed from that now. I explained my current circumstances. She listened sympathetically and was very empathetic. I can honestly say I didn't feel like I was good enough to date her, although she never once gave me that impression. I felt intimidated by her success and I guess I then subconsciously just started to sabotage the whole idea of meeting anyone…ever. Then to finish off our time together the heavens opened and big fat rain fell from the sky. I had no coat so I ended up getting soaking wet. Emma had cleverly worn a rain jacket, not the most glamorous of looks but she was dry. She's definitely the clever one. I walked her back to the car soaked to the skin. Then, as we approached her white VW Golf, she surprisingly offered to give me a lift. I said it was fine but she insisted. We laughed about the weather as she drove me home. As we pulled up I thanked her for a great afternoon and expressed how nice it was to catch up. I didn't expect to see her again. I thought we would remain friends and check in with each other once in a while via text, or I hoped that would happen. But in my mind, I had convinced myself that like most people the texts would slowly dry up, she would then meet someone and then that would be that.

I had always been very confident in myself and was never intimidated by anything, but I was now not so confident and lots of things scared me. The last couple of years had slowly sucked it out of me, leaving a shell of what I once was. I was so focused on getting better both physically and mentally that I dare not let anyone in. Nobody was going to destroy all the hard work that had got me to where I was at that very moment. Meeting with Emma had made me feel inferior, not because she had made me feel like that, Emma was great and that was the problem. I realised I wasn't finished rebuilding myself. I was trying to drive a race car before I could walk. I was not going to put myself in a position to feel like that again. I had nothing to offer somebody like Emma, I had ruined my first marriage and the ink had barely dried on the marriage certificate before the second ended. I was on benefits, I wasn't allowed to drive, I didn't have a penny to my name and I had epilepsy. Who in their right mind would take all that on? I decided that for my own protection and well-being to just be an ear if she needed it. I typed out a message thanking her for a great afternoon and that it was great to catch up. I ended with a polite invitation for dinner expecting her to either not reply or to decline politely. Unexpectedly she text back suggesting a pub lunch, next time the boys were at their dad's for the weekend. I had to read it several times to make sure I was reading it correctly. This was not how I thought things would go.

The following week I had a consultation via video link with a dentist regarding a tooth that needed to be extracted. I had been suffering now and again with a toothache on an upper molar. An emergency visit to the dentist revealed that it had to come out, no problem, actually yes big problem as it turns out. When you have epilepsy dentists are a bit cautious about poking around in your gob with their fingers, I guess just in case you have a seizure. A human can bite anywhere between one hundred and twenty pounds per square inch and one hundred and sixty, easily more than enough to remove any digits working away in your mouth. It was decided that I needed to have it removed under general anaesthetic, yet another complication. Everything in my life now seemed to be complicated, nothing was straightforward. But was it me making everything complicated, was I overreacting to every minor incident that was happening in my life? I was stressing myself out and stress is one of the major triggers that bring on my seizures. It was like a vicious circle, a self-fulfilling prophecy. I had to be mentally tougher and stop overthinking and stop overreacting. Life is tough for everyone. I don't own the patent on hard times and suffering. We all experience tough moments in our lives. I am not unique and nor did I want to be. I just wanted to be normal.

I was trying to make consistent progress, hitting little speed bumps and analysing my response, asking myself "is this the right reaction?" Most of the time we have no control over what happens to us, but we are in control of how we respond and react. I needed to learn to calm myself down, think before I reacted. When life slapped me in the face, I needed to get up, grit my teeth, dig deep and move on. Not run around complaining to whoever will listen that life isn't fair. "Newsflash" nobody else can do anything about it and most people don't care anyway. I trained hard, stuck to my routine and tried to be a calmer version of myself. What I learnt was, if you can suppress your initial instinct to a stressful situation, then as you move further away from the point of origin your reaction is a lot more sedate than if you were to react straight away. An example of this would be when my computer crashed one afternoon while in the middle of editing a video. I lost around seven minutes, which then needed to be reloaded and edited again. This equated to around three hours of work, importing the clips, editing them together, adding transitions, colour grading them and then rendering it all. As I sat looking at the blank screen I started to fill with rage. My next move would have been to explode! After the chaos, I'd probably have to ring around a few friends to see if anyone had a laptop I could use, as mine would be laying on top the garages adjacent to my office window in several bits. The stress would probably have brought on a seizure and that would have written off the day, probably the next as well. Instead of going ballistic I calmly left the office, went downstairs to the kitchen, made a cup of tea and watched The Punisher for an hour on Netflix. After which I rebooted the laptop, imported the clips and carried on editing. Yes, I lost some time and yes it was inconvenient, but just giving myself some space made me react completely different. In the first instance, I felt like the world had ended, after an hour I'd pretty much forgotten it had happened. I now see no point in wasting any energy on insignificant situations which you have no control over. Life is too short.

I was starting to see a connection, as my physical health and conditioning improved then so did my mental health, for once things were starting to look up. This started to play on my mind, because every time something good started to happen, sooner or later it would all turn to shit. I was busy training and getting ready for Scotland. The YouTube channel was doing well and Turtle and I were always out wild camping. I'd also been out with Emma several times, although I still wasn't sure what she saw in me or even if she liked me. She was a hard book to read. The upshot of all this was I was starting to feel a certain amount of anxiety creeping back into my life. I'd left myself open and exposed and it made me feel a bit uneasy. I guess this was understandable considering everything that had gone on before. I'm sure Emma's lack of emotion was probably derived from her husband leaving her. When someone leaves a relationship the other is undoubtedly left feeling that they were the one that failed, that it was their fault.

I had two choices really, embrace the world and all that it had to offer and maybe risk some failure along the way, or play it safe and remove as much risk from my life as I could. This sounded like a very lonely existence to me, almost like quitting, I don't want to be that person. I'd already taken some pretty significant knocks and always managed to get up so why stop now? I should learn from my failures and as I've said before perseverance precedes success. I mean what is the worst that could happen now? I could fall while out training? Well, I've fallen down a whole flight of stairs, several times in the space of a couple of weeks, I was a bit battered and bruised but I'm still here. I could find myself in a relationship with Emma and then she leaves? Well, I've been left before, it's shit for a few weeks, then each day after it gets a little better. We are often afraid of what we don't know. Once I'd figured out what I already knew, which was knocks and bumps heal and heartbreak over a girl is only temporary, there wasn't anything to be afraid of. And when you're not afraid you look at every opportunity differently. Now it was not if or why I should do something, but when and how. I realised that no matter what I did there were always going to be people who expected and wanted me to fail. The kind of people that would rather see me sat in the street with a bin liner of clothes, than see me enjoy any form of success, no matter how minor it was. The irony is, it's those people who get me up at four-thirty in the morning to hike ten miles through the forest. It's those people who push me through that final kilometre on a five-kilometre dreadmill run. It's great to have the support of friends and family, but it's the ones that want to see me in the dirt that fuel my 'fuck you' tank. The ones who want me to fail are the ones who make me succeed.

I wasn't the only one who was needing constant medical attention. In June my best mate Neil the Tash underwent a hip replacement and was convalescing at home, so I decided to invite myself over to keep him company for a few days. Being the great mate that he is he wouldn't have me travel on my own to Norfolk where he lived, so he sent Sarah his wife the two hundred miles to collect me. What can I say about Sarah? Well, she's a fantastically talented artist who sells her work in local galleries. She's quite outspoken, she swears a lot, she's a little bit mad, a little bit scary and she doesn't know how to work the sat nav in her Freelander.

Sarah pulled up outside my home and came in for a quick cup of tea before we loaded up the car and headed off. She'd had a little trouble on the way as her sat nav was set to avoid motorways, this meant she'd driven from Norfolk to Sussex without touching a motorway, coming through central London! She immediately blamed Neil for her late arrival, I agreed with her. Neil wasn't in the car and so he was the obvious choice to lay blame. The journey was a great way to catch up on everything that was going on; we were like a couple of kids. We gossiped about my new 'lady friend' and completely slagged everyone else off who we thought deserved it, and some who probably didn't. We laughed till we cried. It was a car journey I'll always remember and one that was over before I wanted it to end. We rolled into their driveway late afternoon. The house on top of the hill, miles from anywhere, a pimple on the ass end of the world. Norfolk is the flattest county in England and the only slight hill in that county has two houses on it, one of those is Neil and Sarah's. It's always windy there, I even think it generates its own weather. I walked in, made myself at home and made Neil make me a cup of tea, while I joked about his fragile state. It was good to be in the company of true friends. They really are like family to me.

I had known Neil the Tash (as I call him, due to his light ginger lip caterpillar) for nearly twenty years. We had come up together working for a very large American company where we had learnt our fieldcraft in consultative selling. When that company decided to close its UK operation, we both moved to the same company based in Scotland. Neil ended up being my boss, which meant I always felt I had to work that little bit harder, as I didn't want others to think he was doing me any favours.

I spent the week hanging out with Neil, taking the piss out of his limp and having a great time. We ate takeaways every night, drank our own weight in gin, and shot guns in the garden. I seem to recall Sarah putting a hole in the corrugated roof whilst firing a BB gun from the hip whilst trying to shoot a tin can off a ledge, Annie Oakley she was not. Neil in a previous life was an armed forces sniper and guns were his hobby. He took this hobby very seriously. I've always said that should society collapse and we enter the time of The Road Warrior (Mad Max reference) Neil's fort is where I would head to.

It was great to see my friends and to hang out. The evenings however were spent texting and having late-night conversations with Emma. I think we were both missing each other, but neither of us at that time was willing to admit it. The walls on both sides were slowly coming down, but both of us were very wary about entering into a new relationship. Looking back, I'm sure we both appreciated the other being on the fringes of each other's lives, a sympathetic ear to unload the day's woes. It was then suggested during one of these late-night telephone conversations that we should get away for the weekend. I couldn't quite believe this was happening. Dare I even believe for a second that things were starting to hook up and connect for me? I was so used to everything turning to shit in my life, I don't think I was prepared when the roses finally pushed through the manure and started to blossom.

Chapter 8

"Life is not fair; life can be cruel and life can suck the life out of you. But there are moments when the world will show you how beautiful it can be, especially with you in it."

Occasionally in life, you get a glimpse of what might have been, a peek through a dusty curtain at a possible future that you missed or somehow avoided. We all make thousands of subconscious decisions every day that all have an influence on our lives, most of the time we don't understand or know how important those decisions are. When bad things happen, we blame misfortune and when good things happen, we put it down to luck. We never see the possible outcomes of an event should we have chosen a different path. We never look beyond misfortune or luck when things go right or wrong, which they inevitably do in life. There is a certain amount of comfort in our ignorance.

I had almost forgotten about the day, that day when I had decided my life wasn't worth anything. The day when I thought my worth could only be measured with things. Such as material possessions, holidays, social standing and bullshit. The day when I decided not to be here anymore. Because lying on the floor having a seizure, or laying at the foot of the stairs in my own piss waiting for someone to find me, or waiting for an ambulance, or sliding into a CAT scanner, or sitting at home frightened to step out the door, or having your wife dress you because you were incapable of doing so was no life at all. What if my life had ended that day, what then? I was just about to peek behind the curtain.

Kayley Taylor is my cousin Allan's daughter, she's my first cousin once removed if you want the technical term. She's one of three kids with an older brother and sister. I knew them all but I didn't if you know what I mean. I had grown up with Allan as the family on my mother's side (Allan's aunt) was always very close.

Although he was a little older than me, we would quite often hang out together in our youth. As always once girlfriends, wives and kids come along we all drift apart as you have families of your own to look after. I'd bump into them now and again over the years at family occasions. I saw from afar as Allan's children grew from babies to toddlers to kids and then teenagers and so on. Then on June seventeenth twenty twenty-one, Kayley took a piece of rope, left her home and headed to a nearby playing field. She climbed one of the larger trees, tied the rope to a branch and hanged herself. She was fourteen years old.

Whilst Kayley was family, I can't claim to have known her, only that she was my cousin's daughter. I didn't know what music she liked or what her favourite flavour of ice cream was, nor did I have any idea why the world to her felt impossible to live in. Maybe I'm not qualified to write about this or her for that matter. Maybe I'm being selfish by comparing my own experience with Kayley's, after all, I'm still here and she's now sadly dead. I couldn't possibly imagine how her dad must have felt and is still feeling. As her world ended, I'm sure he feels his has too. The thought of anything like this happening to my own children is unbearable to think about. I attended the funeral, I looked at the tear-stained faces of family members and those of her friends. The devastation and broken hearts of those left behind who now somehow have to continue on with their lives without her. I stared at the coffin which was laden with flowers which spelt out her name. Would this have been what my funeral would have looked like, lots of crying and family members not able to understand why? Having to live the rest of their lives wondering whether they could have done anything to prevent this from happening. The reality was, there was nothing anyone could have done and nobody to blame.

I wish that I had known Kayley better. I wish that I had taken the time to speak to her at those family functions. I wish that I could describe her infectious smile from my own experience and not from the pictures in her obituary. I learnt after she had passed away lots of things about her, like her love for playing cards, her hatred of spiders and a love of Marvel movies. I wish I had learnt these things from her and not from reading them in tributes posted on social media. I learnt that she suffered terribly with anxiety, I can only assume that the anxiety was probably what pushed her over the edge. I wish I could have shared my own experience and struggles with anxiety with her, maybe even told her about my own near-death experience. I wish she was still here.

I wanted so much to have the right words to comfort my cousin and his remaining son and daughter. I wanted to let them know that I was there and that should they need anything just message or call. I didn't have the words. I didn't know what to say. It could have been my funeral. It could have been Allan thinking or saying those same things to my mother and brothers. I could feel the pain in his face as much as I could see it, then I could imagine that pain in my own mother. I was watching this all happen in front of me. Someone that I knew, people I grew up with and family members broken by the hole that was now left. I was standing on the outside looking in, wracked with guilt.

Looking back now and thinking about all the reasons I rationalised in my head for trying to speed up my exit from this mortal world, they were nothing. A set of misfortunate circumstances that over time would get better. At the time they seemed insurmountable to me and consumed every thought I had until I felt I didn't have a choice. Kayley was a beautiful fourteen-year-old girl who is deeply missed by those that love her. Although she will never know the legacy she leaves behind, it will always be a reminder to me that my life (like all life) is precious, and in some ways it doesn't just belong to me.

The sun grew warmer as the spring flowers started to wilt and summer was soon here. I have to say that whilst I enjoy the warmer weather, I feel that autumn and winter are my favourite months, why? I don't know. The school holidays came at the end of July and as Emma was a teacher, she would be enjoying six weeks off work. It was at the beginning of that six-week holiday that we decided to go away for the weekend. I felt quite nervous about the mini-break, I kind of felt like I was being tested. We had been getting on great and enjoying each other's company but both of us were holding back. I guess we both needed to open up a little and let each other see the person under the hard exterior shells, exterior shells that had been forged by failed relationships and broken hearts. I found this very difficult to do. I thought that if I showed Emma who I was then she would leave. Even though I'd unpacked a lot of my own 'baggage', I still harboured some resentment towards myself. If you don't like who you are, how can you expect anyone else to like you?

We booked a small shepherd's hut in Dorset and travelled by car the two and a half hours to the coast. I had the most amazing weekend. We sat drinking beer by the firepit outside of our small hut eating a pre-prepared ploughman's lunch. We laughed and joked and then sat in our wooden retreat watching the most horrendous rainstorm until we retreated, tired and a bit merry to bed. We didn't hold out much hope of getting out the following morning, but we were both surprised to see the weather had cleared up and the sun was trying to push aside what cloud was left. After breakfast we decided to head to the beach. We found a small cove not too far away. We enjoyed the good weather and spent time swimming in the sea. I couldn't remember the last time I had gone swimming. It's an activity that doesn't suit epileptics, you know with the likelihood of drowning should you have a seizure. The day melted away along with the world as we sunned ourselves on the beach.

That evening we ate at a local restaurant, enjoying great food and great company. This was what I had been missing, plugging back into society, connecting with someone and enjoying life. I was finding pleasure in the little things. The big stuff that used to fuel my drive and ambition no longer held any sway over me. A glass of cold beer and good conversation now meant more to me than a new car or a nice holiday. I was less angry; I wanted to embrace the world and not hide away from it. Hanging out with Emma was good for me. Looking back, I now believe this was when our relationship started to blossom and I started to believe in myself again.

Inevitably the summer came to an end. I started to feel the cold crisp air of the imminent autumn during my early morning training sessions in the forest. The trip to Scotland was drawing closer and I wanted to make sure that I was as fit as I could be. I was anticipating possibly having to help Turtle. He was not training and I knew that at some point on the trip, he'd start to struggle. I switched between long hikes in the forest and time on the dreadmill, building up my endurance and stamina. But was it enough? I didn't want to struggle in Scotland. I wanted to be able to soak up the environment and enjoy every experience. I knew from my last outing in the highlands how rubbish you can feel when you're not prepared; I didn't want to feel like that again. It was time to see if I was up to the challenge. I needed to test myself.

The south of England where I live is not blessed with many mountains in fact, we have none! What we do have is some very picturesque countryside, none more so than the South Downs. This national park stretches from Winchester in the county of Hampshire, all the way to the town of Eastbourne in Sussex. An area of picturesque countryside and chalk hills, which run east to west along the south coast, extending for two hundred and sixty square miles. Crossing the South Downs is a small footpath along a disused railway line called the Downs Link. The path starts near Guildford in Surrey and heads south for thirty-seven miles, finishing in the port of Shoreham by Sea. The link passes very close to the market town of Horsham where I live.

At the end of September, I decided to catch the train to the coastal town of Shoreham and hike back home along the Downs Link. I worked out from the Ordnance Survey map that it would be around twenty miles. I planned to hike this over two days. Day one would be around fourteen miles, finishing off the last six miles the following day. I had decided to do this trip alone, with no one to help if I had a seizure other than my fall-alert band, which would locate my whereabouts via GPS and alert my emergency contacts. This may have been a selfish act on my part, but I had to try. I knew I was fit enough; I just needed to find out if I was mentally strong enough to cope with the level of anxiety that I may suffer. I put on my Oakley sunglasses, plugged into my ear pods and shut out the rest of the world, as I journeyed up to Gatwick. I would then catch a connecting train south to Shoreham. Shutting out the world always helped to control my anxiety. It's not however always practical to do so, especially in places such as the supermarket. Walking around listening to Guns N' Roses whilst sporting a pair of sunglasses when it's dark outside tends to make you stand out from the rest of the shoppers, adding even more unwanted attention. On the train, as most commuters will testify, this is the standard uniform on any journey.

We rolled slowly into Gatwick Airport train station; I stood patiently by the sliding doors as we cruised to a stop. The doors slid open and I stepped out onto the platform and made my way past holidaymakers, who were either returning from or going on vacation. This was the first time I had been out on my own, properly on my own and I was feeling a little apprehensive, maybe a bit lonely. My connecting train pulled up to the platform, I stepped through the open doors, took off my pack, placed it on an empty seat and sat next to it. The train headed south carving its way through the Sussex countryside. It wasn't long before my destination came into view and it was time to see what I was made of.

Now you may be thinking that a twenty-mile hike in two days is nothing, and if you're fit and healthy you would be correct. But for anyone that has relied on other people for help and support for any reason for any amount of time, it's a big step to step out on your own. My little adventures into the forest had helped but I was never very far away from home. I was always in direct contact with a loved one, and most of the time Turtle was keeping me company. The challenge wasn't really whether I could cover the twenty miles in the time frame given, but whether I could hold it together mentally. There are lots of factors to consider, not just the threat of possibly having a seizure. I was used to that. I was going to have to deal with potential anxiety issues and the side effects of the medication I take, which often left me feeling sick, lethargic and with an overwhelming wave of tiredness. I have come to realise that doing anything when you have uncontrolled epilepsy adds another factor into the mix. It's a bit like when I was a kid and wanted to go play football (soccer) with my friends and my mother would tell me to take my younger brother. It's that feeling of being responsible for something or someone unpredictable. Should the worst happen, like they disappear or get hurt then it's your responsibility. You're the one who gets the blame. You're always on tenterhooks and you never relax, ultimately it breeds resentment. I did, (and still do) in those quiet lonely times resent my epilepsy, which then causes stress and more anxiety which usually triggers a seizure.

The weather was good. It was the end of September but this particular day it was warm enough to just be in a t-shirt. I headed out of the station and checked the map. The start point for the Downs Link back to Horsham was about half a mile away. I quickly worked my way through the streets and side roads of the small coastal town. The afternoon shimmered off the river Adur as it emptied itself into the sea. I crossed a busy road adjacent to a small roundabout next to a nice-looking pub/bar/restaurant. I thought how nice it would be to sit in the beer garden drinking an ice-cold lager. I have to admit for a few seconds I was almost tempted. A small wooden sign with blue lettering pointing to the north read "Downs Link". I didn't stop to mentally bookmark the moment. I just headed north along the path which ran alongside the river. It wasn't long before the sights and sounds of the town faded into the glorious green countryside of the South of England, a mixture of hedge-lined paths and trees which opened up on either side revealing the rolling fields and hills of the South Downs.

The miles passed beneath my feet with considerable ease. My pack although filled with all the necessities of an overnight camp felt like it was filled with feathers. After a few hours, the path found its way back to the river which meandered under a brick bridge, so I decided to stop. I dropped down the left side and leant my pack up against its brick-walled side, then walked to the river's edge to collect some water. I filtered the water and made a cold drink of army ration fruit juice powder, (or screech as it was called back in the day). This was basically orange-flavoured sugar and would keep you wide awake for most of the day. I'm sure many a battalion has rolled into combat with a big mug of screech inside them.

I sat staring at the water as huge majestic white swans glided down the river. I munched on a Snickers bar washing it down with an ice-cold screech. It was mid-afternoon and I needed to get moving, but I was motivated and didn't feel like this was a chore. I carried on along the wide path which soon carved its way through arable farmland. Corn was growing in the fields on both sides of the path. It was just about ready to be harvested making it much taller than I was. The close proximity made it feel like I was pushing through the cornfield itself, dwarfed by the crop that loomed over me which blocked out the horizon. As the cornfields ended the path opened out revealing the most amazing sky. The sun was setting, the world seemed to be ablaze with deep reds and oranges melting into the Sussex countryside. I stood for a time just soaking it up. Just me on my own. Nobody else was sharing this moment with me. I was alone and I wasn't anxious or scared at all. The light was fading fast and I needed to find a place to camp so I grudgingly moved on, a solitary figure silhouetted against a fire in the sky.

Further on the track closed in again. On one side was thick forest whilst on the other side more open fields that stretched all the way to the South Downs, which loomed in the distance. I moved off the path and down a steep slope into the woodland and found a flat spot to camp amongst the tall trees. I pulled my small one-man tent out of my pack and went about pitching it. The light was fading fast casting long shadows in the congested thickness of the woods. The small hiking tent was very quick and easy to erect and was up in no time. My thoughts then turned to food. I sat in the opening of the tent watching the metal military mug on top of a small hexamine cooker, the water in it slowly coming to the boil. Dinner that night was curried noodles with a big mug of hot chocolate. As I sat watching the last of the light vanish from the broken sky, I realised that that day would have been my third wedding anniversary. I felt a little sadness at this revelation and the reminder of the spectacular failure that was my second marriage, but I also had a feeling of pride. It had been just over a year since my wife had left and I felt proud of the way I had conducted myself. I didn't fall apart or resort to blaming anyone other than myself. I had chosen to get on with life, move on and work towards my own happiness. I had taken on challenges I never thought I would. I was looking forward and not back. I hadn't thought about my estranged wife for quite a while until that day, our would-be wedding anniversary. As I sat in the woods looking up at the stars flickering between the small gaps in the trees, my mind moved on to thinking about something else. It had just been a fleeting memory of somebody I once knew. The memory had faded enough that it now felt like it had never happened. I crawled inside my tent and then into my sleeping bag, took my medication and slipped peacefully into sleep.

I slept well that night and was only awoken by the birds calling to each other. It was still dark, just on the cusp of daylight. I took my morning cocktail of anti-seizure medication and hunkered back down to sleep off the worst of the side effects. Effortlessly I fell back to sleep. I awoke gently, but the warmth of my sleeping bag kept me in my slumber for longer than I intended. It was time to move on. Coffee and breakfast fuelled my motivation as I shrugged off the last of the nausea and tiredness from the medication. I folded everything away and stuffed it into my pack and before long, I was back on the path heading north, heading for home.

It was only a few miles and I ambled the morning away with my thoughts, the Downs Link path coming to an end as I came off the track and headed back to civilisation. As I walked along the familiar streets of where I grew up, I spotted my mother and stepfather waiting at the end of their street. They had been tracking me via my phone. I sat in my parents' house drinking tea, telling stories of rolling hills and amazing sunsets. In that moment, I finally realised that anything was possible, provided I committed and trusted my own experience and abilities. I was ready for Scotland and the South Loch Ness Trail.

It took a couple of days to get all my kit washed and cleaned ready for the trip to Scotland. I also ordered all the dehydrated meals and drinks for the trip, along with some energy gels. I wanted to pack light and not carry too much weight. This would make the miles a lot easier underfoot. I also wanted to make sure I was adequately equipped. I agonised over every detail and piece of equipment I was taking. I felt prepared both mentally and physically and was now just counting down the days. Then, ten days before departure things took a turn for the worse.

I awoke in the night with sharp agonising pains in my stomach, so painful that I lay in the foetal position with my arms wrapped around my waist. After an hour of agony, the gurgling started. I leapt out of bed and staggered into the bathroom. I just about made it onto the toilet before my body purged itself. I felt terrible. The night was spent repeatedly opening my bowels. By the time morning came I was sure there couldn't be any more moisture left in my body. The following day was spent in bed, in and out of sleep and off and on the toilet. I wasn't sure how this would impact the effectiveness of my anti-seizure medication. After taking it would it just be ejected out my rear end rendering it useless? I took it anyway in the hope that it would continue to work. The thought of having a seizure whilst harbouring a severe case of the shits was quite frightening. I was in terrible pain and finding it hard to get comfortable. The cheeks of my ass were now numb from the amount of time sitting on the toilet. I reckoned that I must have picked up a stomach bug or virus. Hopefully after a couple of days it would clear itself from my system. However, after several days, I was still no better. I was keeping the fluids up and I also refrained from eating for twenty-four hours. This didn't help as I was now just passing clear liquid from my rear end. I still had stomach cramps and I was now getting weaker due to the lack of food. I couldn't believe it! Of all the ways that I could potentially go out, S.U.D.E.P (sudden unexpected death in epilepsy) or a fatal bang on the head after a seizure, I was now going to end up shitting myself to death.

As the week went on, I slowly started to feel better, but could still only eat dry crackers, anything else would restart the violent shit machine. I was worried now that the trip would have to be cancelled. It would be irresponsible of me to go in the condition that I was in.

I couldn't work out where I had picked this bug up from. Then it occurred to me that I did filter some water from the River Adur on my hike along the Downs Link. Could I have not filtered it correctly and possibly picked up a water-borne virus or worse, a parasite? Very slowly I started to recover. I would still have bouts of diarrhoea, but the painful cramps had started to subside. In eight days, I had lost ten pounds in weight. I was, however, feeling better in myself and was confident that I would make the trip. I resisted the urge to take any form of Imodium, choosing to let nature take its course. The only real relief I got was from taking regular dosages of Pepto Bismol. This alleviated the cramps and pain. A few days before departure I started to expand my menu from dry crackers to white bread and potatoes, which for the most part, my body managed to process as it should. I made an appointment with the doctor just to be on the safe side. A stool sample proved that any nastiness that may have been present had gone, which was good news.

The final preparations for Scotland were done; I was packed and ready to go. I had organised for Emma to drive Turtle and me to the station the following day. It was almost time. I rechecked my kit list, made sure the route was saved in my phone and cross-checked it with the map. I don't think I could have been any more prepared. I went off to bed looking forward to the adventure ahead.

Chapter 9

"We are in some ways like magpies, always drawn to a shiny penny. I have since learnt that in our pursuit to collect shiny pennies, we are often blinded and unable to see what is really valuable to us on this earth."

I got out of the car, kissed Emma goodbye, grabbed my pack from the boot (trunk) and slung it over my body pushing my arms through the straps. Turtle was doing the same, but not with the same sense of urgency as me. He was trying to hoist his pack on whilst attempting to light a rolled-up cigarette, getting that last smoke in before boarding the train to London. He had this unique way of being unusually unorganized and clumsy in his attire and kit, but at the same time being overly prepared for any situation. Forgotten a piece kit? Chances are he'd have a spare to lend out, a walking talking oxymoron.

The journey to London was uneventful, a forty-five-minute train ride to Victoria Station and then the Underground Tube to Euston, where we would board the overnight Caledonian sleeper to Inverness. We had arrived in plenty of time and had a few hours to kill, so we decided to grab some much-needed fodder. Burger King was the choice for our afternoon fare as we sat on one of the many tables outside Euston Station stuffing our faces. Evening came as we sat people-watching and discussing the itinerary for the next couple of days. The overnight train would arrive in Inverness the following morning. We would then store our bags with our travelling clothes into a hired locker at Inverness Station. A bus ride to Fort Augustus would get us close to the head of the South Loch Ness Trail, but we would still have to walk roughly four miles to the start.

The sun was setting over London as we boarded the sleeper, its narrow corridors only just wide enough to move through with our packs on. We found our cabin and opened the door. I squeezed in with Turtle following behind. On the left were two narrow bunks. A small sink and window were situated at the far end. It became evident very quickly that I was going to have to sort out my kit first, then get on my bunk before Turtle could enter the cabin properly. Although small, our habitat for the night was more than adequate and it wasn't long before Turtle was on his bed scrolling through his phone, myself on the top bunk watching a downloaded movie. Then a sharp jolt alerted us that our journey had started. I watched out the window as the station drifted out of sight. The outside world then plunged into darkness as if entering a wormhole to another dimension.

It wasn't long before the eyelids started to get heavy, so I took my cocktail of meds and got ready for sleep. Turtle I assumed was already in the land of nod. I had followed his descent into Never Neverland from nodding off to a full-on coma by listening to his snoring get progressively louder. After ten minutes of trying to fall asleep listening to Turtle's violent snoring reverberating off the walls in our tiny cabin, I could take it no more. I took my pillow leant over the edge of my bunk, and smashed him in the face with it! Needless to say, this had the desired effect and the snoring stopped. Turtle however was none too amused by the manner in which I voiced my complaint. He rolled onto his side angrily stating that sleeping on his back was why he was snoring. This was a lie! Eventually, the medication pulled a veil of darkness over my eyes, and I too succumbed to sleep.

The morning sun shone a beam of light through the curtain of the window; bouncing rays of light off the chrome tap on the sink, filling the cabin with the dull natural light of morning. I sat up slowly, being careful not to bang my head on the ceiling as I slung my legs over the side of the bed. Placing my feet on the cold aluminium ladder I descended from the top bunk, leaned over the sink and pulled up the blind on the window. The rolling mountains of the Scottish Highlands eased by, framed by the small glass window through which I viewed. Every minute a new landscape would settle into view, all worthy of being painted and hung in some elitist art gallery or Royal household. We were here! We had arrived. I don't believe that any of my family on either my father's or mother's side has any connection to Scotland, but I feel in my heart that part of my spirit is here. Embedded in the solid granite of its mountains and Munros is a part of me. A kinship of mutual appreciation. This remote land of mountains, hills, lochs and glens does not give quarter or stand me nor anyone else for that matter easy passage through its beautifully harsh world. My journey is the same as everyone else's. You stand or fall by the same standard regardless of age, gender or ability.

The train started to slow giving us the nod that we were pulling into Inverness. Turtle had decided not to wonder at the splendour of the Scottish Highlands out of the window, but instead vented his anger about the unsatisfactory cup of coffee he had been served on board the train. I wanted to get out into the fresh air and mountains and all Turtle could think about was finding a Costa Coffee. This is just one of the many things that makes Turtle so unique. He is not at all impressed by anyone or anything. He appreciates life and the world around him, but he's not fazed or amazed by it at all. We opened the door to the cabin, dragged our packs out into the narrow passageway and waited by the door for the train to come to a standstill.

The green light flashed on the illuminated panel, I pushed it and the door opened. Turtle and I spilt out onto the platform with all of our kit. We slung on our packs and picked up our overnight bags and headed towards the station building. In the top corner of the concourse was a room which was filled with various-sized lockers. We stuffed our overnight bags into one, collected the ticket and exited out of the station and onto the streets of Inverness.

It was still early and the streets of Inverness were empty. Although it didn't feel cold the air had a certain crispness about it that you don't get in the south. We headed out along the deserted cobbled streets towards the bus station. It was a short walk and it wasn't long before we were standing outside of the bus depot, staring through the window. It was shut, due to open at nine a.m. We unshouldered our packs and sat down on a wide ledge below the large shop front window, waiting for opening time so we could purchase our tickets to Fort Augustus. As the minutes ticked by more people arrived milling about in anticipation, like racehorses trapped in the starting gate. We waited patiently for the doors to fly open. They eventually did a little after nine a.m. I expected a stampede but it was more of an amble as everyone filed in and started to patiently queue. Being the first in line I was first to purchase tickets. I gave Turtle his and we wandered over to the relevant stand and sat down in the bus shelter waiting to start the next leg of our journey.

The bus arrived shortly after and we boarded. We had the pick of seats as the bus was empty. Before long we were heading out of Inverness taking in the sights as we trundled slowly out of town. We would be travelling south on the north side of Loch Ness, along the A82. This gave us our first amazing views of the legendary body of water. None more so than when we passed the small village of Drumnadrochit and the famous Urquhart Castle. This famous ruin has been the background of a thousand Loch Ness Monster pictures. I love the legend of the Loch Ness Monster. I scanned my eye across the water, imagining the giant leviathan swimming just below its surface. Every ripple and wave caught my attention as I snatched glimpses through the gaps in the tree-lined shore. It was a typical Scottish day, overcast with chances of rain, but as we stepped down off the bus in Fort Augustus, none had yet to emerge.

I checked the map and plotted a route to the head of the trail. The adventure was about to start and my whole being buzzed with anticipation. This was short-lived however as Turtle announced he had a little turtle's head of his own to take care of, so we now had to find somewhere for him to have a crap. Surprisingly, we found some immaculately clean public toilets close by. So, with Turtle now a couple of pounds lighter we headed off. Adventure awaits!

The Caledonian Canal waterway flows up from Fort William into Loch Lochy and then into Loch Oich. Splitting Fort Augustus in two it then snakes its way into Loch Ness, carving its way through Inverness and into the Morey Firth, eventually emptying out into the North Sea. We crossed over the road bridge to the east side and followed the canal past its lock gates, small shops and cafes until it flowed into the south end of Loch Ness. It was only then when standing on its south bank looking north, did I truly understand how large this body of water is. It was like looking out to sea. The loch appeared to go on forever. Time was ticking on, but both Turtle and I took a moment to stand quietly and just look, absorbing it all in. The silence was abundant, apart from the sound of a light wind that crossed the loch and the small waves lapping over smooth pebbles on the shore. We could just make out Fort Augustus to our east as we followed the old military road towards Loch Tarff, where the trail officially started. We were slowly leaving civilisation behind us and heading out into the cuds.

Turtle was leading the way and it was always enjoyable watching his short stature waddling along, his rucksack covering his whole body with just a short pair of legs sticking out the bottom. He had one speed; a bit quicker than slow. But that was okay, because I knew that it didn't matter how he was feeling he would maintain this speed till his legs fell off. Even if he felt great his speed would still be the same, a bit quicker than slow. If he was about to drop dead, same speed. We trundled on upwards along the military service road until we hit a snag, well a high metal mesh fence to be more accurate.

We could see on the other side of the road Loch Tarff and the car park at the start of the trail, but weren't sure how to get to it. We travelled along the fence line which separated the road from the open fields we were in. I looked along the fence line hoping to spot a gate or a gap, but I couldn't see one, the fence just disappeared into the distance. There was only one option, we had to climb over. I could already see the sweat start to bead on Turtle's forehead. The look on his face was priceless! He said he was okay with this but his face said otherwise. Being six foot and an experienced rock climber, the fence posed no problem for me. I picked a spot by a thick wooden post, as this would give the fence some rigidity and made short work of its five-foot, pack and all. I stood looking at Turtle through the wire mesh from the comfort of my position. Turtle looked back, not amused at the task at hand.

Now Turtle is short and maybe a little overweight and in his fifties. He has several loves in his life, a love of photography, nature and the outdoors in general. He also however loves cigarettes and beer which I am sure at this moment in time he wished he didn't. He frantically looked up and down the fence line hoping that a miracle was going to happen and a gate would appear. It was no good! He was climbing…end of. In the spirit of friendship and camaraderie… I had left him to get on with it and was crossing the road, heading towards Loch Tarff carpark. However, I was lucky enough to turn around and witness the struggle that ensued.

First off came the pack, then lifting it off the ground like an Olympic weight lifter Turtle edged it up the fence, eventually getting it to the top. It was touch and go but it was now finely balanced on the thin wire on top. He held onto one strap and tried to lower it as far as he could down the other side. The pack weighed just over twenty kilos. Turtle's arm now bore the brunt of the entire weight of his pack, as the top wire dug into his armpit. It looked to me like a stalemate as he stood motionless on his tiptoes, pack dangling over the other side trying to drag him over with it. Even from where I was standing, I could see he was starting to shake. I'm ashamed to say I started to giggle. He eventually dropped the pack onto the soft grass on the other side of the fence. All that tension was now released like an elastic band stretched to breaking point before finally snapping. Now the difficult bit. Like a golfer practising his swing he placed his foot several times on and off the fence, psyching himself up I imagine. Then without warning, he went for it! Reaching up and grabbing the top of the post he jammed his foot knee high into the fence and stood up. The fence wobbled back and forth. Turtle wobbled back and forth. The other foot came up to meet the first and was jammed in alongside it. The wobbling intensified. Like climbing a ladder, he moved both feet up a notch and lent over the top wire, gripping the fence post like his life depended on it. I was transfixed on the action that was occurring and couldn't take my eyes off it. I should have rushed over to help him but I was frozen in the moment giggling like a schoolboy. Some mate I am! The wobbling continued and at one point I thought this might bring down the entire fence. Turtle went for broke and threw his left leg over the top wire, which then upset the fine balance between man and fence. "Shit he's going to fall" I thought laughing uncontrollably as he straddled the thin tight wire. He wasn't going to go down without a fight, nope not Turtle. He gripped that post with both hands and threw over his right leg to join the left. The right leg however did not clear the wire and appeared to be stuck, his knee resting on the top wire as he struggled to stay on the fence (ironic I thought as Turtle never sat on the fence about anything) as it tried to violently shake him off. Slowly the right leg was precariously dragged over to meet the left. He was going to make it! He stood for a few seconds, composed himself, then let go. He dropped to his feet, put on his pack and waddled across the road to meet me as if nothing had happened. I'd wiped the tears from my face by the time he joined me. He was sweating uncontrollably, wheezing heavily and understandably was looking a bit dishevelled.

"All right?" I said.

"Yep" replied Turtle as he walked on and through the gate and into the carpark, the official start of the South Loch Ness Trail.

We moved to the far end of the carpark dropped our packs and sat down to rest. I was still giggling a little from the events of five minutes ago. I undid one of the side pouches on my pack, reached in and pulled out my brew kit, then pulled out a small foam pad to sit on. The brew kit consisted of a one-litre army issue Osprey plastic canteen which nestled into a steel mug, which then nestled into a small dish. The dish acted as a solid fuel cooker and has a small wire frame which folds over allowing you to stand the mug on it. Flammable hexamine blocks are used in the dish, which when lit provide the heat to boil the water in the mug. Also in the kit was an assortment of hot drinks such as coffee, hot chocolate and some Cuppa Soups. I opted for soup. Turtle took the plunge, diving into making some soup also.

It was early afternoon and the temperature was dropping. This was compounded even more as we were now not moving. Coats, hats and gloves were dug out of our packs and put on as I sat watching the flames of my cooker lick the sides of the mug. I stared out onto Loch Tarff. I could only tell where the Loch finished and where the sky started from an island which drifted silently on top of the glass-like water. Its reflection made it appear larger than it was. A perfect mirror image of sky, clouds and island reflected in the flat calm water too beautiful to put into words. It was a perfect moment.

As the water in the mug boiled, I tipped in the powdered soup and began to stir. As I cupped my hands around the hot mug to warm them up the tranquillity was then shattered.

"MATE, OI MATE!" an English voice carried across the carpark dragging me from my moment, I stood up and looked over to see a man standing beside a running car at the entrance of the carpark.

"YEAH," I shouted back.

"YOU LOST A DOG?" I turned to Turtle who in turn was looking at me just as confused as I was.

"NO MATE" I responded; the guy looked around scratching his head. We were in the middle of nowhere; he paused for a minute and then shouted,

"LOOK I'VE FOUND THIS DOG IN THE CARPARK ABOUT HALF AN HOUR AGO. I'M GOING TO DROP IT OFF AT THE POLICE STATION IN FORT AUGUSTUS IF YOU SEE ANYONE WHO'S LOST ONE" he screamed. I nodded my head in acknowledgement and got on with drinking my soup. I watched as he drove out of the carpark and on down the road. That was random I thought. We finished our soup and packed away our kit, shouldered our packs and took a look at the map before heading onto the trial.

The trail was literally that. A worn path that steadily headed east and up onto open hills. No sooner had we started than a massive flock of sheep came over the horizon being herded by two border collie sheepdogs, it was pretty impressive. Bringing up the rear was the shepherd who had complete command over his dogs and therefore the flock. To see this work being done up close was amazing. I thought it may be worth mentioning the lost dog just in case someone was up on the hill looking for one. As we got closer the shepherd lifted his head, a gent's unspoken "all right". I took the opportunity to break the ice with "Seen anyone wandering about missing a dog?" The shepherd stopped, whistled and the dogs lay down and the flock was brought to a standstill.

"How come, ye braw yin?" he replied in a thick Scottish accent. Shit this was going to be a difficult conversation.

"A bloke found a dog in the carpark earlier and was looking for the owner," I said. The Scotsman looked a bit puzzled and paused for a second.

"That's wis mah dug, Tis a young yin,'n,' whin it gets a sniff o' th' trailer he bolts fur th' carpark 'n' whit's by th' Land Rover." I just about understood what he was saying.

"Well, a tourist has picked it up and he's now on his way to Fort Augustus Police Station," I said, which agitated the man even further.

"Fur fucks sake, a've hud a tit stowed oot o' that dug" he then reached into his jacket, pulled out his phone and made a call. "Cheers pal fur letting me ken," he said. And as he wandered down the hill, he stood the dogs or "dugs" up and the flock moved on. As we passed, I could hear him on the phone to his wife.

"That pumpin' dug run o' ti th' Land Rover again and some pumpin' Sassenach teuk it th' polis station, a'm aff tae be pumpin' late." I got the gist of what he was saying and sympathised with his dilemma. We headed up the hill and soon we were the only ones in view.

It was quiet, even the wind that funnelled through the valley and up onto the hills although present felt quiet. We were a few miles in and had already climbed up the track to where it levelled out. We wandered alone along the undulating path atop the hills. There seemed to be no civilisation in any direction, just hills and valleys. It was autumn and the first snow had yet to fall. The entire landscape merged into a cacophony of browns. The sky, although blue and draped in light clouds was losing its shine, its turquoise hue slowly turning grey in anticipation of winter. I stood on the top of a small summit waiting for Turtle to catch up. I took a moment to just enjoy the solitude. There was no thought of epilepsy in my mind; no thought of the pressures back home. I stood silent in the breeze, thinking everything would be okay. Sure, life had been challenging, but I was living it as best I could.

Turtle joined me on the hill and took a short break. He was struggling, but he wasn't complaining. We moved on, descending into a landscape of open woodland scattered with felled trees and fresh stumps. The deforestation was a visible sign the area's timber industry was thriving. The descent was quite steep and the trail was quite slippery. Several times I nearly lost my footing on the damp pathway. I looked behind to see how Turtle was faring, but he wasn't there. I waited for several minutes. Still nothing. I sat down thinking he'd come waddling over the brow any minute, but he didn't. I pulled out my phone and tried to call him but I had no signal. I was now getting worried so I got up and started to climb back up the hill, trying not to be a casualty myself whilst trying to find another potential casualty. I'd climbed about halfway up when a dark figure appeared silhouetted against the sky, it was Turtle. He hobbled slowly down to meet me. Taking his time, he navigated the steep path until he got within earshot.

"I fucking fell over!" he said angrily. He then proceeded to explain in detail how it all happened. Anyone would have thought he'd been trapped for days in the wilderness. Essentially, he'd tripped over. The weight of his pack had made it nearly impossible for him to get up. An upturned Turtle, laying on his shell, waving his flippers in the air. Eventually, he managed to get to his feet and tried calling on his phone, but like me, he had no reception. Anyway, disaster averted we soldiered on navigating the steep path down to a tarmac track that would eventually lead us into a small settlement, where we would cross back over the main road.

It was quite obvious after a few minutes that Turtle was suffering. He was unsteady on his feet and his face would now and again contort with pain. Whilst the recantation of his little trip was made out to be of epic proportion, he reported only a slight "twinge" to the ankle and a dent in his pride. We had covered approximately eight miles over some steep and undulating terrain. I decided to push on for another mile and then lay up for the night.

This would give Turtle time to rest up ready for a longer day the following morning.

The terrain levelled out and the track was easy walking for the next mile. We crossed over the Cumrack Burn River via a small wooden bridge and started to look for a place to camp. We circled around a couple of times before we found a small wooded glade close to the river. Pitching our small one-man tents, we settled in for the night.

The last light of day was still hanging in the air as we started to boil water for our evening dehydrated meals. Faint clouds crept across a blood-red sky as the blackness of night edged in. I started to unroll my sleeping bag and inflatable mat in my tent, making sure to keep all my kit neat and tidy. I had tried to scale down the amount of gear I brought to keep my pack weight light. This also meant I didn't have lots of kit strewn about all over the place. Turtle was doing the same, pushing his sleeping bag into his tiny one-man tent. His kit however was strewn across the entrance of his tent like an outdoor jumble sale. I couldn't help but think "How the hell did he manage to fit all that gear in his pack!" Like a time-lapse film, it slowly disappeared into his temporary abode.

Steam started to emanate from my mug indicating that the water was now boiling. I took the mug off the stove and poured the water into the Mylar bag of dehydrated food, stirring it in before sealing it back up. Turtle was still rummaging about in his tent, like a badger building a sett. It was dark and the small patch of woodland was now only illuminated by the light of our head torches. The quiet noise of the river winding past our impromptu campsite was the only sound. I finished my meal and began to get ready for sleep. I chatted intermittently with Turtle, retelling the story of his epic climb over the fence, the fence now growing in height as the story was retold. Turtled sparked up the last cigarette of the day and sat by his tent. Enjoying his smoke he melted into the scenery, his face only visible briefly as the cherry on his cigarette illuminated his face as he took a drag.

When I first pitched the idea of a trip to Scotland Turtle didn't need any persuading at all, he just said he'd go. He'll be the first to admit that he isn't in the greatest of shape or health for that matter, but he came anyway. And as I watched him disappear into his tiny tent, I realised that he is one of life's last true characters. A bastion of a bygone era, born one month before Neil Armstrong walked on the moon. He doesn't care what people think of him. He talks without thinking and doesn't care if that offends you. He's no slave to fashion and doesn't need his life validated with likes on social media. Nor does he covet material things in a desire to make himself happy. He leads a simple life on his own terms and is not influenced by others. He is unique and I feel extremely lucky to be able to call him my friend.

I felt a sudden pang of guilt as I remembered the time he took me abseiling. I was around twelve years old. Turtle (who was just a teenager then) and a couple of his friends "borrowed" some abseiling kit from the Scout troop he was a member of. We all went down to the river by my grandparents' house and set the rope up over a large brick bridge known as Cattle Bridge. It was the school summer holidays, we spent the day taking turns to abseil down the side of the bridge's brick walls, laughing and joking as kids do. I remember it being hot and the day just seemed to go on forever, like they did when you're a kid and having a great time. We spent the afternoon playing hide and seek in the corn fields over the other side of the bridge before heading home at dusk. As a kid, it was an amazing day. A great memory. As I got older, I saw less and less of Turtle. Eventually I moved into my own house and started a family. Over the years I would on occasion see him waddling down the street or in town, but I never stopped to see how he or his family were. I just carried on walking. I was living a different life, caught up in the corporate world of turnover, profit and loss. I would only associate myself with others like me. I probably thought I was better than him. He and his friends looked out for me when I was a kid growing up, like the older brothers I never had. Being the shallow prick that I was, I was only too happy to dismiss it all and forget about it, like it meant nothing. Yet here he was, looking out for me, making sure I was okay like I was twelve years old again. Those professional acquaintances that I held in such high esteem are nowhere to be seen now, I really got it wrong. I don't deserve to have a friend like Turtle. I give him a lot of grief about his health and lifestyle. I continually moan at him about his smoking and drinking, but it's heartfelt and out of genuine concern for him, because this new life that I am trying to build for myself would be a very sad one without Turtle. Loud snoring started to emanate from Turtle's tent, the pang of guilt quickly evaporated.

We slid gently into the Scottish morning as soft grey clouds slid across a dark grey sky. Turtle lit his stove which sounded like an F15 taking off from an aircraft carrier, breakfast being on both of our minds. I walked down to the river, collected some water to filter and soon had it on the boil for breakfast. Turtle and I were preparing the same; dehydrated scrambled egg and cheese. After pouring in the boiling water and stirring it in we then sealed up the bags, both waiting respectively for five minutes so the water could rehydrate the meal. I was starving and had already demolished a couple of peanut butter Clif bars. I couldn't wait to get stuck into scrambled eggs. Five minutes felt like five hours but eventually, I pulled apart the opening of the bag, eggy steam wafted out preparing my stomach for food. I dived in with my long-handled spoon and excavated a large mound of cheesy egg and shoved it into my gob. It took a second or two for the rubbery substance to circulate my taste buds. "Bloody hell," I thought "This is terrible". I couldn't taste the egg or the cheese. It just felt like warm rubber-tasting jelly invading my mouth, but it was food and I needed the calories. I sat quietly forcing myself to digest the horrendous mess, the consistency of rubberised goo was starting to prove difficult to keep down.

"What the fuck is this shit!" Turtle yelled out as rubberised egg flew out of his mouth. I started to laugh. I wondered how long it would be before Turtle would come to the same conclusion as me. He looked genuinely angry for a few seconds before he clocked me, rolling about with laughter. He too then proceeded to erupt in laughter. Rehydrated egg sprayed from both our mouths as we laughed uncontrollably. Eventually, we both composed ourselves. I let out a last little sigh and took a sip of coffee when Turtle quietly said "I feel like a gorilla just shit in my mouth". I sprayed coffee everywhere and kicked off another round of uncontrollable fits of laughter. Those dehydrated egg and cheese meals still haunt me to this day as a few bags made it back from Scotland. Now and again I will come across one in a cupboard and I have a little giggle to myself.

Turtle on the climb up from Loch Tarff

"Turtle" The legend himself

Chapter 10

The morning was starting to get away from us; we hustled to pack away our kit and then to get going. It was a mild day so no need for wet weather gear or jackets. We moved out of the shaded area of trees which had been our home for the night and out into the morning light and back onto the path. It was obvious straight away that Turtle had not recovered from his fall the previous day. He was in pain and it looked to me that any forward motion on his part was an effort. He gritted his teeth and kept going, as I expected him to do. We had around fifteen miles to cover that day and I knew he was going to feel every one of them. To pick up a slight niggle on a long-distance hike is horrible. Whilst not too painful to begin with, as the miles move on a small ache or pain gradually magnifies. Even a label on a pair of underwear can cause some discomfort over a long distance if it's rucked up against the skin.

The woods and streams gave way to what I can only describe as farmland. The gravel road we were now on was at least, for now, level and straight. This carried on for a few miles, passing several farms and outbuildings. Turtle was unusually quiet as we carried on our way. I managed to get him to take some ibuprofen which he washed down with an energy gel. This seemed to help for a while and he perked up slightly, but it wasn't a fix. As we got to the end of the gravel road, we took a break. While he was resting I unloaded his pack, stuffing as much of it as I could into my own. Hopefully, a lighter pack would make it easier for him to carry, he should at least then get to the next camp, which would be on the banks of Loch Ness.

I forced another energy gel into Turtle and helped put his pack on, before hoisting on my own exceedingly heavy pack. We carried on. However, Turtle was struggling to keep in a straight line. His bad ankle was making walking very uncomfortable for him. It was putting pressure on the good ankle as it was now bearing most of the weight. I desperately wanted to finish the hike but it was becoming all too clear that Turtle was not going to last another three days. I looked at the map and started to formulate a plan in my mind. We were several miles away from the picturesque waterfall situated in the village of Foyers. I was sure that a bus service ran from Foyers into Inverness. This was our best option. Turtle was struggling and I wanted him to enjoy his trip to Scotland and not look back on it as a disaster. My only dilemma was should I go with him or did I dare carry on, on my own? I kept the plan to myself and tried to motivate Turtle with words of encouragement. I thought that if Turtle knew that his nightmare was ending at Foyers, he'd start to slow down. If we took all day to get there then that would be the end of my hike as well. I wasn't sure what to do. I desperately wanted to carry on, but I was scared of doing so on my own. All my old anxieties started to creep back in. What would happen if I had a seizure? Those feelings of being useless and not being able to look after myself made me feel angry. I was pissed off at myself. I'd worked so hard to get into shape both physically and mentally and I hadn't even managed to get halfway through the hike. It wasn't Turtle's fault that our adventure was coming to a premature end, it was mine. I was letting myself get overwhelmed with the thought of failure. This black hole that was forming in my mind was sucking in all of my motivation and discipline. All the planning and expense of getting to Scotland was for nothing. Why did I bother? I didn't want to finish the route sat on a bloody bus, and I hated the fact that I had to rely on someone to keep me company while I did something as easy as a hike along Loch Ness. I was now falling back into being a victim. All my confidence left me and I resigned myself to the fact that my life from now on would be adventureless. I would catch the bus to Inverness with Turtle, find a hostel for a couple of nights and then catch the train back to London. The YouTube channel would get deleted along with everything else. Big Grizzly Indoors I don't think would work as a concept. I had big ideas and dreams, but I must have been out of my mind if I thought that I could achieve any of them. The darkness started to fill the corners of my mind and I now didn't care. Epilepsy had won...again.

I looked at Turtle as he carried on through gritted teeth and determination. He was in absolute agony and still thought that he was hiking to Inverness. I didn't want to carry on now and couldn't wait to get into Foyers, catch the bus to Inverness and head to the pub for a belly full of beer and food. I'd given in and I didn't care. I quit.

How easy it had been to talk myself out of carrying on, using Turtle as the excuse. I had validated the easy option, the path of least resistance and all because I was scared. I'd been in much worse situations before, life-and-death situations. The type of situation where making the wrong decision means you would not make it home.

Way back in June two thousand and five, I had travelled to Italy to climb in the Italian Dolomites. There were several routes that I and the friends I went with wanted to climb, but the main climb would be Cima Catinaccio, a three thousand metre summit which had five hundred meters of vertical climbing. The five-day trip culminated in an attempt to climb the monster slab of rock. The day started well and my climbing partner Stuart and I made quick progress up the first few pitches. Mad Mike was climbing with another of our friends James just ahead of us. We would meet at certain points on the route and have a laugh and a joke, all testosterone fuelled banter. As the day wore on, we didn't see Mike or James anymore as they had backed off the route, (which we didn't know at the time). The day got later and later and we ran out of water. It then started to get dark and cold. The last pitch to the summit was a large wide crack in the rock known as a chimney. This shielded us from the wind, which by now had picked up substantially. We came out of the chimney in the pitch dark, left exposed in cold high winds on top a knife-edged ridge which led to the summit. I remember thinking that I might actually die. A strong gust of wind from the wrong direction and we'd both be hurled off the ridge and into the air, until we hit the ground five hundred metres below. We gritted our teeth, didn't panic and moved slowly along the ridge to the summit. We then made the long abseil down in stages in the dark until we reached the bottom. At no point did we quit. It didn't even cross our minds. We just thought "Oh well! This is a bit shit. How are we going to get out of this?"

I was again now in an awkward situation that I didn't want to be in, but whilst I was feeling shit mentally, physically I was feeling great! I wasn't tired, nothing ached and I was in good shape, (other than dragging myself downwards into the pit of despair). I was quitting, but I didn't want to quit. I'm not a quitter. I'm a stubborn asshole that will stand firm. I could win any war of attrition for no other reason than out of sheer bloody-mindedness. I'm not giving up. I'm not going home to tell people I failed. No bloody way. Once I had decided to carry on, on my own, I started to feel much better. Life is too short to fill it with regrets I thought.

We were getting close to Foyers and I was now really worried about Turtle. He could hardly walk and was looking terrible. I kept expecting his internal defibrillator (a device implanted into his chest to jump start his heart if it were to stop) to kick in and give him a kick in the ass. It never happened, but I must admit I was slightly curious to see it go off, in a macabre sort of way. I expected it to be like something you'd see in a cartoon. He'd get slower and slower and then BAM! A bolt of lightning would hit him and he'd be revived and reinvigorated like the Energizer Bunny.

The sound of falling water gradually got louder as we neared Foyers. Turtle could barely walk by now. The weight of his pack was too heavy for him. Add a twisted ankle into the equation and understandably moving was excruciatingly painful. He limped along the stone bridge, crossed the river and stopped to look at the small waterfall of Foyers.

Turtle slowly dropped his pack to the ground. Relief was written all over his face. As we stared into the crystal-clear pool watching the waterfall break its surface like a stone falling through a mirror, I delivered the news.

"Mate, I think your hike is over. The terrain from here starts going up, even with the best will in the world I don't think it would be very sensible for you to continue." Turtle looked like he had just won the lottery. "I think you should catch a bus from here into Inverness, then try to find a hostel. I'll meet you in Inverness either tomorrow or the day after depending on how far I get today." The look of relief on Turtle's face confirmed to me that it was the right decision to make. Turtle didn't even have the energy to reply. He just nodded in agreement. The amount of effort to walk from the previous night's campsite to here for him was immense. I don't think many would have been able to complete the eight miles we hiked that morning in the same condition.

I left Turtle still standing on the bridge propping himself up against its stone wall and catching his breath. I picked up the pace and headed northeast and through the village of Foyers. I was now on my own, isolated from the chaos of life and moving under my own steam.

Upon leaving the village the trail moved upwards and onto an old road that cork-screwed its way up into a forest. It was quiet and the tall pines that surrounded me on both sides closed in, like I was being held by mother nature. It was as if the trees and the surrounding fauna knew my fate and were gently ushering me through its world. Loch Ness seemed a world away from the Scottish pine forest I was now climbing through. The quietness was only broken by the gentle breeze that whispered past the trees or the odd call of a bird trying to attract another. I was in another world, a world with just me and my thoughts. Effortlessly I swallowed up the miles.

As the forest started to open up and the land started to level out, I decided to stop for a brew. It was great to take the weight off the feet and just relax for a moment, absorbing the environment, fading into it and becoming part of the scenery, of which I was now in a symbiotic relationship with. I sat, leaning back up against a large pine and slowly sipped a mug of hot coffee. Time stood still and I just sat, waiting, for nothing. There was nowhere I needed to be, no one I needed to see and nothing I needed to do. My time was my own. I could have sat there all day if I wanted to, pitched my tent and watched the sun set through the breaks in the canopy. I did however want to get on. I was enjoying my solitude and my loneliness now felt like a privilege rather than a punishment,

Coffee break over I moved on. It wasn't long before civilisation came into view. I navigated my way through the small village of Inverfarigaig and continued to head north-northeast, catching glimpses of Loch Ness as the trail moved closer to the edge of this mysterious body of water. The track seemed to move from a dirt path to a logging road as it carved its way through an area of deforestation. A left turn saw me once again head steeply upwards, skirting the forest and passing small streams that trickled from above. I checked the map and could see that I was now starting to climb back up and away from the loch. I would, however (after reaching the peak) then descend back down towards the loch, on the infamous Fair Haired Lads Pass.

The logging road continued up and as I looked around, I thought I could be anywhere. I could have been hiking on a logging trail in Northern Canada. It was picturesque. A combination of natural beauty and man in perfect harmony was there to see, working the land for mutual gain. The timber provided sustainable building materials for the world and injected life into the local economy, while logging allowed for new regeneration, promoting biodiversity in tree species which enhances wildlife habitat. When managed correctly this industry encapsulates self-sustainability.

The road seemed to go on forever. I was now feeling the miles of incline in my legs. I came upon a small stream that ran down the side of the track; this had created a small pool in a ditch by the side of the road. I took the opportunity to collect water and filtered a couple of litres into two water bottles, before once again continuing upwards. I was isolated and alone, miles from anywhere and loving it. Don't get me wrong, Turtle is great company and I did feel saddened that we were not going to finish the hike together; however, I was now on my own adventure. I wasn't worried about having a seizure; nobody was here, who would know? I'd fall over, wake up, feel terrible, maybe be a bit bashed up but I'd manage…somehow. There was freedom in that thought, an escape. My seizures are more worrying for those that care about me than they are for me; I have come to live with the inevitability that at any moment one could happen. I never witness my own seizures and hardly ever have any recall of them happening, other than slowly fading back into consciousness. So it's understandable that those close to you want to protect you. This however can sometimes be stifling. I was now free and loving every minute of it, I was feeling a happy kind of tired.

As I reached the top of the logging road, I took a moment to catch my breath. My pack was feeling heavy, but I had plenty of daylight left and wanted to make the most of it. A blue sign pointed up towards a track which came off the road, it read "Fair Haired Lads Pass". At last, I was now heading downwards instead of upwards. The pain in my thighs from hiking uphill would soon be replaced with pain in my knees from hiking downhill. The track cut between some trees before opening out and revealing spectacular views of Loch Ness. I stood in awe. I was high up looking down across the water. Urquhart Castle on its plinth on the far shore stood out in all its glory.

It didn't seem that long ago that I was welded to my sofa, losing the will to live and disenfranchised with life. Looking and feeling terrible I had been slowly giving up on the world. I felt that the universe hated me and past misgivings were the reason I was being put through unrelenting torture. But here I was, standing, alive and still breathing, looking across at one of the most famous scenes in the world.

It was then that it all came out, the dam I had built to hold back all my emotional pain broke and I cried. I cried the type of uncontrollable sobbing that doesn't stop. I was releasing all the hurt, rejection, anger, self-loathing and pain. It just poured out of me. Here on a hill overlooking Loch Ness my body finally decided it was time to start healing. I was overwhelmed with emotion and it was relentless. I was reliving the last couple of years all over again and then purging it from my soul, releasing it into this wide-open space. It was being drawn out of me like poison from a wound and when it was over, I felt different, relieved, the metaphorical weight I had been dragging behind me for the last few years felt a lot lighter. It was like the universe had opened up a space for me to exist in again. I wouldn't call myself a religious man, however in that experience I felt that I was given permission to let it all go, to forgive myself and to allow hope to enter back into my consciousness. Although this outpouring of emotion paralysed me, I felt it was cleansing me also. Some may say it was divine intervention, others may say it was just being in that particular moment and space. Standing there alone, my body decided to free the mind of all my misery. Whatever it was, something happened to me right there on that hill that I can't explain.

I'm not sure how long I was standing there but it must have been a while, as I suddenly became aware that the sun was now getting lower in the sky. It was time to descend to the eastern shore of Loch Ness. I snapped a selfie and started the descent. I've never spoken about that moment to anyone, until now. Later on, after returning home I was showing Emma the photos of the trip, upon seeing that selfie on top of the Fair Haired Lads Pass she said "You look happy and content".

I edged down the pass turning left and then right as I negotiated the switchbacks. The terrain was steep and I remember thinking that I was glad to be taking the trail from Fort Augustus to Inverness and not the other way round. It would have been murder to be travelling up the Fair Haired Lads Pass and not down as I was doing. After what seemed like an eternity I popped out at the bottom of the track and onto the main road that runs alongside the loch. With Loch Ness now on my left, I wandered slowly along the path next to the road and started looking for a spot to camp.

On top the Fair Haired Lads Pass

As soon as a gap appeared in the fence, I moved off the path and into the small wooded shore of the loch. A small footpath ran between the trees and after a few minutes of walking a natural open space came into view. It was obvious that this area was used a lot for wild camping, as fire scars and the odd can were scattered about. The ethic of leave no trace is evidently lost on some of those that had enjoyed the space. I decided to carry on a little further along the water's edge to see if I could find somewhere a bit more secluded. Soon a great spot presented itself, a small clearing on a raised mound right on the water's edge, it was perfect. The tent went up and I carefully arranged my sleeping bag and mat inside. It was then time for dinner.

The light was starting to fade as I tucked into my dehydrated meal. Lights from buildings on the other side of the loch started to blink like coloured stars as dusk appeared. The water lapped against the shore and a gentle wind rustled the leaves of the trees, nature's lullaby was rocking me to sleep. I'd covered nineteen miles that day and was now staring out across Loch Ness. It seemed surreal. I watched dusk turn into night and when I couldn't see the water's edge from my tent, I decided to slide into my sleeping bag. The temperature had dropped and it felt good to entomb myself in the warmth. I lay there with the door open just staring out into space. The twinkling lights across the loch were now much brighter in the blackness. Car headlights in the distance would look like shooting stars as they passed the few lit buildings. The water was dark, like a black mirror that extended into the distance. Now and again the moon would reflect off the water and highlight the tips of the small waves. I was tired but I didn't want to miss a second of this experience. I tried to stay awake but nature's lullaby had other ideas and eventually coerced me into sleep.

I awoke to the relaxing sound of the water lapping against the shore. I lay for several minutes just enjoying the solitude and warmth of my winter sleeping bag. The previous day, as I emerged from the cuds and into cell phone reception, I started receiving texts from Turtle. He had made it by bus to Inverness and had found a great hostel to lie up in. I reached for my phone and sent a text to Turtle stating that I would be at the hostel later that day and to book me a bunk. I have to admit I was looking forward to a shower and a McDonald's. I was starting to get fed up with dehydrated food. To keep the cost of the trip down we tried to save money by making our own. We had a couple of shop-bought meals like the cheesy scrambled egg which we both enjoyed so much, but the staple diet on this trip had been king sized pot noodles decanted into silver Mylar bags. This worked well! Breakfast was two packets of Quaker porridge oats (golden syrup flavour) again decanted into a Mylar bag. Lunch was an assortment of protein bars that I had purchased in bulk from a wholesaler which were very close to their sell-buy dates. I would estimate that this saved us around fifty pounds each in total. However, the truth is, sitting down to a king size curry pot noodle in the evening is not as exciting as sitting down to a dehydrated potato hotpot or macaroni cheese. My body was starting to crave real food, like a cheese burger.

I emerged from the tent and into the wind of the morning. Sat on a small rubber mat, I brewed up some coffee and sat staring across the loch. I loved the mystery and the possibility of a giant leviathan cruising just under the surface, a species of fish that had gone undetected for hundreds of years. I took the opportunity to do some Nessie spotting of my own. It's easy to see how you can get caught up in it all. Every adverse ripple or a distant bird just sitting on the water sparks your imagination. Like lots of things in life, if you truly believe in something then of course it's real. Loch Ness is truly a magical place.

I wanted to while away the hours trying to catch a glimpse of the beastie, but it was time to leave and meet up with Turtle in Inverness. Before packing away the tent I decided to take my small drone out for a flight over the loch and record some film for posterity. It was windy but the little robot handled it well. After about ten minutes of flight time, I turned the drone around and started its journey back to the home point. The wind however had pushed the drone further down the loch. I watched the monitor as it approached the shore, but it was obvious it had been blown off course. I flew the drone close to the shoreline hoping to visually pick it up or even hear it, but alas it avoided detection. The controller started beeping informing me that the battery was low. In the event that you don't then land it, the drone will automatically return to where it took off. This was a great fail-safe and I would have just allowed the autopilot to take over, but I was situated very close to tall trees and the drone that I had didn't have automatic avoidance. I had a drone stuck high in a tree before and had to get the help of Paul to retrieve it. He climbed up in crampons to get it. It was a right ball-ache; one I didn't want to repeat. I fixed my gaze on the screen and concentrated hard. I eased the drone over the shoreline and remotely landed it, setting it down gently on the beach. I activated the "find my drone" function which made the drone give off an audible beeping sound and headed up the shore to retrieve it. It took me an hour to find the thing. After reviewing the footage when I got home you could see how far it had been pushed off course. Add the fact that I had flown the drone a considerable distance, it wasn't surprising it had gone AWOL. I eventually found the tiny aircraft patiently waiting for me about half a mile away.

It didn't take long to pack up the gear and I was soon heading down the B852 road towards the village of Dores. The trail from there broke off the road and once again headed into the hills. It had started to spit with rain and I was keen to keep moving and get to Inverness before the heavens opened. A light mist was washing over the green rolling hills and sporadic flocks of sheep were heading for cover. I was not concerned with the impending rain storm but rather the need to vacate my bowels. I had been hoping to make it to the hostel but the situation was now desperate. I quickly moved off the path and into some scrub surrounded by bushes. I took the poop kit from my pack (which contained biodegradable toilet tissue and a small titanium trowel) and quickly dug a hole. I pulled down my strides and assumed the position letting gravity take over. As I squatted alfresco the cloud lifted to reveal the most amazing rainbow. The colours were so vivid it looked like it had been painted across the sky. I dug out my phone and took a picture, right there squatting amongst the gorse. Every time I look at that picture I'm reminded that there is beauty everywhere, you just have to look, even when you're in the shit.

Crisis averted I hastily carried on. I only had a few miles left to go but it was now raining steadily. This abated a little as I headed into another section of woods and was slightly protected from the weather by the canopy of trees. The path meandered on through, then all of a sudden no more path, just a country road in the middle of nowhere. The big blue sign just before the fence that marked the boundary of the woods read "South Loch Ness Trail". It was over. I'd done it.

It was a massive anti-climax. I'm not sure what I expected. I guess on reflection I was experiencing a valuable life lesson. It's not about the destination but the journey. Whilst it wasn't a hike of great distance, the journey had ended up being more of a spiritual experience than anything else. I'd even go as far as to say it was more like a pilgrimage. It started as an adventure with a friend and ended up being much more.

The three-mile hike into Inverness in the rain, along the main road was grim. I staggered through the door of the hostel called "Bazpackers" threw off my pack and slumped into a chair next to a warm fire. Turtle had excelled himself in finding this gaff, it was perfect. The rooms had built-in bunks with a curtain you could pull across which gave you some privacy. They were more like pods. The showers were great and the hot water eased my aching muscles. It was probably the longest shower of my life. Upon returning to the communal area feeling clean and refreshed, I found Turtle sitting at a table next to the window. He looked a lot better than when I had last seen him. As I sat down, Turtle reached under the table and produced an enormous brown bag stuffed to the brim with food from McDonald's. Exactly what I needed.

I finished up one of the best meals of my life and retired to bed. Lying in my pod I started to reflect on the last few days, trying to put into context everything that had happened. I thought that I had unpacked a lot of my issues in the months before Scotland, the reality was I had just buried them deeper. I hadn't worked through my emotions or feelings as I had thought, I had just figured out a way to ignore them. The distraction of being in a new relationship had helped to facilitate my ignorance. This gave the illusion that I was feeling better about myself, but it was essentially a lie. The premise is that if you ignore something long enough it will eventually go away, I had been good at this. I'd ignored the fact that the mother of my daughters had been unhappy; I'd ignored the people who were telling me I was acting like an idiot; I'd ignored the fact that I was sick; I'd ignored the fact that my second wife was looking for an exit strategy and I ignored the fact that I was suppressing my feelings. What I now realise is that when you ignore these things for long enough they don't go away; they eventually explode causing massive devastation and casualties. Was I now cured of all my insecurities and negativity? I would have liked to think so, however, I had the feeling that as one journey ends, so starts another.

My thoughts soon centred on Emma. It was only then that I realised how much I was missing her. I took out my phone and sent her a text to see how she was. I ended it with a love heart emoji, the first time I had ever acknowledged how I felt about her. Funny how one tiny thing can mean so much.

Chapter 11

"Nobody likes pain, but sometimes it's necessary to move on."

I leant back on my faux leather office chair. It creaked under my weight as if to say, "Fuck me, get to the gym will ya." I stared blankly at the dirty screen of my laptop. Inspiration that day was eluding me. I was going through the process of updating the website and trying to write a blog. However, I just couldn't think of anything interesting to say. I'd been back from Scotland a few weeks and was still feeling a bit low after such a big high. I was trying to be more productive and was also trying to push myself back into some form of regimented work ethic. One thing I realised when I was away in Scotland was that I wanted to work. This however was difficult in my current medical condition. The problem wasn't that I wasn't willing to work, the problem was due to my seizures still being quite regular. Most, if not all employers don't want to take on that kind of liability. I could potentially be off work sick at least once a week on average. There are times when I would go nearly two weeks without a seizure which was great, but then there are also times when I would have two or three in a week. A doctor told me I should try and find a job where I could work from home and work my own hours. I think the entire planet would love a job like that.

At a three-monthly meeting with a work coach at the local job centre, I was told it was unlikely that I would get a job from an employer. She then told me to possibly start looking at self-employment opportunities. When I asked about funding for a potential start-up, I was told there isn't any and that you don't really need any capital to start your own business. She then went on to give me an example of a woman she had dealt with who sat at home, working her own hours knitting tea cosies to sell. Is that what my life had come to? Was that all I was worth? Don't get me wrong I'm not knocking it, because at least she's doing something and trying to get by on her own. I however wanted to turn what I love doing into my job. I wasn't worried about earning a big salary, but if I could just survive and not have to rely on government benefits and family for support, I would be happy. To do that I had to pull my finger out and start putting in some real effort. I couldn't just sit, wish and hope for things to happen. I had to start making things happen.

The YouTube channel was building okay and I had just reached one thousand subscribers. That was one of the prerequisites for monetization (receiving a percentage of the ad revenue). The other was to have four thousand hours of watch time in a rolling twelve-month period, which I didn't have. The key element for YouTube success was to be consistent in creating and uploading content, once a week at least. I was going to have to do better, not only in uploading consistently but also in making sure the content was as good as I could achieve. I also couldn't just rely on YouTube as my only source of income. It takes years to build up a channel that pays enough to live on. I could start doing some Big Grizzly Outdoors merchandise, hoping that as the channel grew so would sales of merch. The answer (to me anyway) was to build several potential revenue streams, each bringing in just a little bit of cash. All this ran through my head and seemed plausible, but putting it into action however was another matter.

I opened up the calendar on my phone. It was blank. I had nothing planned for the foreseeable future, no wild camps, no events and no trips away. This meant I had no content to create, and if I didn't have any content then the channel wasn't going to grow, therefore my dream of being a professional content creator was over before it started. I closed down the calendar and started scrolling through my social media. I was bored and unmotivated. I desperately wanted to find the motivation to do something different, something that tested me, something that would push me further than I ever thought possible.

I had recently read Chris Ryan's book 'Bravo Two Zero', the story of the ill-fated SAS mission in Iraq during the first Gulf War. The eight-man team had set up an observation post in a dried-up river bed (or wadi) and were compromised by a young boy herding goats. In their escape, three members lost their lives and four were captured. Chris Ryan, showing phenomenal endurance and perseverance, walked one hundred and ninety miles, across the desert. Moving only at night to avoid detection. It took Chris eight days, with no food or water for three, to cross the border into Syria and safety. It was the longest-ever 'escape and evade' in SAS history. I had been fascinated recently by all things SAS and Special Forces in general, watching a lot of content on YouTube. I liked the idea of having to push past your physical and mental limits and having the tools to adapt, learn and survive. This was something I wanted to learn. A way of fighting my physical disability and strengthening my mental capability. I'm pretty sure however the SAS wouldn't want a forty-something epileptic, with a history of 'mental illness'. I googled Chris Ryan to see what other books he had written, in the hope to draw some more inspiration. I dived into the rabbit hole of websites and social media, before ending up on Facebook. Facebook however was not giving me any sort of relief from the brain fog, or any useful information either, in fact, I was getting infuriated by the number of suggested posts that Facebook was putting in my timeline. Then BOOM, I happened to read an advertisement for an endurance event, The Fan Dance.

The advert was from a company called The SF Experience, SF standing for Special Forces, as in the Special Air and Special Boat Service, or as they're known around the world the SAS and SBS. The company is run by former members of the armed services, and the Fan Dance was just one of several events that they ran. Part of the selection process for the UK special forces is a TAB (tactical advance to battle) or ruck (running with a rucksack/bergen) over the mountain of Pen Y Fan in the Brecon Beacons, South Wales. I studied the advert intensely, learning as much as I could about the event. The twenty-four-kilometre route heads up to the lower summit of Corn Du and then along to the summit of Pen Y Fan, the tallest peak in the Brecon Beacons. The route then drops down the back of the mountain on a steep descent known as Jacob's Ladder. This is then followed by a long slog along a Roman road to the halfway point, where you are then turned around and sent back the way you came. Nothing to do with dancing at all. This has to be completed wearing military kit including boots, whilst carrying a thirty-five-pound bergen (rucksack)! Plus, the additional weight of any food or water you take. All in all, the pack would weigh around forty pounds.

I looked at the pictures of competitors snaking their way up the mountain, all loaded down with kit. This must be one of the hardest endurance events out there. I mean to get into the SAS you have to complete it. I desperately wanted to enter. I wanted to show people that what you think is unachievable is actually achievable, if you're prepared to put in the time and effort of course. You just have to grit your teeth, dig in and get it done. I laughed at myself, bloody hell just because you've walked the length of Loch Ness, doesn't mean you're now Chris Ryan and capable of taking on the SAS selection course…does it? I read on. The more I read the more I started to get invested. I could do this, bollocks I'm going to do it. I didn't have to read anymore, I went straight to the page where you sign up, paid my money and I was in for the summer Fan Dance in June twenty twenty-two. It was an impulsive and spontaneous decision. I had now signed up and was going to take on the SAS selection course. I was smiling, I had something in the diary and something to train for. Hold on, how do you train for an event like this?

I decided to keep this to myself for a bit. My poor family and girlfriend had just gotten over the anxiety of me hiking in the highlands on my own. Now I was going to be racing over mountains, not to mention all the training that would have to go on. I know that a lot of the time it's hard being me. There are days where I just feel rubbish. Whether that's because I'm recovering from a seizure or suffering from the effects of the anti-seizure medication, it's a way of life that I have had to get used to. As I've said before, I can be quite selfish. So, when I'm not feeling great, I lock myself away, become distant. I remove myself from society and selfishly hide from the world until it passes. I forget that other people in my life worry and care about me. I forget that whilst I'm dug in at home they are also dug in, waiting for a call or text saying I'm okay. I never got this until I started dating Emma. She would quite often text "Are you okay?" I'd always reply at some point saying I was fine, scratching my head thinking how odd. Until she explained, that when nobody hears from me for a while and I don't reply to a text or answer my phone, people naturally think the worst. The penny dropped. I myself get frustrated when people don't reply promptly. I then imagined how I would feel if it were a loved one with a medical condition. I think I would panic. At some point, I was going to have to break the news that I was taking on one of the toughest challenges in the UK. I would also have to do more outdoor training, a lot more! As much as it's sometimes tough being me, I think it's a lot tougher having to be my mother, brother or girlfriend.

I guess the starting point to this adventure would be to see if I could run with a pack on. I mean I can run without a pack and I can hike pretty fast with one, so how much harder could it be? On the morning of the third of November twenty twenty-one, I found out.

The night before I packed my military bergen with the mandatory kit list from The SF Experience website. It was kit that should something untoward happen en route you'd be able to take care of yourself. Stuff like a bivvy bag, first aid kit, additional food and water, spare clothes, map and compass. (You get the picture). I dug a pair of hand-held digital scales out of the drawer and hooked them on to the pack. It weighed thirty-nine pounds, including two litres of water which I would drink en route. I hoisted it onto my back and bounced up and down the hallway. It didn't feel that bad. Maybe this wasn't going to be as bad as I thought.

The gentle ambient sound of relaxing music emanated from my Alexa alarm, gradually coaxing me from my sleep and into a state of awakeness. It was four thirty a.m. and it was still dark, cue Bill Conti's theme to Rocky. It was time to get up drink six raw eggs and then pound some pavement. The reality was after limping out of bed I was then sat on the sofa struggling through a bowl of porridge, thinking to myself "What the hell am I doing?".

My early morning hikes into the forest had sort of prepared me for what was to come. I had all the right kit, clothing and boots etc. Instead of hiking around the forest I was now going to have to run, or at least run as much of it as I could. I let Lemmy out for his morning ritual and then prepared to leave. I was going to run my forest ten-miler route. I thought this would be a good test of my fitness, as it was flat in parts and hilly in others. A good route I thought, a benchmark to work from. I strapped on my bergen, opened the door and stepped out into the darkness of the morning.

I limped back to my front door two hours and thirty-seven minutes later a broken man. How much harder was it running with a pack on? The answer was unimaginably much harder. I was in bits. I was now wishing I had never seen the advert for this event. People sign up for this voluntarily. Are they all insane? My feet were blistered to hell. I knew this without even taking off my boots. The boots which had been broken in over miles and miles of hiking and which had not caused me any pain at all, had now destroyed my size eight trotters. My thighs were on fire and kept cramping. My calves felt like overstretched rubber bands just before the point of snapping. My shoulders ached so bad and my lower back sent electric shocks up my spine every time I leant a certain way. It had been muddy up in the forest so I was covered in crap. I was also cold and wet. I dropped the bergen off my back and just let it fall to the floor. I stared at it with contempt and would have given it a good kick, if I didn't think in doing so would snap my toes off. I opened the front door and just sat on the step trying to catch my breath. I was breathing heavily and producing some kind of strange wheezing sound. This time I had bitten off more than I could chew. I was out of my depth. I realised then that I knew nothing about tabbing or rucking. This was a level of fitness and mental toughness that I had never had to deal with.

Lemmy joined me on the step and gave me a good licking of the earhole. He then trotted out onto the grass and laid a massive turd, great. I cleared up the mess and then started the process of cleaning myself up, stripping in the hallway and placing my wet clothes in the washing machine. The climb up the short flight of stairs to the bathroom was brutal. I stepped into the shower and turned on the water. I watched as the dirty brown mess that was pouring off my body drained away. I placed both hands against the tiled wall and let the hot water soak into my tired broken body. My feet were stinging like hell as the open blisters on my mangled feet came into contact with the water. This was no fun, no fun at all. I washed and dried myself, took my anti-seizure medication and crawled into bed, where I then slipped into a self-induced coma.

I awoke late morning and ate brunch. The rest of the day was spent tumbling down the YouTube rabbit hole learning about the art of tabbing, or rucking as it is known in the U.S. Like all forms of sport once you break through the surface you will find that it's not as simple as just pulling on some boots, strapping on a pack and then going for a run. What boots are best; should I use aftermarket insoles; what socks are best; should I wear two pairs of socks; do I need to tape my feet; if so what tape and what's the best way to tape; what pack should I be using; which is the best way to load it; should I use a water bladder or just carry bottles? It was a minefield of information which I had to learn and learn quickly!

I decided to start at the bottom and then work my way up. My feet needed sorting. You cannot run carrying any form of load if your feet are torn to pieces. The difference between hiking and rucking is the latter produces much more pressure on your feet, therefore increasing the chances of blisters and general wear and tear. I learnt from the Tube that blisters occur due to moisture and friction mainly, along with ill-fitting boots of course. As your feet get hot, start to sweat and swell, this creates friction and so on. I watched hours of videos on how to tape your feet, which socks to wear and how to lace your boots differently to allow for the swelling of the foot. I wrote a list of stuff that I thought would help and then dived into Amazon ordering some Luekotape, moleskin patches, foot powder and some more merino wool socks. The following day I decided to rest, then try again the next morning, putting my newfound knowledge in foot care to the test. This was not going to beat me.

The alarm dragged me out of bed at zero four thirty. It had been a couple of days since my last painful attempt to ruck the ten-miler. The last few days had seen the pain in my feet, legs and back fade, I was now ready to take it on again. I packed my rucksack in between eating breakfast and taking on fluids, after which I started to prepare my feet for the slog ahead. The blisters on both feet had deroofed and had left open wounds. I had kept these clean and they had now dried out. I cut small circles of moleskin the size of each blister and then stuck them over the affected areas. Moleskin is like a soft plaster that acts like a second skin. This would add an additional barrier, not only to help prevent blisters but to protect the ones I already had. After applying the moleskin, I moved onto the taping up of toes, heels and over the moleskin to protect it. I sprinkled my feet with foot powder to help absorb any sweat, then slid on a pair of thicker merino wool socks, pulled on my boots and carefully laced them up. I walked to the kitchen, poured a large glass of water and popped a couple of ibuprofen for good measure. It was November, it was early, it was cold and it was wet, but these are the days that count.

The light in the forest was a subtle shade of pink. You know that time when it's no longer night but too dark to be day. It was still muddy and whilst it was cold, it wasn't cold enough to freeze the earth, so I was ankle-deep in wet mud. A small flashlight clipped to the sternum strap of my pack cast its light through the blackness, highlighting the small section of disused road in front of me, just wide enough to catch the edge of the trees on either side. It reminded me of the epic trench run in Star Wars, although at the end of this road was a right turn deeper into the forest and not an exhaust port to blow up the Death Star.

I'd been going for around an hour and to my surprise the feet were holding up well. My legs however were in extreme pain, especially my thighs. This was surprising to me as I thought it would have been my knees that would start to give me pain, however, I seemed to have dodged that bullet. I was running, loaded up with nearly forty pounds in weight on my back, although you can't really call it running. It's like a cross between jogging and speed walking, but without the silly wobbling hips. I kind of scooted rather than ran. The pain in the legs was now starting to trigger the "let's sack it off and go home" response, but I tried to ignore it and carry on. That voice however got louder and louder. As the pain and discomfort increased so did the internal voice which screamed to stop. I was breathing heavily and wasn't sure how much longer my legs would keep me upright for. Maybe diving head-first into this kind of training was not a good idea. A gradual increase in weight and distance would probably have been a better option. Anyone will tell you however, that is not me, that is not what I do, I dive in head first and at full speed.

A short descent at the far end of the forest offered some respite, but not for long. The sun was now high enough to cast ribbons of light through the trees. If I wasn't in so much discomfort, I would have appreciated that exact moment. Today however, it was lost in a world of pain and suffering.

Strange things happen to your psyche when under that much stress. I was starting to use the pain. When it got to the point that it was almost unbearable, I'd think back to a moment when I hadn't been the best person I could have been. I started to couple the pain I was feeling to an event where I wasn't so proud of myself, or a time where I had experienced some emotional trauma. I used the pain as fuel to keep going, taking an emotional feeling I had experienced and then making it painful in reality, like a punishment. I'd never pushed this hard before, whilst the pain was always present it now served a purpose which made it slightly easier to live with. I'm not sure how healthy it is mentally to do this. You may say it's a form of self-harming, be it a less aggressive version. All I know is that when it got too hard and I was being screamed at internally to stop, when the pain was almost overwhelming, I'd dive into the archive and expunge a particular moment which I could share my pain with. Don't get me wrong, I was not flying around the forest like a man possessed. If you'd happened to catch me on that morning, I'm sure my appearance would have been enough to warrant calling an ambulance.

I trudged on. I was a mile from home. It's always the last mile which is the hardest. I was out of the forest and onto the pavements of my hometown. The world was just waking up. I looked at people in their cars heading off to work. While they had been sleeping or eating breakfast, or trying to wake kids up for school, I had been in the forest, breaking my body and mind, just a few short miles away. They would stare back with an air of curiosity. I was an odd sight, different to the normal monotony of their morning. I crossed over a road and onto a traffic island, waiting for the path to clear of traffic before I could get to the pavement on the other side. When I thought it was clear I stepped out from the island. A car screamed around the corner and upon coming face to face with each other we both stopped suddenly. I waved to say thank you and sorry at the same time. The guy behind the wheel didn't acknowledge this, at most he gave a quick glance and maybe a moment of wondering. His attention was then diverted back to the traffic and the school run. I was slightly pissed at this. My day was just as important as his. I'd slogged myself to near extinction while he was sat in a nice warm comfortable car, prick! However, I realised nobody can feel your pain, nobody can experience your emotional state just by a brief moment of locking eyes. I then wondered as I ran up the path if the guy who just nearly hit me, was he okay? Was he happy, maybe he hated his job or maybe he felt trapped in a life he no longer wanted? Was he just about to lose his shit with the young boy in the back seat who was so preoccupied with his phone, that he didn't even notice the near miss? The one thing I was sure of, he was not looking at me asking the same questions. He had just simply looked at me with utter contempt. I could have given him the finger or shouted some obscenity at him, I can be quite intimidating if I choose to be. That would have been my response at one time. I carried on the last few hundred metres home, sincerely hoping that his day got better. I hadn't reached in through the car window and dragged him out by his neck! I think that's what you would call personal development!

I pushed the stop button on my G Shock watch, fumbled in my pocket for my keys and then opened the front door. I didn't care what time I had done; I didn't feel that it was that important. I was tired, a bit sore and soaking wet, but I had gotten around. My feet felt better. In fact, in general I felt better all over. It was a million miles from the effort of a few days ago. I went through the next stage of the routine, undressing, shoving my kit in the washing machine and then showering. I took my medication and went to bed, waiting for a wave of tiredness to wash me to sleep. I came to realise, in my half-dream-like state, that whilst I was torturing myself in the forest, I could allow myself to go to those really dark places in my mind, accepting responsibility for the things I had done wrong, but also forgiving those that I felt had hurt me. I'd found a way to process all this emotional trauma, a way to manifest it into something real and tangible, something that could make me feel those things, where previously I felt nothing. I was healing. On the hills above Loch Ness, I had given myself permission to move forward and let go of the hate and self-imposed suffering. In a dark wet forest, I had found a way to do it. I drifted away, not thinking whether I should put myself through it all again, but when?

A few days passed and those sore muscles soon forgot about the slog through the forest. Although my newfound hobby of running around the woods, loaded up with kit was still on my mind, other distractions were taking up time. I'd decided (after a meeting with my job coach) to retake my English exam. The English exam I had spectacularly failed in school some thirty-three years ago. Fortunately, because of my financial and medical situation, I qualified for free funding, I think I would have been stupid to pass up this gift horse. As with all things though, I had to sit a test to see if I was smart enough to take the course. A test to be able to take the test so to speak. Things like this always worried me, as I am often plagued by self-doubt. My spelling and grammar had always been atrocious and I had forgotten the very little I had learnt at school, but I wanted to take on new challenges, so I pressed on. I had the time so why waste it by being a lazy slob. Anyone can do that.

The morning arrived of the test. I logged into the online portal via a link I had been emailed. I felt pretty nervous and worried, if I fell at the first hurdle, I'd again feel that sting of failure that I hated so much. I wanted to be a person that succeeded, not failed. I'd had years of failure that I was now trying to methodically work through and recover from emotionally. To fail is to learn and I was learning, the curve was not only steep but near vertical. I wanted desperately to do this, to take the course and pass the exam.

As the test started, I worked my way slowly and carefully through the questions, some were pretty basic and some I found difficult. I'm not a very fast reader. This had been exacerbated after I tried to break a solid oak table with my head. I often have to read things twice to fully understand the content and this was slowing me down. I eventually managed to get to the last question, surprisingly with time to spare. It was a large paragraph of text with no punctuation and with spelling and grammar mistakes. I found this almost impossible to correct, but I tried. Working methodically through it line by line. I read through my work, made a few alterations and then was out of time. I just hoped that I had done enough to have passed. Later that day I received an email saying not only had I scored high enough to take the course, but I also qualified to be put on the intensive course. Instead of being on a course that would take a full year, I would be on the shorter, more intense six-month course. This would start in January with the exam being taken in May. I felt a feeling of overwhelming pride, a feeling that I hadn't felt for as long as I could remember. I was working hard in all aspects of my life and it was starting to show, small steps and little victories that all add up. I was starting to think of myself as a survivor and not so much of a loser. I was setting goals, working hard to achieve them, then setting more, all forward progress. Very slowly it felt like the tide was starting to turn. I still had a long way to go, but every little win inspired me to keep up the hard work. I realise now, that a lot of the time change isn't noticeable. It's also not chronological, as you don't sort out one issue and then move on to the next. Like a painting or a picture that appears in random parts, it slowly fades into view. One small corner becomes recognisable and then a section in the middle will slowly form until it too is recognisable. All of a sudden you wake up and realise that what you are doing is working. It takes time; it takes effort, and a lot of the time you feel like it isn't working, but very slowly it all starts to come into focus. It's only once you determine that idleness intensifies the suffering, do you then realise that consistent productivity and hard work precede any form of success.

Hill training on the "Dreadmill"

Chapter 12

"I don't think I can ever be content, it's like another word for giving up?"

I carried on the training, but more importantly, I was learning something from every training run. I was making minor adjustments to the set-up and tweaking the kit in an attempt to make those long rucks more comfortable. Taping my feet had helped, but due to the amount of training I was doing my feet were still getting sore, toenails were turning black and on occasion when a blister did arise, it was taking ages to heal. This prompted more research into foot care. I was reading as much as I could and watching far too much YouTube in an attempt to unlock the secrets of pain-free rucking. One piece of advice was to wear a very thin pair of liner socks under your main pair of socks, to reduce friction. Even better I discovered were toe socks, a pair of very thin socks with toes, like gloves for your feet. This proved to be a great bit of information and drastically reduced the number of blisters I was getting. I did feel though that maybe the heavy boots I was wearing were not best suited for the task in question. I had been wearing a pair of British Army-issue boots by an Italian company called Aku. These were great boots but heavy. I had read that one pound of weight on your feet is equivalent to carrying five pounds in your pack! Each boot weighed six hundred and fifty grams, or two point nine pounds a pair. That's the equivalent of carrying fourteen pounds! If I could reduce the amount of weight I was carrying, not in the pack, but about my person (clothing and boots etc) then surely that would be a massive help in reducing fatigue.

I needed some lighter boots. There was only one person I need ask when it comes to boots or packs or anything military, ex-Army sniper and my best mate…Neil the Tash. And when it comes to boots there is only one brand that Neil wears, Danner Boots. I checked out their online store and scanned through the rows and rows of boots that Danner sells, finally settling on a pair of Danner Tachyon boots. These lightweight military boots weighed only one point six pounds a pair. That's one point three pounds lighter per pair on the foot than my Aku boots, working out at six-point five pounds lighter in the pack. If you go by the one pound on the foot equals five pounds in the pack equation. It doesn't sound like much but believe me it counts, especially once you start getting past the ten-mile mark. It was all starting to come together, a little tweak here, a small change there and progressively the rucks started to get a little easier. Easier didn't mean easy though, oh no, no. It just meant you went faster. I was still tearing out my emotional demons in an attempt to exorcise them from my being, using those feelings to acknowledge the physical pain I was in. When it was over, I felt that I had not only worked my body hard but had also managed to burn some of the emotional baggage I was carrying about. The ten-milers were doing the job, I was getting fitter. I was feeling more emotionally stable. I felt I was becoming a better person; it was time to up the ante.

I wanted to put all that I had learnt to the test, I also wanted to test myself. The forest ten-miler was giving me a good foundation and a great level of base fitness, but could I go further? The Fan Dance was twenty kilometres of undulating terrain. The forest ten-miler was sixteen and I was on my feet for around two and three-quarter hours. The Fan would see me out in the hills for over four. I needed to see if I could cope with that amount of time on my feet. I wasn't worried so much about the terrain. I just wanted to see what five hours felt like, fully loaded, pushing it. I decided on going ten miles down the Downs Link road, turning around and doing the ten miles back. I had hiked this route before, from the coast back up to my home town. I was familiar with the terrain and knew what to expect. So early one cold November morning I strapped on the pack and again, headed out the door to see what I was made of. I didn't want to kill myself in the process, so I decided that rather than try and run or ruck as it is called, I would walk at a fast pace, somewhere around the fifteen-minute mile mark.

The first few miles flew by. A quick jaunt through the town, past the old secondary school which I attended (now converted into posh apartments,) up the hill and out towards a large village where I picked up the disused railway track, which is the Downs Link. I was keeping up a steady pace, pretty much bang on the fifteen-minute mile mark. I was happy with my progress at that point. I pushed on, past a disused railway station, through a couple of tunnels, until I reached a main road. The track then ran alongside the road before turning left and back into the country, heading towards the River Adur. The enclosed disused railway tracks now opened out into wide open agricultural land. It was turning out to be a great morning. I wasn't in any discomfort, my feet were holding up well and I was feeling good, so I couldn't believe it when the watch beeped to say I had completed another mile, mile ten.

I did a one-eighty and started to head back in the glorious morning sunshine. Although it was November and the air was crisp, the low sun was keeping warm as I headed home. Around mile twelve things started to slightly ache, my breathing was getting slightly heavier and I was now having to concentrate on what I was doing. No longer could I just amble along, soaking up the rolling fields of the gorgeous Sussex countryside. I was now having to work. As I progressed, the harder the work became. I was soon starting to suffer. I wasn't sure why the sudden increase in effort, because up until halfway I had been cruising. Now, I was battling with myself. Negative thoughts flooded my mind, and everything was starting to hurt. Mile fifteen and I was sure it was over; I was moving on willpower alone. My back hurt, feet hurt, shoulders hurt, even my head was hurting. I resorted to conjuring up images of all the people who wanted to see me fail. Those who wanted to see me sat on the curb with my life in a bin liner, not surprisingly there are many. This kept my legs moving and stopped me from just giving up. I wasn't going to give those who wish me ill the satisfaction of seeing me quit.

At eighteen miles I reached the end of the Downs Link track and was now on the pavement, heading home back through the village. I so desperately wanted to sit down, but I couldn't. I wouldn't let myself. The last mile was a blur. My mind was totally focused on motivating my body to move. Every time I started to slow down, I silently screamed at myself to keep moving, until eventually I arrived home.

It was several days later and after I had recovered that I decided to look at the data captured from my watch. It all became clear then, why the sudden increase in effort. Heading south on the Downs Link felt great. This was because it was ever so slightly downhill, all the way to the ten-mile mark. So obviously the return leg was ten miles uphill. No wonder I had suffered so badly. You wouldn't notice the difference in incline. It was barely noticeable to the naked eye. I learnt a very valuable lesson! It had taken me five hours and twelve minutes to complete twenty miles. That wasn't good enough, I needed to be faster and I needed to train harder.

I wasn't just running about in the woods like an extra from Rambo, I was also putting time in on the dreadmill as well. I had four routines I would use for training. A five-kilometre sprint with the dreadmill set flat, a ten-kilometre ruck loaded with thirty-five pounds, dreadmill set at a two percent incline and the dreaded ten-kilometre loaded uphill slog, dreadmill set at ten percent incline. All this plus the ten-miler around the forest. I would try and get through all four routines in a week. This happened most weeks but not all, (I am only human after all)!

It was bound to happen sooner or later and in early December it did. I was midway through the ten-miler. The sun had yet to crest the top of the trees in the forest so it was cold and dark. My fitness levels were slowly improving and the ten-miler didn't grip me with fear anymore, like it did on those first few rucks. I felt in control. If I wasn't in any sort of discomfort, I would think I wasn't training hard enough, so I would up the pace. I turned right off a solid logging road and onto a wide muddy path that bent around the back end of the forest and descended into the blackness. My small chest light was just about bright enough for me to avoid any big puddles and the worst of the mud. As I reached the bottom of the small hill the lights went out completely.

I'm not sure how long I had been unconscious. It may have been only a minute or it could have been much longer. I had no idea. It took a while for me to work out what had happened, as I slowly tried to open my eyes. For some reason, this felt difficult and I couldn't understand why. I managed to free an arm which had been pinned underneath me and tried to rub my eyes. They were thick with mud; in fact, my whole face and mouth was full of it including up my nose. I'd had a seizure. The forward momentum and the speed at which I was travelling, meant I had ploughed a deep furrow in the wet mud with my head. Normally after a seizure, I would take it easy, lay back in bed and go to sleep for the day. Someone would be alerted via my fall-alert wristband and check up on me, but not this time. The band works by connecting to my phone and like most forests, there was no signal. The band had gone off but couldn't connect. I was on my own. I didn't panic. I lay waiting to see if I had injured myself, or whether there was pain somewhere in my body which would slowly develop as I moved out of the postictal stage. I wasn't badly hurt. A few aches and pains but nothing to write home about. I rolled onto my side and started to unclip the sternum and waist straps on my pack. I wouldn't stand a chance of getting to my feet with that still on.

Once undone I rolled onto my back. This was harder than it sounds and took several attempts. Slipping my arms out of the shoulder straps, I very slowly sat up. I was a mess and caked in mud. It was still dark, so I grabbed the small light off my pack and shone it around to get my bearings. The small beam scanned the area and I looked hard for anything that I could recognise. My woolly hat lay about eight metres away. This kind of marked the impact of where I went over. It also highlighted to me how far I had been a human plough!

I sat for a good thirty minutes just trying to get myself together, fighting off the urge to sleep, which would have been deadly in the cold conditions. I was now extremely cold and was starting to shiver. I needed to get moving. I dragged myself to my feet, staggered up to grab my hat then staggered back. I reached down and stood my pack up, turning it facing outwards away from me. I rearranged the straps and with one big effort lifted it, pushing my arms through the loops, just like that cool way of throwing on a jacket or coat. I stumbled a little but didn't fall over. I felt very weak and not completely sure of myself. I think if I had just fallen over without having a seizure, I would have been more worried and concerned. But my current loopy self didn't register the gravity of the situation I was in. My brain was still recovering and everything was a bit weird. I think I was just on autopilot. I knew I had to get home and so home I went. I headed back the way I came as that was the most logical route, slowly creeping back up the hill. Now and then I'd have a little rest, then I'd carry on. Progress was painfully slow as my body wasn't responding well. Each step was a massive effort. It was well into morning and daylight by the time I reached the country road, which intersected with the main road leading into town. The hours ticked by and eventually, I dragged myself to the front door, placed the key in the lock and pushed the door open. I dropped the pack, removed my boots, staggered into the living room, collapsed on the sofa still caked in mud and slept for hours. I could have called someone to come and pick me up when I had got cell service, but could you imagine the panic and worry that would have caused. My family wouldn't let me out of the house again! Whilst limping home had drained me of all energy and pretty much near on killed me, it was still better than the alternative. Which was calling Mum or Emma to come get me, then receiving a telling-off and lecture about how I was doing too much and needed to take it easy.

It was late afternoon by the time I woke up. The mud had dried and I was now stuck to the sofa. I slowly rose and checked the data on my watch as I hadn't stopped it upon my return, so it had continued to track my route. I fell at zero-five twenty-five and I arrived home at eleven forty-seven. I had been stationary (laying in the mud) for fifty-one minutes, which meant it took me five and a half hours to walk four and a bit miles home. I cleaned myself and the sofa, ate some food, let Lemmy out for a wander and then went to bed, vowing to myself to never tell a single soul about what had happened.

I decided to take a few days off from training. The wipe-out in the forest hadn't shaken my confidence one bit. It just went to prove in that situation, I could just about manage. I think I just needed a little rest. A break to collect my thoughts. I did think that maybe I should work on a contingency plan should it happen again and started looking into satellite communication. The price on these units had decreased dramatically. Several companies were now offering small units which allowed third parties to track you and allow basic text communication via satellite (no cell service needed) with selected contacts, all for a monthly subscription. Christmas was fast approaching and so maybe this was a good gift idea.

It was shocking how quickly Christmas had come around again. The year had sprinted by and so much in my life had changed. I was filling my time constructively. Gone were the days of loafing on the sofa feeling sorry for myself. I was now a man of action. In the new year I was going to become a mature student, going back to school again, albeit remotely. I had also been in contact with an old climbing acquaintance Keith, who was a fully qualified mountain leader instructor whom I had met when I was at school. Keith ran several courses, but it was the mountain leader course I was interested in. If I could get this qualification then it would be another string to my bow, a potential small revenue stream.

In my last year of secondary school, my PE teacher Mr Parnell asked if I would help out on a residential school trip with a younger year group. Mr Parnell had the previous year introduced me to rock climbing, a sport that I had carried on after school and only stopped after Mike's accident on the Troll Wall in Norway. I guess that Mr Parnell thought my enthusiasm and dedication to being a better climber and general outdoor enthusiast, would be put to good use helping other kids find the same enjoyment in the outdoors as I did. Upon reflection and looking back at those years with adult eyes, it's probably fair to say that Mr Parnell was influential in instilling that never give up attitude in me. A substitute father figure during those crucial teenage years. He was the school rugby coach and pushed me to not only play for the school but for my home town as well. The first time that I ever saw the hills and valleys of Derbyshire, where I would spend many years climbing the Gritstone, was because Mr Parnell had taken me. I'm not sure whether he felt sorry for me. The opportunities for me as a teenager were slim because of our financial situation. My mother couldn't afford for me to go on residential school trips. I was also not the most academic of students, leaving school with basically no qualifications. Maybe he wanted to send me out into the world with a productive work ethic and a positive "can do" attitude. An athletic man of steadfast principles, who took no nonsense from any of us. He wore a thick 'Magnum' moustache, smoked

Rothmans cigarettes and married my geography teacher. They don't make teachers like that anymore. what a legend!

It was at that residential school trip that I met Keith, who was working for the company that ran the camp. I bumped into Keith ten years later when he did my single pitch award training, a qualification I needed to become a rock-climbing instructor at the local wall I would train at. And now, twenty years later I was booked on another of his courses the following August.

There was lots going on. Academic courses booked, mountain leader training booked and to keep the momentum going, Turtle and myself booked another trip to Scotland in March of the following year. I needed these things in my life, goals to shoot for. It kept me focused and motivated.

As the Christmas trees and lights started to appear, I was looking forward to the holiday season with some trepidation. Although last Christmas was good, it had been a Christmas I hadn't looked forward to. It had been the first Christmas without my estranged wife and a seizure had caused me to lose my speech. It had been hard to get excited and stay positive. This particular year I was determined for it to be different. I was in a new relationship; I was healthier due to the amount of training I had been doing and I just felt a lot better about myself.

The build-up to the big day was great. Emma and I saturated ourselves in the holiday spirit and made plans to spend some quality time together once her boys had left to spend time with their father. Emma spent Christmas Day and Boxing Day with her family and I with mine. After which I then went to stay with Emma for a few days. I can't describe how great this was. We lit the log-burning stove and spent days lying on the sofa under a blanket, watching Christmas movies and eating and drinking far too much. I felt that my life was starting to resemble some sort of normality, and I took great pleasure in being able to enjoy the simple things. We did of course exchange gifts and lovely they were too. But for me the best gift was spending time with Emma, just enjoying Christmas.

It's a strange thing happiness, 'being happy', feeling happy. We often tell people that we're happy, because well, telling someone that you're not happy is usually a conversation-ender. It's almost seen as a sign of weakness, or you're looked upon like some kind of moaning whinge bag. I believe that our brains compensate for this by masking a lot of our misery, convincing us that we are happy when we are not. Encouraging us to look for quick hits, usually in a spending spree on nice new things, or a vice that will give us that rush of dopamine that we crave. This feeling of fake happiness is often short-lived, after which we then hunt for our next fix. At some point in our lives, we have been truly happy. A memory that you can recall, where in that moment, contentment and happiness merge and you feel warm, loved and appreciated. Where you look out unto the world and realise how lucky you are. I'm pretty convinced that it wasn't when you were dropping fifteen grand on a Rolex, or handing over your credit card to pay for a pair of Gucci sneakers. Spending Christmas with Emma was one of those moments. A moment where I remembered how to be happy.

We spent New Year's Eve with my brother Michael and his husband David at their home in the country. It was a quiet and sedate evening compared to our last visit in the summer, when my brother (possibly trying to increase his potential inheritance) tried to kill me with alcohol. I'd been on the gin and tonics, until the tonic ran out, when my brother then substituted the tonic with vodka. Yes, that's right; my drinks were then gin and Russian rocket fuel. I passed out. The mixture of my brother's cocktails of death and my epilepsy medication knocked me out cold. Once I was poured into bed, Emma and Michael then danced their way into the early hours of the morning to the music of Belinda Carlisle and Cher. Michael, no doubt at some point would have removed his t-shirt and waved it about his head. It took me two weeks to recover fully. I've not touched a gin and tonic since. I was more careful on New Year, avoiding the long pours and not drinking like I was on a rugby tour. We all saw the New Year in and went to bed.

I was looking forward to twenty twenty-two. The sharp broken shards of my life were slowly being put back together, piece by piece. I didn't feel so lost anymore, but I still wasn't sure what my purpose was. I had found peace in the woods and forests around my home, I had found fulfilment in the mountains of Scotland, I had found a reckoning and self-healing in those long-loaded runs, I had found true friendship in the unlikeliest of places and I had found love. I had seen moments of happiness which made me believe not only that I could be happy, but it was okay to let myself be happy.

The new year heralded a new routine and the start of a busier schedule. I was now a mature student with online classes twice a week. I was also keeping up with the YouTube channel and dropping a new video roughly every other week. This took a couple of days out of the week, a night out wild camping and then a whole day of editing. I was also keeping up with my training, I liked the feeling of being busy. It wasn't a proper job in the sense of the word, but I was starting to treat it like it was. The schedule would however be derailed at regular intervals due to my seizures. I'd lose a couple of days out of the week recovering. My epilepsy had improved with some tweaks to my medication but I was still averaging about one seizure a week and several absent seizures, when I would just stare into space for a minute or two, before returning to Earth. It was frustrating. Between the doctors and myself we just couldn't get over this final hurdle. The search continued. The vast myriad of drugs I was taking constantly was being shifted up or down in dosage, in an attempt to reduce my seizures further.

As we approached the end of January Emma and I decided that we would book a short break away in February, for my birthday, which coincidently falls on Valentine's Day. We would also take the opportunity to visit Neil the Tash and his wife Sarah, that was the plan anyway. A few days before departure, I received a phone call from Sarah. Neil had caught Covid! We still packed up the car anyway and headed to the seaside town that time forgot, Cromer. We'd booked a very quaint apartment on the coast, overlooking the high street lined with small tourist shops, fish and chip establishments and small independent art galleries selling the work of local artists. Set very close to the beach it was idyllic, well it would have been if it wasn't blowing a gale and throwing down big fat rain all weekend! It didn't bother us. We spent the day in a bar perched just above the sea and ate and drank till we staggered back to the apartment. The following morning, we headed out for breakfast. Frustratingly due to the school holidays the town was busy with tourists and everywhere was full. No problem, Emma offered to cook breakfast at the apartment. We headed to the local supermarket to collect supplies. I remember walking in, I remember suddenly feeling the urge to leave and then the next thing I know I'm waking up lying opposite the self-checkout tills, with Emma talking into my ear, coaxing me back to consciousness. As the world started to come back into focus, I felt severe pain in my left side. I waited till the fog had dissipated and then managed to get to my feet. Emma tried to hold me up as best she could, we struggled out into the carpark and then limped back to the apartment. The pain in my side started to fade away, but when I took a deeper breath, it would instantly shoot back. I played it down as I didn't want to worry Emma, although I was starting to worry myself. What if I had broken a rib? Although I only have basic first aid knowledge, I knew there was nothing that could be done medically. I also knew these types of injuries take months to heal. Emma set about cooking breakfast, whilst I sat uncomfortably on the sofa convincing myself I wasn't in any pain. I was sure it would be fine by the following morning. If I sat perfectly still and upright,

I hardly felt any pain at all, but lying down was very painful. I didn't sleep much that night. Every time Emma asked if I was okay, I'd say I was. I didn't want to spoil our trip. I carried on as if nothing had happened. We went for a walk along the beach, getting sandblasted with salt water in the mini hurricane, before seeking refuge in the beachfront bar and grill, again. We stayed most of the day and then into the evening, drinking porn star martinis with our hamburger dinners. The drink helped massively with the pain and I was quite happy to while away our time drinking and just generally having a good time. It was a great evening, considering the whole weekend from an outside perspective would've looked like a complete disaster. We travelled home the following morning.

As the days went on my rib didn't seem to be getting any better, frustratingly this was stopping me from training. I was getting increasingly worried as I was heading off with Turtle to Scotland in a few weeks, hiking the Great Glen Way. I wasn't sure that I would be able to manage it with the amount of pain I was still in. I reluctantly took myself off to the local minor injuries' unit, just up the road from where I live.

After a quick check-up, it was concluded that I had probably cracked a rib, possibly two. I could have then travelled to the next town to get an X-ray for confirmation. I didn't see the point in this. There is nothing you can do with this kind of injury other than rest. The rest of February just saw me sitting, willing myself to heal. Around this time, the tooth I was waiting to have extracted in hospital was also causing me terrible pain. It never rains! It was so bad that I even contemplated removing it myself, watching YouTube tutorials on how to do it. Emma convinced me that it was probably the most idiotic idea to ever have come out of my mouth. An emergency appointment at the dentist was then booked. The dentist took one look at the tooth and said it needed to be removed, obviously, but she wasn't prepared to extract it. It had to be done under a general anaesthetic due to my epilepsy. She took pity on me and gave me a shot of Novocaine. As the area around my tooth went numb, the pain instantly disappeared. Heaven! She then removed the nerve from my tooth, put in a temporary filling and I went home. The tooth never bothered me again.

The rib was healing very slowly and the pain now and again would catch me out, reminding me that I wasn't completely healed and still needed to take it easy. I spent the next couple of weeks just prepping for the next trip to Scotland. Turtle and I were again heading to Fort William, home of the highest mountain in the United Kingdom, Ben Nevis. From Fort William I would then hike to Inverness along the Great Glen Way. Turtle would catch a bus to Inverness and whilst waiting for me to arrive would spend the days photographing the area. I couldn't wait to get back out and into the highlands of Scotland. I wasn't however looking forward to carrying my twenty-five-kilo pack seventy-eight miles with a cracked rib. This time I was going to be tackling the whole route on my own, with Turtle in the area for support in case something were to happen. For Christmas I had been gifted by my parents a satellite GPS communicator. This allowed me to be tracked via satellite and also send pre-programmed text messages. The device also had an emergency S.O.S. button which would alert the emergency services should I need them. This was all done via satellite and didn't require any cell service. I could be tracked and could communicate at a basic level, all via satellite. This added another layer of security and gave everyone that cared for me some peace of mind. I don't think it stopped anyone from worrying about me, but I was doing all I could to make sure that I was as safe as I could possibly be. Emma and my mother were given a copy of the route and an A4 sheet of details, such as how long I expected to take, where I was looking to camp each evening and some relevant telephone numbers. Another mini adventure was just about to start.

Chapter 13

"There are several types of loneliness, not all are a sign of desperation, some can remind you that you are loved."

The familiar sound of Turtle's snoring started to emanate from the lower bunk. The gentle rocking of the carriage as we travelled to Scotland from London had lulled him to sleep. The journey by train was now well rehearsed, which meant that it was just that, a journey, a necessary distraction. I lay on the top bunk rehearsing the next four days in my head, visualizing possible scenarios and what to do if the wheels suddenly fell off.

The Great Glen Way is a long-distance path which follows the Great Glen, a geographical fault that runs in a near straight line from the Moray Firth (a large triangular bay just north of Inverness) to Fort William, and is around seventy-four miles in distance. I was going to start at Fort William and over a few days hike to Inverness. Turtle was going to spend his time in Inverness, visiting wildlife parks and doing some photography. He was, in sorts, a one-man support crew should I need assistance. The image of Turtle bolting into action, organising a recovery, liaising with family, and generally taking charge of the situation in the event that something were to happen to me, was hard to imagine, as he lay flat on his back, in his bunk, snoring and dribbling out the corner of his mouth.

After an uneventful night, the train finally pulled into Fort William Station, the gateway to the Highlands. We exited the Caledonian Sleeper and stood on the platform sorting out the array of bags and rucksacks we had brought with us. I handed my overnight bag to Turtle and watched as he struggled down the platform, laden down with not only his kit but half of mine also. Turtle was going to check the overnight bags (along with his pack) into a locker within the station, then head out to get some shots of

Ben Nevis. After which Turtle would retrieve our bags from the locker, then catch the bus to Inverness, where he would wait for me at his favourite hostel, Bazpackers.

I left Turtle taking care of the admin and exited through the automatic sliding doors of the station and into the Scottish morning sun. The start of the Great Glen Way was situated just outside the station, next to the main road, close to McDonald's. It was strange to stand looking at the tall blue monolith, which marked the start of the trail, cars rushing past. It didn't seem a fitting location for such an epic journey to begin.

I headed off, northwards following the well-signposted trail. It wasn't long before I was out of the town. A snow-capped Ben Nevis loomed in the rear view in all its glory. I passed the abandoned ship known as the Corpach shipwreck, which rests on a sandy bank where Loch Linnhe meets Loch Eil. I had seen this maritime carcass on several YouTube videos before departing, so it was great to meander past it with a feeling of familiarity. The trail was easy to navigate and after passing Inverlochy Castle, I crossed the river Lochy via the soldiers' bridge (built by soldiers in the sixties as a goodwill gesture to the town of Corpach, hence the name soldiers' bridge) and carried on northward on a wide-open path, escorted by the river Lochy on one side and the Caledonian Canal on the other. The canal was a major part of this trail and I would be in sight of this massive man-made feat of engineering all the way to Loch Ness, as it flowed into and out of several lochs on my journey. Constructed in the early nineteenth century by Scottish engineer Thomas Telford, the whole system was dug out by hand and took nineteen years to complete. It has twenty-nine locks along its length, with eight of those situated just outside Fort William in the small village of Banavie, which are known as Neptune's Staircase. I stood at the first lock, mesmerised by the creative engineering that went into designing this famous set of gates. Imagine the conversations that were had when trying to work out how they were going to raise the canal seventy feet! In my head I had a vision of a massive bearded Scot in a kilt saying "Na problem, hand me ma shovel!" I had never really taken much interest in these things as a child, but now as an adult, I find myself fascinated with not only the engineering of the canal itself but also of the many locks along the way.

I would be on this towpath for quite a while, all the way up to Loch Lochy. It was late morning and the sun was unusually warm, well unusual for March in the Highlands anyway. I drifted in and out of my thoughts and soaked up the amazing scenery. The snow-capped mountains of the Highlands hung from thinly draped clouds in the morning sun to the northwest. I was happy in my own company and before I knew it, I had wandered into the afternoon. The sun had crossed the yardarm. I had left civilisation behind and had the towpath to myself. The few miles which had passed by had travelled beneath my feet unnoticed, the canal and the odd assortment of barges were my only company. My pack weighed around twenty-five kilos. I was carrying everything I needed with me, total self-sufficiency. It didn't feel heavy though. I had conditioned myself with all the training that I had been doing over the last few months. It felt like a breeze. I was used to running with around eighteen kilos, so a gentle walk carrying twenty-five was easy, for me anyway.

During the last few weeks I hadn't done much training, on account that my rib had still been healing. A remnant from the seizure I had in Cromer's Co-op back in February. I now wasn't in any pain. I felt good, so I decided that while I was on the flat towpath, I was going to run a couple of miles. I waited for my GPS to round up to the next mile and started running. I was going to run a mile and then see how I felt, but the first indications were good. I had no pain in the ribs and the towpath (which was as flat as a pool table) made it easy. I kept up a steady pace and it wasn't long before I'd ticked off another mile. I stopped running and decided to walk a mile before running the next. The rib was giving me no pain at all and this boosted my confidence. I had been worried that I may have had to cancel the Fan Dance due to my injury, but now I was sure I'd be fit enough. Another mile ticked by and off I went again. Keeping a steady pace, I cracked on. This mile felt a bit tougher, not because of the rib, but because I was lacking a bit of fitness due to the time off. The second mile was not as comfortable as the first and as I reached the end, I was blowing…hard. Maybe tabbing with a twenty-five-kilo pack wasn't the greatest way to test if the rib had healed?

Before long I had reached the point where the canal flowed into Loch Lochy. The loch, which is around nine miles long and five-eighths of a mile wide shimmered in the afternoon sun, like the Mediterranean Sea, which caressed the golden sands of a deserted beach. It was hard to believe I was in Scotland and not in some faraway country. All that was missing were the coconut trees. I wandered along the trail which hugged the shoreline, until I decided to sit. I'd been on the road for several hours and thought I deserved a rest, where better than the picturesque place I now found myself? I made a hot drink and sat on a large tree stump. Looking across to the far side of the loch, my gaze hit the snow-capped mountains on the horizon and then onto the deep rich blue sky. There are places on this earth that are too beautiful for words, this was one of them. I was tempted to camp right where I was for the night, but I felt the beauty of where I sat was intoxicating me, willing me to stay and keeping me from moving on, like the sirens of the sea tempting sailors to the rocky shores. I finished my brew, packed up my kit, shouldered my pack and set off. I will never forget the tranquillity and beauty of that moment, ever.

I hiked on, rather briskly if I remember correctly, with not a care in the world. It was well into the afternoon. I continued alongside the loch and under the canopy of trees which hugged the shoreline, until the path moved slightly further away and closer to the road. I was now out of the shade and into the sun, which was still reasonably high. I felt the warmness on my neck as I negotiated between the path and the road. Dusk was still a few hours away, which meant the soft warm rays would be accompanying me for a few miles more.

As the road intersected with the trail, I came upon another very significant waypoint. Now and then, along the route, you'd come across small blue information boards. These boards would tell you about historical sites at the location you were in. This board caught my eye and I stopped. Just off the path was a rectangular concrete base. In front of the concrete base was a large rectangular hole, approximately twice the size of the base. This had been filled in with shingle. I knew instantly what this landmark was from the research I had done prior to leaving. It would have been easy to miss so I was glad to have spotted it. The concrete base was the remaining remnant of a dummy World War Two landing craft, the type of craft that landed on the beaches of Normandy on the sixth of June nineteen forty-four. The wooden structure that would have been built up and around the base had long since perished, the trough which would have held a large volume of water had also been filled in. Soldiers who were training for the Normandy landings would have been crammed into this replica. The wooden drawbridge would have been raised and on a given signal would have been dropped. Soldiers would have then exited down the ramp and into the trough of water. Smoke grenades and explosives would have been going off to simulate the landing, along with instructors firing live ammunition over their heads. I felt very humbled reading the information which was screwed under a clear Perspex sheet. The picture of one of these training exercises was next to the written information and depicted the true nature of the task ahead. My grandmother's first husband (and father to my oldest auntie, now sadly passed away) was killed at Arnhem in the Second World War, we believe that he was part of the Normandy landings. He's buried in a war grave in the town of Uden in Holland. A picture of him in uniform hung always in my grandparents' house. I stood and gave my own minute's silence.

The road beckoned and so I continued, northeast along the loch. The small village of Clunes was well behind me and as the sun hit the peaks of the mountains to the west, I decided to look for a campsite. No sooner had this thought crossed my mind than I came upon one of the purpose-built wild campsites, which are situated along the route. An area allocated for wild camping with the addition of composting toilets. I'd covered just under twenty miles that day and was three-quarters of the way along the loch. I would have been a fool to pass up this location. I passed the wooden shack that housed the toilets and headed along the shoreline. An open space emerged. It was however littered with rubbish and the large remnants of a fire, so I decided to move further along. Eventually, I found a flat spot to pitch, right on the shoreline with great views of the loch. As the sun hid behind the hills to the west, it splashed the sky with a fiery red phoenix, rising from behind the mountains as if lifted from the pages of Tolkien himself. It was there I pitched my tent.

The first day was over. I sat in the doorway of my small one-man tent, boiling water on my stove for my dinner, watching the myriad of colours fall from the sky and settle on the smooth surface of the loch. The stars gradually revealed themselves one by one. It was as if the sky had fallen into a deep sleep and had woken the stars from theirs, as dusk transitioned into night. I crawled into my sleeping bag and zipped it up, but left both tent doors open so I could watch the stars staring at their reflections in the glass-like water, which stretched out before me. I slowly ate my rehydrated noodles. It wasn't much, but it felt like a banquet fit for a king.

Dawn shifted into the morning and the sky was ablaze. The sun had risen above the horizon but was still in hiding behind the mountains. I drank coffee and sat on a small rock at the water's edge. The morning was cold and my exhaled breath mirrored the steam emanating from my mug. Unusually my feet were sore from the previous day, I wasn't sure why as my boots had been well broken in. A couple of small hotspots had developed on the toes and the balls of my feet. I soaked them in the freezing water of Loch Lochy, dried them and then taped up the affected areas, before heading back to the tent to deconstruct my temporary home.

It took slightly longer than I had wanted to pack away my kit. I was a bit sluggish and maybe a bit reluctant to leave this perfect campsite, but I had a long way to go that day and needed to crack on. I headed out of the small paradise I had camped in and back onto the path, it wasn't long before I reached the village of Laggan and the end of Loch Lochy. I was then again back on the towpath of the Caledonian Canal, heading towards north Laggan and Loch Oich. After a mile or so I started to develop some pain in both feet. As I passed north Laggan and headed along the shores of Loch Oich towards the village of Invergarry, I was in severe discomfort. I should have stopped, checked and possibly retaped my feet and changed my socks, but as per usual my stubbornness prevented me from doing so and I pushed on. By the time I reached Invergarry, I was in lots of pain in both feet and was struggling to walk. I wanted to take my boots off and sort my feet out, but was worried that once the boots came off my feet would swell, then I'd be unable to put them back on. I popped some ibuprofen and hobbled on, hoping that either the painkillers would kick in, or my feet would just numb up on their own.

I made it to the end of Loch Oich and was now back on the towpath of the canal, barely able to walk. I found a shaded spot, took off my pack and slumped to the ground. Was this the end of the road? I couldn't see how I was going to continue in my current condition. I decided to remove both boots and assess the damage. I pulled off the boots, then removed my socks. The tape that I had applied in the morning had held, so I slowly and carefully peeled it off. Blisters had started to form on my toes, heels and on the balls of each foot. Both feet had also started to swell, which was my worst fear. I stared down at my trashed feet, red and sore, like my feet had developed some sort of jungle rot infection. Why had this happened? What had I done wrong? Although taking my boots off had given me instant pain relief, it didn't resolve the situation. Do I continue, or do I hobble into the next town and quit? I decided to just sit and enjoy a moment of a pain-free existence.

As the pain subsided, my attitude improved. The swelling had started to go down and in doing so a tiny bit of hope started to appear. If I could protect the blisters I already had and prevent any more from forming, I should be alright. I pulled out my first aid kit and started to arrange the components I would need on the grass, scissors, moleskin, tape and foot powder. I cleaned both feet with antiseptic wipes and then let my feet dry in the morning sun. Whilst my feet were drying, I started to cut pieces of Luekotape and moleskin to the sizes I thought I would need. I also pulled the laces out of my boots. Once dried I applied the sticky moleskin to both heels and then covered them with tape. I then individually taped up my big toes and the pinkies next to them, placing a piece of moleskin in between, before taping the two toes together. I then taped up my little toes. My toes were where most of the damage had been done. Lastly, I placed a strip of tape across the balls of my feet, before giving my heavily taped feet a good dusting of foot powder. I'd done about thirty miles, but my feet looked like they had done three hundred. I took some more ibuprofen, packed away the first aid kit and stuffed it into my pack. I took the opportunity to rehydrate and take on board some sustenance in the form of a protein bar, then pulled on a new pair of fresh socks. There I sat, contemplating sticking my ham trotters back into my boots. I had a theory that my boots had been laced up too tight and as my feet swelled, they got hot (which they will undoubtedly do on a long-distance hike). This had caused more friction, which was compounded even more by my sweaty wet woollen socks. I placed my boots in front of me, and stood up. A slight soreness started to return. I wiped any debris off the bottom of my socks, then stepped into my boots. An all too familiar feeling of uncomfortableness returned. I proceeded to re-lace my boots from the bottom up. However, I decided to lace them up like my Danners (the boots I use for tabbing). The laces didn't cross over from the second eyelet to the third, but threaded from the second eyelet and then up to the third eyelet on the same side, continuing to lace up to the top in the standard cross pattern. This allowed for some cross-lateral movement in the width at the widest part of my foot, allowing the boot to give a little. Both boots now back on and re-laced, I paced up and down the towpath. Disappointingly the pain returned, not quite as bad as before the retaping of feet and relacing of boots, but bad enough that I'd probably have to call it a day when I reached the next town, which was Fort Augustus.

I slowly carried on down the towpath. I planned to make it to Fort Augustus and catch the bus to Inverness. I knew where the bus station was as I'd done that bus journey before, albeit in reverse, from Inverness to Fort Augustus when I hiked the South Loch Ness Trail the year before. Again, it was an unusually warm day, but I wasn't enjoying the weather or the scenery for that matter. My eagerness and enthusiasm to get going and get to Inverness (nearly eighty miles away) in three days, had seen me make the schoolboy error of not taking care of my feet. This wasn't the first time I had made this mistake. I should have learnt.

I was several miles away from Fort Augustus and making okay progress, the pain in my feet however was starting to subside. Whether that was because the ibuprofen was doing its job, or the taping of feet and relacing of boots was helping, I wasn't sure. Either way, things were starting to look up. By the time I reached Fort Augustus I was feeling much better. I walked along the pavement on the west side of the canal, past the tourist shops and cafés. It was a glorious day and lots of people were out enjoying the weather, sitting at tables outside, drinking teas and coffees and enjoying the odd cream cake or ice cream. There was a mini supermarket at the end of town, situated at the roundabout where three roads converged. I decided to enter and resupply with more ibuprofen and tape. I was going to need it. I picked up what medical supplies I needed along with a sugary soda and a chocolate bar, paid and exited the store. I sat on the wall outside and washed down a couple of ibuprofen with the soda and chocolate bar. It was mid-afternoon.

The route would now take me out of town, where I could either take the low road or without sounding corny, take the high road. The thought of quitting had long exited my mind, looking back I now realise that I was never going to give up. That was never an option. It was a momentary lapse of discipline that manifested itself into the default mode of thinking quitting was an option. It wasn't, I don't give up. I wanted to complete the route in three days. I had however given myself a fourth day as a buffer should I need it. Worst case scenario, I had an extra day, which I could spend resting my feet.

Drinks and chocolate finished, I hiked out of town and picked up the trail. As I headed up the road a familiar blue post came into view. This was crunch time, low road or high road? I didn't even question it. I turned left off the path and headed upwards and into the forest. I was now moving parallel to Loch Ness, however it would be a while before I would be able to see the fabled body of water. On the map, the climb up through the forest didn't look like much, but with a twenty-five-kilo pack and slightly sore feet, it took a concerted effort to keep heading upwards. The twisty path that snaked its way up through the mass of trees seemed to go on forever. Then, and without warning, the terrain levelled out. I was again now moving parallel with Loch Ness and heading out of the forest. I had reached the top of the path, the forest now dropping away to my right. This gave me the first stunning views overlooking the loch. It was a clear day and I could see Fort Augustus where I had just come from in the distance. Even the canal was now visible from the high elevation, as it meandered into obscurity. It was these moments that motivated me to venture outdoors. The majesty of the arena in which I stood added more fuel to the tank. The soreness in my feet dissipated and for a moment, time stood still. The only sound was a gentle breeze in the air and the breath being exhaled from my body. It was then that I felt a feeling of loneliness. To stand and look out across the mighty Loch Ness would have only been better if I were to be sharing it with someone.

I am often surprised and dumbfounded at how difficult it is to share my passion for the outdoors, especially with family. Michael, the older of my younger brothers, has a passion for travel and has visited many parts of the world, all from the comfort of business-class air travel and exceptionally nice hotels or private villas. Emma and I had discussed that we'd both like to hike the Inca Trail to Machu Picchu, the famous Inca ruins in Peru. Michael also mentioned that this is a place he would love to visit. Great I thought. A trip we could all do together? It turned out during the discussion that Michael was not interested or had any intention of hiking to the Inca ruins, but rather his preferred method would be an organised excursion from the comfort of his hotel. There is nothing wrong with that. He works hard and deserves to enjoy these luxuries, but for me, I feel I would miss too much. The journey is just as important as the destination. Michael would argue that he'd still be able to see it all from the window of an air-conditioned coach.

I couldn't hang around much longer absorbing my surroundings, time was ticking on and it looked like the weather was in a state of change. The wind was picking up and darker clouds loomed on the horizon. I didn't much fancy having to pitch up in the rain, it was time to get going. As I struck out, I remembered it was Emma's youngest son's birthday. Bertie was turning eleven that very day. I had met both of Emma's boys for the first time several weeks before. I guess this was her way of acknowledging that our relationship had legs and was (for want of a better expression) serious. Alfie was the older of the two boys, he was fourteen years old and reminded me of his mum when she was his age, tall, extremely slim and all arms and legs. He was quiet and very polite. As we've got to know each other he's now not so quiet, but he's still very polite, to me anyway. A stereotypical teenager, any parent will understand the challenges of raising these creatures of raging hormones. Bertie on the other hand is just a ball of energy. He's either at one hundred percent or asleep. I'd say he was more communicative with me than Alfie, but that's because Alfie is cool and doesn't want to associate himself with the uncool, namely adults. In fact, by using the term "uncool" I am by definition being uncool. Both boys however are good lads and along with the rest of Emma's family have made me feel very welcome. At the time of booking the trip, I had yet to have had the pleasure of meeting the boys. If I had, I would have pushed the trip back a week as to not miss Bertie's birthday.

The wind was picking up slightly, although I wasn't very high up in terms of metres. I was halfway up the valley and quite exposed. I recorded a short video message for Bertie, wishing him a happy birthday, sent it via WhatsApp to Emma and then got a hustle on. The views remained amazing as I carried on up the trail, I'd almost forgotten about the pain in my feet. After around a mile or so the high road intersected with the low road. Both now pushing northeast. I was now starting to get very conscious of time. The sun was low in the sky and I still wasn't sure where I was going to pitch up for the night. The terrain where I was didn't lend itself to wild camping. Trying to find a flat spot would be difficult. I needed to push on and get to the next village of Invermoriston, then at least I would have dropped down from the higher ground and out of the elements. It seemed a big ask. I had wasted a big chunk of time earlier in the day trying to sort out my feet, which I was paying for now.

The terrain started to undulate the further I went on, up and down, down and up. It was starting to take its toll. The first spots of rain started to fall from the darkened skies. This gave the landscape a sinister appearance which was further infused by the disappearing sun. Life was now dull and grey. Gone were the rich greens and browns and the shimmering sparkles on the water of Loch Ness. She was now just a dark mass of water. This part of the trail felt like it was never going to end. The rain was holding off for now, but I was sure at some point the angry skies would drown me in their hatred. I persevered and carried on. As dusk set in I started to descend a dark narrow trail back into the forest. Darkness had crept in without me noticing and I was now having to use my headtorch. Tall trees overshadowed the narrow path the further I descended, closing in and blocking out the sky. Eventually, after what felt like an eternity I was spat out from the downward funnel of trees and onto the dark streets of Invermoriston. There was not much here. A few properties and that was it. It was now proper dark and I still had no idea where I was going to camp.

As I wandered aimlessly down the dark street, I spotted a property on the left-hand side of the road. It appeared to have several cabins on a plot of land and looked like they could be holiday lets. Maybe they had an area for camping, it was worth a punt. I crossed over the road and headed down the dark driveway, past a set of bins and towards the first property. This was starting to feel like the beginning of a horror movie.

A weary hiker walks alone in the dark looking for somewhere to stay. Trying to shield his face from the rain he stumbles across a wooden shack in the middle of nowhere. He climbs up a short set of wooden steps and onto the weather-beaten porch. As he approaches the door, the sound of laughter emanates from inside. A loud television set is playing a game show which is amusing the occupants, then very hesitantly, he knocks on the door...

The television set was either turned off or the volume turned down, as it was no longer audible. There was a significant pause. I knocked again. I then heard some movement from inside. I was now feeling very apprehensive about who or what was going to open the door. If it's a young kid with a banjo I'm away on my toes I thought. The handle turned and the door was gently pushed open from the inside. An elderly woman stood in the doorway, backlit by the kitchen light, in her arms she held the decapitated head of a young man! Only joking! "Hello, can I help you?" she asked. Relieved that I wasn't now going to be forced into a rendition of Duelling Banjos, I replied.

"Yeah, er Hi! I've just come across the high pass from Fort Augustus heading towards Inverness on the Great Glen Way, I was wondering if there was anywhere I could pitch a tent, I don't mind paying". The lady didn't answer, she just turned towards the lounge area which was just past the kitchen and shouted to her husband.

"Can we let this man pitch his tent?" she shouted. Without noticing a young man suddenly appeared from behind scaring the life out of me. He'd obviously been alerted by the shouting.

"You all right mate?" he asked.

"Yeah, I'm just looking for a place to pitch a tent for the night, I don't mind paying and I'll be gone by sunrise", I nervously replied. The feeling that I might be murdered in my sleep, was now feeling like it was a real possibility.

"Who is it?" came a reply from the lounge.

"A man who wants to put up a tent!" said the wife.

"Yes mate, no problem. We have a small flat bit of land just past the bonfire. You can put your tent up there" interrupted the man who was standing on the porch next to me. A booming sound then erupted from the lounge.

"Tell him to pitch it up on the flat ground, just past the bonfire. He'll need to make donation to charity when he leaves." The young man (who I now realised was the couple's son) started to laugh.

"Follow me mate, I'll show you where you can put up your tent and where the outside tap is if you need water." I followed the man off the porch and past several wooden shacks, past a burnt-out bonfire and towards the back of the property. Is this where I'm going to get clipped, my belongings stolen and my body consumed by a cult of shack-dwelling elderly residents, I wondered? I was shown the area where I could pitch up and where the tap was. The son turned out to be super cool. Further conversation revealed that his parents owned the land and that it hadn't been a holiday let for years. I'd rocked up to a private residence, whose owners had then let me pitch my tent in their back garden out of the goodness of their hearts, plus a small charitable donation of course.

No sooner had the tent gone up and my sleeping kit rolled out inside than the heavens opened. I lay on top of my sleeping bag, sore and tired. I'd covered twenty-two miles. What a day. I ate, made a hot drink and inspected my feet. The tape had held well and showed no signs of pulling off, so I decided to leave it on for the next day. I checked the map. There was a large campsite just off the trail in the next town of Drumnadrochit, home of the famous loch side ruin, Urquhart Castle. It was around fourteen miles away from my current position, which meant a shorter day. If I could get an early start, I could be in Drumnadrochit by midday. This meant I could rest up before the last day, the hike into Inverness. I then wouldn't need to go into my buffer day. I could potentially finish the route in the time frame I had set myself. Plan formulated, I took my medication and let the sound of the rain pull me into sleep.

Chapter 14

"You don't just quit, there is a process, a negative thought that swells in your mind that convinces you that quitting is the only option. To push through, don't follow the process, simple".

I woke several times in the night, probably as the rain got heavier, as it rapidly fired its ammo against the thin fabric walls of the one-man tent. I didn't mind, I almost always instantly fell asleep again and I wanted to make sure I didn't oversleep. The final awakening came around six a.m. I could tell it was still dark outside but the rain had at last stopped, at least for now. As I regained consciousness, I suddenly became aware that I needed to go, desperately, number two. This sprung a mild sense of panic through my body. How was I going to manage this? I was literally in someone's back garden. I hastily opened the inner tent door and was instantly stopped in my tracks. There, laying on my rubber sit mat was a large clear Zip-lock bag, a Zip-lock bag that didn't belong to me. Inside this Zip-lock bag was a small dark rectangular box. I unzipped the bag and pulled out the small box. I lifted the lid and inside was a beautifully made, antler-handled knife. It was around six inches long including the handle, with a highly polished blade. Also, inside the box was a handwritten note. The note was from the owner's son, thanking me for taking the time to talk to him the previous night. We had (as I was putting up the tent) a long discussion about hiking, camping and the outdoors in general. I had given him a brief outline of how I had gotten to where I was in my journey and he described what his life had been like. We had both suffered with depression and it was very cathartic to acknowledge the similarities in each other's stories. The son made a small living by making these beautiful handmade knives, using local materials. It was a touching moment; I hadn't realised we had connected in such a strong way. Even today I still find it hard to talk about my own mental breakdown. I still unfortunately see it as a sign of weakness in myself. I know many of you will now say that I probably haven't come to terms with, or resolved certain issues within my own mind, and you may be right. I had enjoyed my conversation with the stranger the previous night and now, after receiving this beautiful gift from him, it made me feel that I had, in a small way helped, just by listening. I put the knife back in the box and put it safely inside my pack. The large Zip-lock bag, well that was fortuitous and was going to come in very handy.

The sentimental moment was soon shattered, as a sense of urgency gurgled in my belly. I slid into my boots, grabbed the large empty Zip-lock bag and the poop kit, opened the outer door of the tent and stepped out into the sharp crisp air of the morning. It was overcast, a dampness hung in the air from the previous night's rain. I rushed to the rear of the tent, still only in my thermal underwear and boots, and concealed myself behind the tent as best I could. I absolutely did not want to get caught crapping into a Zip-lock bag, by either the owners' of the property or the son. I would then have to murder them all with my shiny new knife, burn their corpses on the bonfire, wipe my prints off the murder weapon, before disappearing into the wilderness, never to be seen again. I rapidly put operation 'crap in a bag' into effect. With the speed and agility of a highly trained ninja, I had soon accomplished my mission. I now had a see-through bag of shit to dispose of! I rummaged around in the vestibule of the tent and found the silver Mylar bag from the previous night's dinner, stuffed the Zip-lock bag inside, and sealed it up.

I crawled back inside the tent and started to get ready for the day ahead. I gave my feet a good dousing of foot powder and put on fresh socks. I now only had one pair of clean socks left, which I was going to save for the last day and the hike into Inverness. After struggling to get dressed in the confines of my small tent, I finally emerged. I would say like a butterfly emerging from its cocoon, but the reality was, I was probably looking terrible and smelt even worse. The campsite that I was heading for that day was loaded with facilities, showers, a laundrette and an on-site shop. A perfect place to consolidate before the last day. I started to pack up my kit and take down the tent. The gentle wind of the morning had partially dried the tent, making it easier to collapse and stuff back into its bag. As I was putting all the kit away into my pack the son appeared. I thanked him for his generous gift and gave him my number and told him he can call any time, day or night. As of writing, I have yet to receive a call or text. I hope he's doing okay. I hoisted up my pack, gave the son a "charitable donation" in the form of a twenty-pound note, said my goodbyes and headed off. As I passed the gathering of bins near the exit, I tossed in the Mylar bag from the morning's ablutions.

I exited the property and turned left onto the road, which in the daylight didn't seem as foreboding as the night before. I crossed over a stone bridge that spanned the cascading water of the River Moriston, which ran out of Loch Ness and headed out of town. As I came up to the junction of the A887 road which headed towards Drumnadrochit, I came upon a small shop. Outside the shop adorning its biggest wall was the most amazing painting of the Loch Ness Monster I have ever seen. Painted in blues and blacks, the scene depicted a tiny boat on top of the loch, adjacent to Urquhart Castle which was shadowed in the background. The scene was dark, depicting a stormy day upon the loch. Underneath the boat the giant leviathan was rising. A long neck and small head pointed up towards the tiny boat, with body, flippers and long tail directly below, reminiscent of the movie poster from Jaws. The head of Nessie had been painted in such a way that you knew this beast beneath the waves was kind, and meant no malice, unlike the shark in Jaws. I was mesmerised by the large painting and just stood, staring, trying to take in every detail. I took several pictures with my phone and entered the shop, which was small and quaint.

I purchased a warm sausage roll and a sugary soda and consumed both in the shop while perusing the rest of the store. Breakfast over it was time to hit the trail again, fourteen miles into Drumnadrochit and hot showers, hot food and an early night.

The trail followed the road for a few hundred yards, then a left turn ushered me up into another Scots Pine forest. The path zig-zagged upwards and was overshadowed by tall trees, the steep incline required some effort to keep going. My feet although much better than the previous morning, started to increase in soreness along with the increased gradient.

It was hard work. I was starting to feel the burn as I puffed and panted up the switchbacks. The day was overcast and colder than the previous one and I wasn't feeling too great. Yes, I had sore feet and was a little tired, but I'd usually shake this off and carry on regardless, but it wasn't that. I felt grey, like the weather. I had no reason to feel like that. I just felt I needed to get to Drumnadrochit, pitch my tent, take a long hot shower and chill. I felt a sense of urgency about it, like I would feel better once I had gotten there. The zig-zag path that wound its way up the hill flattened out and I exited out of the trees and into the wind. I looked down towards the loch which was shrouded in cloud, the wind whipping hard, the bigger gusts making me a bit unsteady on my sore feet. As I crested the hill, I came across another famous landmark on the Great Glen Way. The Viewcatcher. A stone plinth which stands on top of the high path. On top of this plinth is a circle made of wooden branches twisted to form a large ring. It frames a group of Munros to the north when looking through it. I stood for a while and stared hypnotically through its twisted branches and into the distance. The wind had driven out the morning cloud and I could see uninterrupted for miles. After a while I ducked down behind the plinth, opened my pack and pulled out my jacket. I was feeling the cold.

The monster beneath the waves, which adorned the outside wall of the Peachie Ness store painted by Texan artist Oh La La

The trail continued, as did I. Loch Ness down to the east escorting me along the high pass. After a while, I came upon a convergence of trails. A blue post and arrow pointing in my direction of travel marked the waypoint. It read "Drumnadrochit 7 Miles". Seven miles was nothing. I'd do seven miles for breakfast, but today it felt like a long way. My heart sank. Even though the terrain had flattened out, the day was rapidly becoming a laborious slog and I couldn't wait for it to be over. The trail continued, the wind continued and I continued, atop the northwest hill above Loch Ness.

Eventually, the elevation started to drop. The views of the mighty Loch Ness disappeared behind a blanket of trees and the trail turned into a road. A straight road which would stretch on for a few miles before dropping into Drumnadrochit. My feet were now taking a real pounding on the road, once again I was in extreme agony. I couldn't wait for this section to be over. It was gutting, but at least I was out of the wind. Eventually, I reached the outskirts of Drumnadrochit. A large sign on the road read "CAMPING 100 Metres". At last, hot food and a hot shower. I crossed the main road and opened the small gate, which led to a footpath and onto the campsite. There were a couple of motorhomes parked in neatly marked-out bays, but it was empty, and for good reason. It was closed.

The large sign pinned on the office window stated that they were due to open at the beginning of April. There was a mobile number at the bottom, so I decided to give it a call. After a brief conversation with the owner, he agreed I could pitch up at the rear of the site, provided I couldn't be seen from the road. He was worried others might see the tent and then also pitch up. No showers, no toilets and no on-site shop. It felt like a terrible end to a rough day. I was grateful that I was allowed to camp on the property and it was still early afternoon, so I was going to get plenty of rest. I hobbled to the far end of the site, dropped my pack and pushed the message button on my satellite GPS unit. This sent a pre-typed message to Emma and my mother saying I was okay. It wasn't long before the tent was up. I was now looking forward to some hot food, some rest and ultimately sleep. Then, while I was in the middle of arranging my kit, I had a seizure.

I think it was the cold that brought me around. I was shivering. It was then that I instantly knew what had happened. I was lucky. I was kneeling and leaning into the tent when it happened. Whilst my lower legs were slightly damp from the fine rain that had started, the rest of me was dry. I dragged the rest of my body into the tent, removed my boots (which was a struggle) and managed to climb into my sleeping bag. Fortunately, I had inflated my mat and rolled out my sleeping bag just before having the seizure. I instantly fell asleep.

Even though I had slept for a couple of hours it was still only the middle of the afternoon. I was still feeling a little loopy from the seizure, but decided I needed to sort myself, and my kit out. I unzipped the inner tent door and then the outer door. I grabbed my pack which I had left outside and dragged it into the vestibule of the tent. My plan was to undress and get into my thermals. Before removing my socks, peeling the tape off my feet and tending to any blisters. Finally finishing with a hot meal and hot drink, before getting an early night. I struggled out of my damp clothes and into my thermals. I tentatively pulled off my socks, then slowly and meticulously I peeled off the tape on both feet. It was a horror story. I had big blisters on both heels as well as on the balls of my feet and toes. My left little toe had developed some kind of blood-filled haematoma on it. All the blisters were still intact, but all were full to bursting with fluid. Minor surgery was now required.

I readied the operating room. Clearing a space, I removed all the items I would need from my first aid kit. Antiseptic wipes, needle, lint-free gauze, tape, scissors, lighter and a towel, arranging everything on the towel in the order in which I was to use them. I then wiped both feet thoroughly with the wipes, took the needle out of its sheath and heated it with the lighter. After what I thought was sufficient time to kill any bacteria on the needle, I gave it a clean with another antiseptic wipe. I started first on the heels, pushing the needle gently into the bottom of the blister, releasing a river of clear liquid onto the towel. After draining both blisters I moved onto the toes, then the balls of the feet, methodically draining the fluid out of each one. The blood-filled haematoma spurted its contest into the air. You'd have thought I had hit an artery with the amount of blood. Surgery complete, I wiped both feet again, then placed lint-free gauze over the empty blisters, before lightly taping the gauze down. I wasn't going to strap my feet up till the morning, but I wanted to cover up my handiwork to avoid infection. Somewhat triumphant in my surgical skills, I took to boiling some water for my dehydrated meal and a hot drink.

The rain had started again. I sat, eating my meal still overwhelmed with tiredness and fatigue from the earlier seizure, forcing myself to stay awake, listening to the symphony of raindrops bouncing off the tent. I was twenty miles away from Inverness and was determined to get there the following day. I didn't want to use my buffer day. I wanted to get there in the time I had set myself. Dinner finished I shuffled down into my sleeping bag, set my alarm for zero six hundred and turned out the light. I started to close my eyes; and was asleep before they had fully shut. It had been a short day in terms of mileage, but it had felt like the longest day.

I slept uninterrupted, only awoken by the alarm. I still felt a little groggy from the seizure the day before, but it was time to hustle. I needed to get a good breakfast inside me, strap up my feet and break camp. I wanted to be back on the trail by zero seven thirty. I opened the inner tent door without exiting from my warm sleeping bag. My cook kit was already laid out from last night's dinner. Picking up the stove with the gas canister attached, I gave it a good shake before setting it back down again and lighting it. I felt the warmth of the lit stove slowly fill the tent. The hypnotic glow of the heated element kind of made the morning feel better. I emptied half a litre of water from my Osprey bottle into the pot and placed it on top of the MSR Reactor stove. I opened the top of the outer door to keep the tent ventilated, (you should never cook inside a tent unless it's well-ventilated.)

Breakfast was a blur, I shovelled warm porridge into my pie hole, washing it down with a large mug of coffee. It looked damp outside. Fine rain chilled the air. The assortment of empty food packets and the cooking kit was methodically packed away, placing it all in a waterproof stuff sack before rolling down the lid and clipping it shut. I took off my thermal shirt and pulled on my base layer, then it was time to prepare my feet for the next twenty miles. Sliding my lower half out of the warm comfort of my sleeping bag, I peeled off the tape and gauze to assess the damage. Both feet looked a lot better than the previous night, but they were still in poor shape. All the blisters had drained nicely. There was no redness and nothing evil was oozing out of them. Over the next thirty minutes I carefully taped up the affected areas. If I wasn't happy with a particular taping of a toe, I tore off the tape and started again. It had to be right. After finishing the prepping of my feet, it appeared there was more tape than foot! I patted myself on the back for a job well done and finished getting dressed.

It was around seven by the time I set off. It was dry but the threat of rain hung in the air. It felt like mother nature's stopwatch. Could I make it to Inverness before time ran out, where I would then get a soaking? I crossed the empty field of the campsite and exited through the small gate and back onto the road. The town of Drumnadrochit was empty as I crept through its deserted streets. I headed towards the top end of town. This is where I would pick up the last section of the trail on the Great Glen Way.

Heading out of town I passed the famous Loch Ness Centre and Exhibition. I was a little disappointed that I didn't have the time to visit, but today was time-critical, I wanted to get to Inverness in good time. Turtle had secured me a bunk at the hostel. The thought of a hot shower, warm fire and a massive McDonald's dinner complete with a large Fanta was now my motivation. Turning off the road the trail once again headed upwards, steep at first but then levelling out. For several miles the trail passed through more pine forests, the gradient still heading upwards, but shallow enough for me not to notice. At some point I must have hit a high elevation, as the last of the winter snow was still blanketed across the trail. Small purple heads of heather were just visible through its crust. I had been alone on this trail. I had only come across one more soul while hiking the actual route. The solitude had meant that the only companion on this trip were my own thoughts, spending time with myself, checking in and making sure I was okay. I'd walked fifty miles in two and a half days. I'd come a long way, but I'd also come a long way in my own development. These hiking trips, where I would spend time alone in the open vastness of the hills and mountains, was like sticking a USB cable into my brain and wireless charging off the earth itself. As I was uploading and saving memories, I was also downloading my consciousness, sharing my thoughts.

My peace was eventually shattered by the sound of a large diesel engine heading my way. It was strange to hear that type of sound out in the remote hills of the Great Glen Way. Then from out of nowhere came two huge juggernauts around the corner. I moved to the side of the wide trail so they could pass, the driver of the lead truck raised his hand to say 'thank you' as they drove by. Two guys out at work, grafting. I'm not sure what they were hauling or where they were going. Wherever it was it was remote.

The trail now started to gently drop. This meant I was now on the descent into Inverness. I still had a long way to go, but the gentle drop made walking easier and lifted my spirits. Several miles later I started to see brightly painted wooden signs. "Café" they read. The Environment Café as it's called is a must-visit landmark on the Great Glen Way. It's literally in the middle of the wilderness and open all year round. More colourful signs appeared until it seemed like there was one every few yards. Eventually, I came to a turning where a huge sign welcomed me to the entrance of the café. It would have been rude to not pop in! The long pathway soon led to a large wooden shack, with a covered deck. It was well weather-beaten and looked a little unsafe, with rusty nails holding up crooked shelves which were adorned with old bits of junk. There were sharp edges everywhere. Tetanus lurked around every corner. I dumped my pack on the open deck, hoping that it didn't fall through the wooden floor. A large metal gate adorned the front of the owner's property, which looked like a scaled-up version of the 'shack of death'. I rang the small bell, several minutes later a lady appeared. She was not what I expected. She was smartly dressed and didn't look at all like she lived in the wilderness. I guess I was expecting to see someone of unkept appearance, possibly dressed in rabbit skins. The very pleasant lady took my order of coffee and bacon and carrot soup. I then returned to the deck on the 'shack of death' to await my breakfast. It wasn't long before she arrived with a large tray with my order on. It all tasted amazing. It was hard to believe that an establishment this remote could produce such great food and coffee. It was just the pick-me-up I needed, a brief respite to take a load off and refuel. There was so much food that I couldn't eat it all, I left cash on the tray and headed back out and onto the trail, full up.

The miles passed effortlessly beneath my sore feet; I was coming to the end of my journey and starting to feel quite conflicted. I wasn't sure whether I was sad it was coming to an end or whether I was looking forward to getting it done. Turtle had been messaging me all morning, checking up on my progress and then organising some resupply for when I landed in Inverness. He'd been out getting packs of blister plasters and more ibuprofen. I wasn't sure what state my feet would be in when I got there, but it was obvious that it wasn't going to be good. Although the trail was still winding its way through small forests, up and over small hills, it was starting to lose its remoteness. Inevitably as I moved out into a clearing, I caught my first sight of Inverness below in the distance. I stopped to take it in. I had three miles to go, all downhill.

The path wound its way down and onto the outskirts of the city. It was strange to now be moving along the streets of a housing estate, when earlier that morning I was wandering along the hilltops of Loch Ness. As I reached the last mile, I sent Turtle a text "I'll be at the finish in fifteen minutes and I'm coming in hot". I had decided that I had gone into this hike tabbing so I was going out tabbing. I tightened up all the straps on my pack and started running. I crossed over the bridge which spanned the river Ness and onto Ness Island, before crossing the north end bridge and onto the path that ran down beside Island Bank Road. A small set of steps took me up and onto the main road. This was it, the final uphill push.

I ran hard up the final incline towards Inverness Castle, which slowly came into view. I could just about see Turtle, standing patiently, puffing on a cigarette. I think I caught him by surprise. As he clocked me running up the road he suddenly burst into action, camera violently clicking away. I ran onto the grounds of the castle and up to the blue monolith. A blue monolith which looked identical to the one I stood at three days previous in Fort William, over seventy miles away. I touched the monument. It was done. Turtle clicked away with the camera, ensuring we had some good shots for social media. It was good to see my pal again. I started pulling his leg about where my McDonald's was. He responded with a quip about how bad I smelled and that I should take a shower first. We headed off to the hostel which was just sixty yards away. I hobbled along on my blistered feet; Turtle waddled along smoking a cigarette. I thought he may have offered to take my pack for me, but no, not Turtle.

The room in which we were bunking was empty. Turtle informed me that we were the only ones in it. So, I picked a bottom rack and dumped my kit. Turtle was going to head to McDonald's with my monster order, while I was going to take a long hot shower. I sat on the lower bunk and removed my boots and socks, then delicately I started to pull off all the tape on my feet. This as you can imagine took quite a while. It was not a good look. My feet were trashed. I had large open blisters on my heels, with big flaps of skin hanging off them exposing the raw flesh underneath. My toes were in no better shape and neither were the balls of my feet. Turtle had kindly put my overnight bag on the bed. I rummaged through it, found my wash bag, my clean clothes and headed to the showers, grabbing a towel from the clean laundry cupboard in the hallway. I picked an end cubical and hung my clean clothes and towel over the door. I undressed out of my kit, dumping it by the locked door of the cubical and then turned on the water. Hot water came through instantly. I placed my hands on the tiled wall and let the water run over the back of my head and neck. I instantly felt better, the hot water and steam soothing tight muscles which had been under constant strain for over three days. Then the water hit my blistered feet! An instant lightning bolt of sheer pain hit me like a truck and I let out a guttural scream. The pain was so bad it had a sound of its own. Like electricity buzzing in my head. I held my breath, gritting my teeth in agony. I had forgotten about the raw flesh exposed on my feet. I stood for as long as I could bear, letting the water clean the open wounds. Tears of pain rolled down my face, mixing with the warm water from the shower. It was times like these that I wished I had called it a day, given up, and caught the bus from Fort Augustus back to Inverness, but I chose not to. I chose the harder option. The option of carrying on, which I was truly paying for now. The truth is that anybody can fail. Anybody can give up, quit, jack it in, throw in the towel etc. The funny thing is, that the instinct to persevere, to push on regardless is not born out of the fear of failure. It's driven by the thought of what others will think of you. There was no way I was going to tell family and friends I couldn't finish, just because I had sore feet. I like to think I'm made of tougher stuff. I finished showering and changed, before hobbling back to the dormitory to retape my feet, which were now starting to swell.

After patching up my feet with blister plasters and tape, I dressed and then went to meet Turtle in the common room. As I hobbled in Turtle was sitting at a table by the window, a big toothless grin across his face. On the table in front of him, a huge brown bag from McDonald's. With the roaring open fire warming the stone room, I sat and consumed around three thousand calories of junk food, not forgetting a large Fanta. I'd like to say that I then retired to bed, totally knackered. I did not. After my McFeast, Turtle and myself then left the hostel via the main door and went next door into the pub. I then demolished several pints of orange juice and a large burger and chips, after which we slipped back into the hostel and I slipped into a food coma.

The following day started with a McDonald's breakfast, followed by a walk around town shopping for souvenirs for our loved ones back home. Loaded up with shortbread and biscuits, I hobbled back to the hostel with Turtle to retrieve our bags, before heading to the station. Our train wasn't due to depart till around eight in the evening, so we set up shop at the pub in the station complex. Staring at the condensation rolling down the outside of my glass of cold lager, my thoughts turned towards the next challenge. Obviously, it was the looming Fan Dance event that was going to be taking place in June, in around six weeks' time. In the back of my mind, I was already planning a return to Scotland; a return to the mountains to resolve some unfinished business. I wanted to keep pushing myself, to keep challenging my body and mind. I wanted to find the line of what was possible, then tentatively step over it. If I kept pushing myself and moving forward, no matter how tough it was going to be, I would always be making progress, never going backwards. I'd had so many rock bottom moments in the last few years. So many moments of thinking things were starting to get better, to then have the rug pulled from under me. I wasn't going to let that happen again.

We boarded the train, jumped into our bunks and fell asleep, only waking as we hit the outskirts of London, another adventure was over.

Chapter 15

"I don't always see a clear path, sometimes I blindly stumble through the day, lost. But it's in those days where we find our strength and determination."

Upon returning from Scotland, I had another small issue that needed to be taken care of. The problem tooth. The day had finally come to bid farewell to the molar that had been causing me so much pain. It had taken nearly two years for the appointment to come through. The procedure was pretty simple. Put to sleep, extraction, woken up, ice cream, sent home, job done.

I was now in full-on training mode in preparation for the Fan Dance. I decided to set up a Just Giving page, so I could raise money for the Epilepsy Society. It almost felt like a full-time job, training and twisting the arms of family and friends to part with their hard-earned cash. I had learnt that being idle did you no good. It drained you of motivation. Like a virus it attacked every cell, leaving you to wallow in self-pity. I felt much better when I had a plan, when I was working towards something. My days were filled with early morning runs, attending my online GCSE English course and continuing with the YouTube channel. The seizures were still happening. Some weeks were worse than others, but that was just a fact of life now. Dr Chan the consultant neurologist had now passed my care over to an epilepsy nurse, a lovely man called David. I was a little sceptical at first, but upon reflection, I now feel that it increased my care. I was able to email David directly if I had any issues and was able to speak to him more frequently than with Dr Chan. Nothing changed however, just more continual tweaks to my medication, which didn't seem to have any effect. But it was comforting to know that I had a direct line of communication should I need it.

As the event drew closer, I started to doubt my level of commitment and fitness, which then triggered some anxiety about the whole event. I'd never done anything like this before. Watching YouTube videos of the event wasn't helping, it made it worse. Seeing people struggle, fit people looking like they were about to break. I was going into this blind, and that was making me uneasy. I'd been confident about this challenge, but now people had donated money, which added to the pressure. If I had a bad training session or didn't achieve a personal best in a run, I'd panic. It was occupying my every thought. On the outside I portrayed an image of relaxed confidence, but on the inside, I was losing belief in myself. It wasn't long before the thought of quitting started to hover in my mind. I could pull out and pretend I was injured. Nobody would know and, in some respects, I was sure some family members would be relieved. It was time I gave myself a good talking-to. I was making excuses. The fact of the matter was, not that I didn't think I was fit enough, I was unsure of the unknown. What it boiled down to, I was being lazy. There was only one answer. I had to go and walk the route for myself prior to the event. That way I would know what I was letting myself in for, hopefully kerbing the anxiety.

One thing that I have learnt over the last few years is to not take people for granted, this had been a behaviour that I had previously repeated over and over again. It was a contributing factor in the breakdown of both my relationships. I learnt, the hard way, as usual. This part of my personality applied to everyone, including family and friends. In the tornado of events that surrounded my epilepsy diagnosis, I reaped the crop which I had sowed. But true friends, those who care about you, will stand by you no matter what. Neil the Tash is one of those friends. The one friend that I can call and talk to about anything, who'll listen without judgment. I gave Neil a call and explained how I was feeling. By the end of the conversation, we'd arranged a trip to Wales. Neil was going to take care of everything. He arranged the date, the transport and the hotel. I didn't have to lift a finger. It's hard to put into words what our friendship means to me. We'd started out as work colleagues twenty years ago and ended up as family.

Neil had taken a few days off work at the end of April for our recce to Wales, this also happened to be just after his birthday. I wanted to get him a gift, something that would show my appreciation for our friendship. I decided on a military sculpture of a sniper, sitting in the prone position. Neil was ex-forces and a very keen marksman, so I knew this would be something he would appreciate. Bronze in colour, the sniper sat cross-legged, camouflaged and placed on top of a wooden plinth. On the plinth was a plaque which had been engraved, it read "To my brother Neil, for always having my back, Bravo Golf Oscar". Bravo Golf Oscar being the initials of Big Grizzly Outdoors, using the phonetic alphabet. When Neil arrived on Tuesday afternoon, I gave him his belated birthday gift. It was a touching moment. He was speechless. He just sat, looking at it from every angle, taking in every detail. It felt good to be able to show how much I appreciated our friendship. I wanted him to know it wasn't taken for granted. That evening I introduced Neil to Emma. We met at a Turkish restaurant in town and spent the night eating good food and drinking, reminiscing about days gone by and just generally having a good time. I took the time to soak up the enjoyment, to make sure I remembered the moment, to make sure that this moment wasn't taken for granted. I didn't want the evening to end, but time ticked on and inevitably it was time to leave. I asked for the bill, but it had already been paid. Neil had taken care of it when he had gone to use the bathroom earlier. We offered to pay our share, but he refused. A true gentleman. The following morning, we loaded up the car and headed off to South Wales.

It's just over two hundred miles to the Brecon Beacons from home but the journey flew by. Neil and I were chewing the fat all the way. The motorway soon gave way to the rolling hills of South Wales. It wasn't long before we were driving through the small town of Brecon and then pulling up outside our hotel. Neil had made a good choice, a comfortable hotel just a few miles from the start line. We checked in, got the keys to our rooms and headed off to find them. The hotel was old, you could tell this from the thick Axminster-style carpet to the multiple layers of paint on the doors. This was highlighted even more when we got to our rooms. After closing my door, I noticed a gap at the bottom. It was maybe half an inch at the handle end and about two inches at the hinge end. I couldn't quite believe that it would have been left like this, but once I started to move around the room it became evident that the floor was not flat either. It ran downhill and slightly to the left, creaking and groaning as I paced about. Upon further inspection, I noticed the bed had to be propped up on one leg to make it level, along with a small table that was pushed up against the wall. The view from the bathroom was amazing though. As I sat on the toilet, I stared out of the enormous window opposite, which had no curtain or blind to offer any kind of privacy. I gazed over the rooftops of Brecon, with the mountains of the Brecon Beacons breaking up the horizon.

Later on, I met Neil in the bar which was situated by reception. We sank a couple of pints, before heading out to get some food. After devouring a curry from a small Indian restaurant in town, we retired back to the hotel and to our rooms. An early night was needed in preparation for our recce the following day.

I awoke around zero six hundred and spent an hour taping up my feet. Although my feet had fully healed, the pain of Scotland was still fresh in my mind and I didn't want a repeat performance. Once I'd sorted my kit I headed to the restaurant for breakfast, knocking on Neil's door as I walked by. It wasn't long before we were tucking into fried eggs, sausages, beans, bacon and toast, fuelling ourselves up for the day ahead. Breakfast over, we headed to the car and then drove out of town and to the foot of Pen Y Fan. We parked the car in the carpark opposite the Storey Arms (which had been an inn until the early seventies, when it then became an outdoor education centre) and the famous red phone box, which marks the start of the Fan Dance.

The Fan Dance has been an integral part of the British SAS selection process. It was introduced after the Second World War by Major John Woodhouse, who was the brains behind the first SAS selection course. It is effectively a speed march over the Pen Y Fan Mountain and back again. Candidates on selection would be loaded up with kit, including their weapon and given a cut-off time to complete the course. I have heard that to pass, the twenty-four-kilometre course needs to be completed in four hours and ten minutes. Whether this is true or myth I wouldn't know. What I did know, I was just about to find out how tough it was going to be.

Neil and myself strapped on our packs, locked up the car, touched the red phone box and then headed upwards. Neil was doing amazingly well considering he was breaking in a new hip! The weather was good for us. It was a bit windy and cold but we didn't have any rain, which meant we had fantastic views of the hills and valleys around us. We eventually reached the peak of Corn Du, then headed across to the summit of Pen Y Fan, where we took some pictures and had a little break. The back section of the course descended down a trail known as Jacob's Ladder. This was steep. In the wet, I could imagine it being very problematic. The track levelled out slightly and then, after about half a mile it intersected with the Roman road. This took us several miles south and to the halfway turnaround point. By this time Neil was a little stiff in the hip and it was decided that he would catch a cab back to the car. This now allowed me to test myself on the return leg. I about turned, started my Garmin watch and headed back. It took two hours and twenty-six minutes to get back to the car, where Neil was waiting for me. I was knackered, but I had learnt a lot of valuable information about the course, which alleviated some of the anxiety that I had been experiencing about the event. I now had five weeks of final prep. Armed with first-hand knowledge, I could now focus these last few weeks of training where it counted.

I spent the next couple weeks cramming for my English exam and training. I wanted to do well in both, so I worked hard to make sure I was giving myself the best opportunity to succeed. If I did well in my exam then I knew it would be down to me, the same with the Fan Dance. If the wheels fell off and it all ended in disaster, I had nobody to blame but myself. For me, it wasn't easy to dedicate myself to this. There were days I didn't want to strap on the pack and run, days I didn't want to revise the differences between a metaphor and a simile. I had my work cut out for me. Some days it was like trying to hiss and yawn at the same time. I started to break it down into small manageable chunks. If I didn't run then I made sure I did some walking that day. If I didn't study then I would read in bed for an hour before sleep. Any progress no matter how small was still progress.

April drifted into May. It had now been a year since I got soaking wet in the forest, meeting some girl I'd met on the internet. I had never expected to meet anyone, let alone start a relationship. I never expected anyone to love me again. I had considered myself damaged, beyond repair, a broken person that was probably best left alone, to be alone. I'm not sure what Emma saw in me. Maybe my vulnerability made me seem less intimidating or less of a threat. It wasn't love at first sight, we didn't rush into anything, we just hung out, getting to know each other and slowly but surely friendship blossomed into romance. I still felt a little intimidated by her. I was always conscious that I had nothing to offer the relationship. It could be that I was stuck in the dark ages, where a man is supposed to take care of his partner and family and be the breadwinner. Having epilepsy and not being able to work was a massive blow to my masculinity. I had always considered myself an alpha male up until then. Is this why I was pushing my body so hard? Was I trying to compensate? Was I trying to show the world how tough I was? How much pain I could take, in an attempt to prove that I was still a man?

The training was relentless. A mix of long rucks in the forest and speed work on the dreadmill. I was giving it my all. I was driven and focused on every aspect of my life, from my training and academic challenge, to my new relationship. There were certain aspects of my life which will always be outside of my control. But the parts of my life which I could control, I was now making sure it was all squared away. It's not hard to be a good person. You instinctively know what is right but it's also very easy to ignore these instincts and make poor decisions, especially in times of stress or conflict. Now, even though I was still focusing on myself, I was making sure I was making good decisions. Emma and her family had welcomed me in with open arms. I wasn't going to do anything to jeopardise that, or let anyone else either. Where once these attachments were not that important to me, they now meant everything to me. I had ignored this critical life skill before my accident. It would be fair to say I'm not very well thought of by my children's mother, or her family and for good reason. We have no relationship and hardly any contact. Occasionally, I will receive a text lambasting me for something I had said to my daughters which she didn't approve of, but it's water off a duck's back. I had always been the type of person who didn't care what people thought of them. I had considered myself a cut above everyone else…untouchable. Now as I understand the world a bit better, I wished that things were different. Maybe myself and my ex-wife could have a relationship which would make co-parenting easier. I think this would also strengthen the relationship I have with my daughters. But as the girls get older, I now realise it's very unlikely to happen. It's only when you sit down and take a long hard look at yourself, that you realise these things are important and shouldn't have been ignored.

A day that had been sitting in my calendar for months, suddenly arrived. It was paper one of my English exams. My eldest daughter was also sitting her English exam on the same day. She would sit hers at her school and I would sit mine at an adult education centre, a thirty-minute drive from my home. It was a warm day, too warm to be sitting in a classroom for most of the morning, but here I was. Unlike most, I was allowed to take this exam on a computer, rather than having to handwrite it. This wasn't because my handwriting was unreadable. Since banging my head I now find it a struggle to write down on paper what is in my head. I get words around the wrong way or write them down twice. Writing a birthday card for instance can be an effort. I sometimes have to write it down on paper first, before committing it to the card. My handwritten exam paper would have been full of crossings out and changes. Being able to use a word processor would allow me to turn in a readable submission.

After waiting in a holding area with the other students for about half an hour, we were eventually taken to our classrooms. Those that were taking the exam on the computer were separated out, then led up a narrow set of stairs and into a small classroom. There were several rows of desks, all adorned with a keyboard and screen. We were allocated a desk each, all of which had small paper nameplates on them. I found mine and sat down. The sun shone in from the double-aspect windows, casting a warm haze over the room. It would have been a great day for camping or running, or even both. I was starting to feel a slight pang of anxiety. This made me feel like I wanted to be somewhere else and not in a stuffy classroom. I was quickly dragged out of my negative mind space as an exam paper hit my desk. We had a brief announcement about how to use the computer and about time management, then we were off. The only sound that could be heard then was the typing of keys, as I and the half dozen other adult students battered our way through the exam. Time rocketed past and I was soon in a bit of trouble. I didn't panic, I kept my head down and I pushed on, just like I would on a ruck. The one hour and forty-five minutes soon elapsed. We were then instructed to stop typing and to print out our work. Paper one was done. It was much harder than the mock exams we had practised on in the lesson. I wasn't sure how well I had done. Had I set myself up to fail? I still had paper two to do, but that was going to be in the second week of June, a week before the Fan Dance.

The training schedule and revision continued. I was fixated on avoiding failure and I pushed myself as hard as I could. I was obsessed. Every conversation I was having with anybody was about the Fan Dance. I'm pretty sure that those close to me were getting bored of hearing about it, but I was excited. I was motivated and above all, without noticing, my life was rounding a bend. I looked forward to those long rucks in the forest and the early morning starts. Watching the sunrise over the horizon of trees, listening to the sounds of the world as it wakes. These simple moments would fill me with hope. I craved the feeling of tiredness that only hard exercise and exertion would create. I pushed myself until I believed I couldn't stand anymore, that was when I pushed harder, digging deep into the dark spaces of my soul. It was almost trance-like. The sound of my feet hitting the path, mixed with my laboured breathing was hypnotic. Some people choose to exercise with music. When pounding the dreadmill I would listen to the band Queen, cranked right up. In the forest, I chose to listen to my thoughts and the sound of my body. It had a weird kind of tranquillity to it, a sound all of its own. The hypnotic pounding I was putting myself through, was not only familiar, but comforting also.

The days rushed by in a haze of training, resting, revising, running, repeated over and over. I enjoyed this. I felt like I was doing something productive. I was stretching myself academically, mentally and physically. It was like I had stumbled across the building blocks of a happy life.

The second English exam paper came and went, pretty much like the first. All I had to do now was wait for the results, which would come in August. My focus now was turned purely on the Fan Dance, which was one week away. I pored over details, wrote kit lists, worked out a nutrition strategy and made sure I had all the provisions I needed. Neil and Turtle would be supporting me on the event. Neil being the chauffeur and moral support, Turtle taking pictures for social media.

Neil arrived on Friday morning from Norwich. We loaded up the car, collected Turtle and once again headed to the Welsh mountains of the Brecon Beacons. The long journey gave me time to think, time to prepare myself mentally for what I was going to endure the following day. Here I was, sitting in the car heading to one of the most brutal endurance events in Great Britain. An epileptic being supported by a chain smoker with a heart condition and a fifty-something with a hip replacement! It was almost comical to think about. Even funnier was the fact that we were all deadly serious about this challenge, none more so than me. I was either going to prove to people that no matter what your mental or physical challenges are, with hard work and discipline, there is always a way. Or I was going to prove that I had no business being at such an event like the Fan Dance. Either way, it was time to put my money where my mouth is, to pony up and put it all on the table. Where previously I had developed some anxiety regarding the event, this was now replaced with sheer determination, a positive mindset where failure would not be an option. That stubbornness and selfish part of my personality was now in control. Where previously it would be driven by personal gain, it was now driven by the desire to succeed and not fail. I was going to show those who had faded away that I was worth something, whilst making those who had supported me proud.

I had booked us into a bed and breakfast for the Friday and Saturday night, which was not as salubrious as the hotel Neil had booked for our recce, when we had the luxury of a room each. We were sharing, the three of us in one room. Cosy. We checked into the quaint terraced house, which some years ago had been converted into a bed and breakfast. It was situated in the middle of a long-terraced street, just outside the main town of Brecon. We passed through a maze of rooms and were shown up a flight of stairs to our room. It was more like a dormitory than a room, with the benefit of an en suite bathroom. Bags were thrown onto beds and we went about sorting out our kit. The mood was quiet as everyone set about rummaging through their bags, preparing for the early start the following morning.

At some point it was decided that we needed food and a swift pint, so we headed out into town in search of a restaurant. Nobody was bothered where we ate, so we settled on a small Italian place on the outskirts of town. We ate, we drank a little and we just generally had a good time. But in the back of my mind, the nerves were starting to creep in. I was running through the game plan for the following day in my head, trying to anticipate any problems. Did I have all the correct kit? Was the dry weight of my pack bang on the thirty-five-pound minimum weight? What was the weather going to be like? What time should we get to the start? What should I eat now? What should I eat in the morning? I was inundating myself with potential problems and trying to over-analyse everything. I needed to relax, enjoy the moment and not think about these things. I had all the answers to these questions, I'd been preparing for this event for six months. There was no point in second-guessing myself now. I'd gone through the routine so many times in training, I shouldn't be panicking over the minutiae.

We finished our meal and headed back to the bed and breakfast, suitably fed and watered. It was early evening and the sun was low enough that it cast an orange hue over the town. I needed an early night, but more importantly, I needed a great night's sleep. I knew that this was most likely impossible due to the company I was keeping. Turtle snored like an elephant and I'm pretty sure Neil did too. It was going to be challenging to sleep through the cacophony of grunts and wheezes. I was also wired with anticipation and worry. It was hard to push it all to the back of my mind and relax, to just enjoy myself with the lads. Eventually we settled into our beds. Slowly the banter and boisterous conversation petered out to the odd bit of hushed chit-chat.

As the sound of heavy breathing started to emanate from the boys (the precursor to full-on snoring). I found myself wishing that Emma had travelled up as well, she is quite often the calming influence. We'd been away a few times together over the last twelve months and always had a great time. She would know what to say at this moment to put my mind at rest, making me feel and believe that I was ready. A softer edge than the adolescent banter that was generated by the current occupants! I'd had a great evening with the boys, which was just what I needed. But what I needed now was the quiet voice of reassurance. I lay in bed, somewhere between dreaming and half awake, the reality of the world around me mixing with the illusory state of sleep.

I'm not an elite athlete. It's not my job. I don't make vast sums of money from endorsements and sponsors. I've paid to be here. I'm here because I choose to be. If I don't finish tomorrow nobody will care other than me. It's not the Olympics. But the moment is significant. It bookmarks the near end of an operation. From concept to preparation to conclusion, a six-month project that I have executed. The training and the setbacks won't mean anything to anyone other than me. To me this is the Olympics and finishing would be like winning a gold medal. I'll line up with everyone else and I'll take my shot, give it my all. Those who stand around me won't know of my struggle. As they have most likely had their own struggle, their own story of how they came to stand shoulder to shoulder on the side of a mountain with over a hundred other competitors. Before leaving, I was wished well by all who knew I was taking part, with a rhetoric of 'do your best'. Several conversations were had about not being hard on myself if I didn't finish. All you can do is 'try your best'. Friends and family almost preparing me for disappointment, making me feel okay with potential failure. Because you know, in the grand scheme of things, it doesn't really matter. Well, it bloody well matters to me. To me it's everything. My days are empty spaces that need filling. I live on my own. I have no job and no purpose, so if the space isn't filled then it's smothered in darkness. I have filled those days with sweat, pain, discipline and tears. I will not be okay with failure. The journey matters and the plan matters. I stand now a better version of myself because I poured everything I had into this moment. If I succeed then I would have found the blueprint to lay over my life, a way to keep focused and to continually grow. I can't think about failure.

I swirled in a dreamlike haze of driven anger and self-belief until I finally fell completely asleep. I didn't dream, I didn't wake in the night with my mind racing at a hundred miles an hour. I slept, in relative peace.

"Neil the Tash" Pen Y Fan

Chapter 16

"A moment in time may only last a few hours, but the impact can last a lifetime"

I was snatched sharply from my deep sleep at zero four thirty hours to the tune of Reveille. I had set my alarm on my phone the night before and thought Reveille would be most appropriate. Neil shot up from his bed as if someone had run into the room shouting "STAND TO STAND TO" and immediately started to hastily get dressed. I guess you can take the man out of the army but not the army out of the man? In stark contrast, Turtle rose very slowly, coughed for five minutes, farted and then eased his legs gently out of bed and onto the floor. He sounded like Darth Vader having an asthma attack. The sight of these two fifty-something specimens moving about in just their undercrackers is something I will never be able to unsee. Whilst they were about as far removed from elite warriors of the outdoor endurance world as you could get, they were my best mates and they were here. I thought about the big social circle of friends I had before my accident and how slowly but surely, they had mostly drifted away. I guess when you're no longer any use to people they move on, what a fickle world we live in. Not these two wankers though. They show up. I'd bury a body in the woods with either of them if they asked.

I rose and started to go through my anti-blister prep routine; I had practised this so many times it was now muscle memory. I pulled a large silver tin which contained all of my foot care products from my Under Armour holdall, grabbed a small white towel from the bathroom and relocated myself into one of the faux leather chairs. The boys had finally got dressed; I was now the only one in his undercrackers. I placed the towel on the floor and opened up the tin revealing a plethora of ointments, medical tape and a pair of sharp scissors. I cleaned my feet with rubbing alcohol and then sprayed the areas that I was about to tape with Benzoin Tincture or as I know it Friars' Balsam. A dark brown liquid that you would add a teaspoon of to a bowl of boiled water. You would then place a towel over your head and lean over the bowl inhaling the fumes, this would ease the congestion of a cold. This acts as a second adhesive, helping to stop the tape from pulling off as your feet sweat and get wet. I proceeded to methodically tape up the toes which were prone to blisters and then, onto taping up my heels. Finally, I dusted both feet with talc before pulling on a pair of toe socks followed by a pair of merino wool socks. Now my feet were sorted I then moved onto my body, applying a thick layer of Squirrel's Nut Butter to my inner thighs and bollocks to avoid chafe. I pulled on a pair of army-issue combat trousers and an olive-green technical t-shirt, then slipped into my Puma trainers (I would change into my boots later).

I couldn't believe that the day had finally come. All those months of training. Early mornings, sweat, blisters and epileptic seizures were now all behind me. It was now the day of reckoning. Lots of things spun through my mind, but it was hard to collate all my thoughts into any kind of coherent internal conversation. We had one final check of kit, filled my water bladder with bottled water and an electrolyte powder, then headed out the door of our room. We made our way down the stairs and into the deserted breakfast room, finally exited the building by the back door and into the carpark. As we walked up the path to the car the first spots of rain fell. Typical. It had been twenty-five degrees Celsius the day before, but now the grey sky was a prelude of what was to come.

We drove through the empty streets of Brecon in silence heading towards the carpark at the foot of Pen Y Fan. This was the meeting and registration point of the event. Registration was to start at zero seven thirty, so we decided the night before to get there for zero six hundred so we could get a good parking space. Our decision paid off. We pulled into the carpark and managed to secure a great spot very close to the finish line. There was already a buzz about the place with people milling about chatting with each other, no doubt talking about how they were going to tackle the day's events. We all stepped out of the car into the misty rain and scoped out the lie of the land, finding the registration tent which was set up at the far end of the carpark and flanked with two SF Experience event flags. More importantly, we found the snack van and toilets.

The fine mist started to turn into rain, so I retreated back into the car to try and stay as dry as I could for as long as I could. Neil and Turtle remained just outside, having their ears bent by an ex-Para who was reliving his army career to the pair of them. Neil loves to chat about his days in the army, however on this occasion he could hardly get a word in edgeways. Neil being the great guy that he is was only too happy to laugh and nod in the relevant places. I'm sure this made the gentleman's day. I sat in the car eating my pre-prepared chocolate and walnut porridge in silence. The porridge recipe had come a long way since that first trip to Scotland. It had, over time, undergone a few recipe changes. I'm glad to say it's now at least palatable. I wanted to be outside soaking up the atmosphere but my anxiety was starting to creep in and it demanded some solitude. I tried to relax and get into the zone, but instead, I just sat and watched the raindrops run down the windscreen. More cars filed into the carpark and it wasn't too long before it was full. It was almost time. Then as if on cue, just as I was thinking about wandering over to registration, my bowels decided they needed emptying. Better now than on the hill I suppose. I had one last crap, went back to the car and got my Danner Tachyon boots from the trunk. These boots had seen some miles in the weeks and months leading up to the Fan Dance. They were well and truly broken in. I methodically slipped each foot into the boot and took great care in lacing them up. Nobody wants to stop midway to relace a boot that has come untied. I paced up and down beside the car ensuring that my feet were snug but not too snug in the boots. Competitors were now starting to head to registration, so the three of us walked slowly up to the tent.

A long queue of people lined up waiting to check in and collect their race numbers and maps. As we got closer, the line split into three and we were diverted into one of the three queues which had been set up alphabetically. As my surname began with D, I was ushered into the first queue and promptly signed in, collected my race number and map then stood about idly waiting for the race brief to start. I was now starting to feel a lot of pressure, all of it self-imposed. I didn't want to let anyone down, especially all those that had donated money. I wanted to do well. I didn't want all those months of training to count for nothing. Both Neil and Turtle had given up their weekends to come and support me, not to mention Emma who had put up with my training infatuation and constant talk of the event for the last six months. I never heard her complain once and she always gave me one hundred percent unconditional support. I wanted to make her proud, she had stuck by me when I was at my worst, looked past the jobless, penniless epileptic and treated me like an equal. Somehow, she saw the potential in me and made me see the potential in myself. She made me feel like I could achieve anything. I wasn't going to fail. I'd crawl on my hands and knees to the finish line if I had to.

The crowd of competitors all gathered on a small plot of land next to the registration tent to hear the race brief, the rain fell inconsistently but nobody was taking any notice. The race director talked through all the key points; I was listening but didn't hear, my mind was elsewhere. This hanging about was doing nothing for my anxiety, I just wanted to get going now. After the briefing, I joined the masses who were moving slowly to the start point. Those that were in the 'Clean Fatigue' category were lined up at the front and were set off first. I watched the fast fell runners take-off up the hill and it wasn't long before they had disappeared. Those of us in the load bearing category were subject to a random bergen weight check, just to make sure we were carrying the minimum thirty-five pounds required. I had double-checked my weight, with additional food and water I was carrying just over forty-two pounds, the average weight of a six-year-old child. My bergen however was not checked. Those that thought they had dodged a bullet would get caught at the halfway point where all bergens would be checked, just in case you decided to ditch some kit on the way to lighten the load. If it was found that your pack had mysteriously shed some weight, you would then of course be disqualified. With the bergen check over we all lined up four abreast down the hill. I would guess there were around one hundred souls eagerly anticipating the start. The rain, which was now more of a fine mist added to the tense atmosphere as it rolled across the Brecon Beacons. I checked my bergen making sure it was high on my back and the waist belt and straps were tight. A piece of advice I had been given by a local legend in my home town and friend Jason, who was ex-forces and had done the route in the eighties. He followed up that advice by saying "rather you than me" which was encouraging. I was as ready as I was ever going to be. The anxiety was now gone, I was now purely focused on the task at hand. I could feel the gentle wave of adrenaline move through my body as I shuffled nervously on the spot, this is fucking it. I thought about how tough the last five years had been, the seizures, the hospitals, the never-ending hardship. I looked back and nodded at Turtle and Neil who were standing with the other spectators, a bloke's way of saying "Cheers lads". Then all of a sudden Jason the race director stood on a small mound of earth and screamed "STAND BY, STAND BY… GO!!!"

The mass of competitors lurched forward in unison like a juggernaut pulling away with a heavy load. I was in the first third of the pack and was determined to stay there, moving at the same pace as those around me. It wasn't long before the herd started to thin as the climb up to the first summit of Corn Du started to get steeper. I was starting to feel the incline and starting to breathe heavily. We'd been going around five minutes and already I was feeling my calf muscles tighten, this wasn't a good sign. I pressed on up the path, occasionally looking up but there was nothing to see. The summit of Corn Du was shrouded in mist and all I could see were a few bright yellow bergen covers (these were given to all those in the load-bearing category to identify us at a distance). After another ten minutes I had settled into my pace, the pack was strung out enough that I was now heading upward on my own. I passed a few of the slower competitors and was also passed by a few myself. I knew I had to race my own race, not let myself get swallowed up trying to keep pace with the front runners. The terrain started to flatten out giving a slight respite as I descended towards a small brook. Crossing the brook the track once again shifted upwards restarting the burn in my calves.

The summit of Pen Y Fan was two miles from the red phone box which is situated at the start line. I knew this from my recce with Neil a few weeks back. I'd been making steady progress and my Garmin watch let me know that I was a mile in. Now and again the curtain of mist would rise slightly allowing you a brief glimpse of the summit. The mountain letting you know you were going to have to continue to work hard, before once again shrouding itself in mist. The intermittent rain didn't bother me to be honest. I didn't feel it at all, though I was starting to become aware that I was slightly wet. I wasn't sure if this was from the wet fog or my own sweat. I pushed on maintaining my own steady pace, determined that I was not going to rest at any point. The initial climb up to Corn Du and then to the summit of Pen Y Fan was crucial. Lose time here and you wouldn't be able to make that time up, on either the descents or the long slog along the flat Roman road. I crested a sharp incline and recognised a wide layby of grass on the left. It was an amazing vantage point to look out onto the valleys of the Brecon Beacons, but not today. There was no time and the mountain…well she was hiding all of her beauty in dark clouds and light rain. Maybe she was helping us. Keeping our attention on the job in hand and not on the beautiful Welsh countryside. I knew now that the gradient was going to get much steeper, but I was struggling. My calves were burning and I was breathing heavily, each step felt like an effort. I was disappointed in myself. Had my training not been sufficient enough? Why was I feeling like this? I gritted my teeth and carried on regardless. The terrain got steeper and steeper until I was almost scrambling up the mountain. Pushing myself as hard as I could I continued upwards into the clouds. Just as I thought that I must be near the top, I spotted a small bearded man sitting on a rock. It was the official photographer, taking pictures of all those competing and reaching the summit of Corn Du. I think he wanted a smile, but it was all I could do to acknowledge that he was there as I heard the shutter on his camera click.

I stepped onto the flat summit of Corn Du. It felt as smooth as a pool table under foot, which put out the fire in my calves. There was no time to hang around. I followed a clear path that headed towards the summit of Pen Y Fan. The peak sitting at eight hundred and eighty-six metres above sea level, the highest point in the Brecon Beacons. The path descended for a hundred meters. I rucked this section before hitting a short steep climb onto the summit. As I ran towards the cairn, I could see people were busy getting pictures of themselves on the summit marker, but I rucked past them all heading towards a small shelter which was the first control point. I gave my race number to one of the marshals who cheered me on, then headed to the extremely steep descent of Jacob's Ladder. I'd overtaken around a dozen competitors on the ruck onto the summit and this had given me a positive boost in energy. It had taken me just over one hour to get to this point.

The steep descent of Jacob's Ladder was next. I carefully stepped down onto the steep ledge and moved slowly down the first five meters. A fall here would be catastrophic. Whilst I was pushing myself hard to get the best time possible, you have to finish to finish. Once past this section I stepped off the rocky path, favouring to descend on the grass verge which ran alongside. It was flatter and would be quicker to descend. I trotted down as fast as I dare avoiding potholes and wet patches. I was making up good time and passing people who had decided to descend using the obvious path. I knew I wasn't strong on the uphill sections of the course, but on the downhill and flat sections, I was going to come into my own. The miles of training would then start to bear fruit. I was concentrating hard making sure every step was solid. As I finally reached the bottom of the valley the long stretch of Roman road lay ahead. This section was roughly three miles long and at the other end was the halfway turnaround point. I knew that if I was to make up any time from the ascent of Corn Du I was going to have to ruck all of it. I turned right onto the path and started rucking. This was what I did. This was my strength. I moved to the left and off the path, choosing to move onto the grass verge, and I ran. It felt good to feel confident, as I started to pass people my confidence grew even more. This is what I had trained for and it showed. As I hit the first mile on the Roman road, I was surprised at how good I felt. This felt easy! Suddenly all the miles of training felt worth it. I was now cruising, even better I was enjoying it. I was going to soak up this moment as I knew that it was going to get much tougher. I was so busy weaving in and out, dodging rocks and finding the best course, I didn't notice the fine mist had once again turned into full-on rain. I was maintaining a perfect rhythm, moving confidently. Until a steep descent into a small stream, which then shifted up a steep incline, broke the pace and snapped me out of my utopian mindset. The halfway point was now near and I was starting to see some of the clean fatigue runners on their return journey. Several minutes later I saw the first load-bearing runner on his return. He looked extremely focused and was moving quickly. To keep up that level of intensity you had to have an extreme level of fitness and the strongest mindset. I wondered if I would ever be able to achieve that same level. Another load-bearing competitor approached on his return leg, as he got close, he threw me half a Mars Bar which was much appreciated. I think it would be fair to say that the Fan Dance is more of a challenge and race against yourself rather than other participants. Along the way people were cheering each other on. These were people not competing with each other, but supporting a community of amateur athletes testing themselves against the course, not other competitors. I headed into the halfway checkpoint. I was not stopping. People were milling about picking up free chocolate bars and chatting. Not me! I was keen to get in and out. I gave my race number to the marshal, took off my bergen, had it weighed, then hoisted it back on, tightened the straps and waist belt, did a one-eighty and was out of there all within a couple of minutes.

The three miles of Roman road which I had just covered were slightly downhill on the approach to the halfway turnaround point. This meant that whilst almost undetectable to the naked eye, heading back to Jacob's Ladder was slightly uphill (a bit like the return leg on the Downs Link during my training run). It wasn't long before I started to feel the familiar burning sensation in my calves once again. The continuous rain was now starting to take its toll and, for the first time, the seeds of doubt were hammered into my mind with every raindrop which struck my head. What was I doing? What was I trying to prove here? Slow down. Why are you doing this to yourself? The inner voice of all my insecurities started to get louder. I then fell into the pit of negativity. One negative thought was fuelling the next and before I knew it, I wasn't thinking about the course anymore. I started to think about my relationship with Emma, more specifically when was she going to leave, because that's what people in my life do? This was a totally unfair appraisal of our relationship, as she had never given me any indication to think that she would. But my body was tired and so was my mind, it was hard to convince myself any other way. Then my legs started to feel strange, jelly-like almost; Oh, please no! Not a seizure, I thought. A sense of panic shot through my body pulling me out of the spiralled descent into self-loathing. What was happening? I was still maintaining a reasonable pace although not as fast as I would have liked, but the slight incline was taking it out of me. I was going down here and I couldn't work out why. Then it dawned on me...I was bonking! Bonking is a term used when you have depleted all of your energy reserves. In other words, the tank was empty and the fuel light was on. During my woe-is-me moment, I had forgotten to take on food and fluids and now my body was saying, "sort this out or I'm shutting down". I quickly shot into action and started to drink from my hydration pack, which was filled with water mixed with electrolyte and carbohydrate powder. I drank enough to get some nutrients into me but not enough that I had a belly full of liquid. I then pulled a couple of energy gels from my strap pocket and squeezed the jelly-like substance into my mouth. Almost immediately I felt much better, not only physically but mentally as well. I could literally feel my body absorbing the fuel and putting it to use. I made a note of the time and set a refuelling programme in my mind. Every five minutes I'd take a big swig from my hydration pack and every fifteen minutes I'd take on board a gel. In between I would munch on a cocktail of Jelly Babies and Skittles, which I had in the side pocket of my combats. These however had got wet, what I was now shovelling into my gob was more a sticky rainbow mess than the well-known confection. No sooner had I sorted myself out, than I came to the end of the Roman road, turned left and started the ascent back up to the summit of Pen Y Fan. The notorious Jacob's

Ladder stood before me and I was sure all I was going to feel now was pain.

I had decided that no matter how tired I was I wasn't going to stop and rest. I would rather go at a snail's pace than come to a complete standstill. The problem with resting is that it makes you comfortable. You have to then summon up the mental strength to get going again as well as the physical strength to keep going. The first incline although steep was short and I moved past this section with ease, keeping a moderate pace. The route then flattened out and slightly undulated for a while before hitting the infamous Jacob's Ladder. I could see mist had shrouded over the summit of Pen Y Fan, but it still seemed so far away. I kept my head down concentrating on every step willing myself not to look up, as this would just confirm my lack of progress and would be a mental mind-killer. My thoughts began to wander and I just let my mind drift into whatever pattern it wanted. I was not concerned with the rain, or the pain that was starting to creep back into my legs. The hardship of the last five years seemed to be encapsulated in the climbing of this hill. Everything that I had been through was fuelling these last few miles, the pain, the misery, the tears and loss seemed to be in symbiosis with myself and the hill at that very moment. Being epileptic has shown me how people treat you differently. The mere suggestion of doing anything remotely strenuous is always met with negativity and an attitude that I was somehow being selfish. I don't want to put myself in harm's way, but I do need to take some risks...Don't we all? The gradient shifted upwards and I knew I was on the final push to the summit and so did my body. I was moving very slowly now and was breathing very heavily, my calves screaming in pain. Every step was one small step closer to the summit. I thought back to a quote from David Goggins' book, 'Can't Hurt Me'.

He says "When you think you're done, you're only forty percent into what your body's capable of doing".

I dug deep and just kept placing one foot in front of the other. I had to lean into it now as the gradient was now so steep. I tried to picture soldiers moving up the same hill on their SAS selection, digging deep, pushing hard to beat the clock on the way to getting that famous sand-coloured beret. The terrain started to get rocky and I knew I was close to the top. Then as I looked up, I could see no more mountain. I scaled over the last few rocks and stepped onto the flat summit. Bloody hell the hard part was over. I felt in bits, my body begging me to rest, but I ignored it and moved swiftly across the flat plain, not even stopping at the summit marker. I did however slow down enough to shout my name and race number as I passed the control point. The race marshal made a funny quip about not engaging in a conversation with him. I wasn't being rude, but I was breathing out of my eyeballs at the time and wasn't capable of holding any kind of conversation.

I picked up the pace and started rucking toward the descent, moving past a few competitors on the way. As I approached the final descent, I caught up with a lad called Josh who I had met earlier at the start line. Josh was a university student and was competing in the Fan Dance Trinity which meant he was doing Saturday's dance, Saturday night's dance and finally Sunday's dance. Three Fan Dances back-to-back. Mental! We decided that we would run to the finish line together, I was glad of the company. The descent toward the finish was about a mile and three quarters and although it was all downhill it wasn't too steep. We kept a quick pace and started to overtake a lot of people. Some were competitors and some were just hikers out on the hill. I was surprised at how good I felt. With any endurance event it's mostly the feet that suffer, but mine felt fine. All those practice miles in boots, which socks worked best and learning how to tape my feet had paid off. We upped the pace and raced toward the finish. We were that close we could now see the small brook at the bottom of the valley and spectators gathered by the fence above it. I was going to make it. I was going to finish. Just as I started to let myself think about crossing the finish line I tripped. My foot hit a rock and I went down hard. I flew through the air and hit the ground landing on my left side, knocking the wind clean out of me. I was running downhill at speed carrying over forty pounds on my back. I waited, expecting to feel the pain of broken bones, which luckily never came. Another competitor who we had passed earlier sauntered by and gave a little laugh. This pissed me off! I raised my hand and Josh helped me to my feet, we then continued running to the finish. The adrenaline of the fall was starting to wear off and it was evident that I had hurt the left side of my ribs again. I blocked out the pain and raced on. I crossed the stream went up the embankment and through the gate to the finish line. A young lady called out my time of four hours and forty-two minutes. I collected my medal and certificate, had my picture taken and was greeted by handshakes and back slaps from Neil the Tash and Turtle. It was over, six months of training and hard work and now that was it.

I felt a little underwhelmed, I thought that I would feel some kind of elation or some form of closure, but I didn't. I'm not sure what I was expecting to feel, I didn't feel how I thought I would. There was no euphoria or feeling of accomplishment. I just felt tired. Turtle took some pictures for my social media, after which we walked slowly back to the car and drove back to the bed and breakfast. It was hard to believe that it was done. On the journey back I started to reflect on the day scrutinising my performance. Although I felt a small sense of achievement, I was a little disappointed in my time if I was being honest with myself. I should have moved faster on both the hill sections and also on the return back up the Roman road. I had trained hard but the result (to me) didn't match the level of input. We headed back to Sussex early the following morning, it happened to be Father's Day and I was going to be spending it with my girls. A fitting end to the weekend.

I decided upon my return to take a week off training to let my body recover. The following week the country was forecast to have a tropical heatwave and I was looking forward to getting out there and grinding out some miles. The universe however would have other ideas. On Monday I started to feel a little unwell. I had developed a slight headache but nothing too dramatic, more of a constant dull ache. Tuesday it had gotten worse and I went to bed early. In the night however I woke up shivering cold and was feeling very unwell. Wednesday I just stayed in bed all day. Then the night sweats started and so did the sore throat. By Thursday I was feeling like death and my throat felt like I was swallowing razor blades. I did not sleep at all Thursday night. My throat was so painful I couldn't even swallow. I was in bits. I couldn't eat, drink or sleep and no matter what I took nothing would touch the pain. To take my Epilepsy meds I had to crush them up to have any chance of getting them in me. I suspected I may have caught Covid, but the headache had now gone and I had no cough or runny nose. It was just my throat. I can't describe the amount of pain I was in. I had never felt pain like it before. The only thing I could tolerate was ice lollies and even those were extremely painful to eat. I managed to get a doctor's appointment on the Friday. I hadn't slept and was desperate for help and almost in tears. A quick look in my mouth and I was diagnosed with strep throat which is a bacterial infection, so antibiotics and strong painkillers were prescribed and home I went. Within twenty-four hours the pain had subsided enough that I could take onboard liquids and could now sleep. It would be a further three weeks before I felt one hundred percent and could think about training again.

I was hoping that completing the Fan Dance would exorcise some demons and give me enough sense of achievement to feel content, to feel like I had achieved something. It hadn't. I still felt the same as I did before the event. A feeling that I didn't push myself hard enough. I wasn't sure what I was looking for. There was still a hole that needed filling. I decided then I was going back next year. I guess I still thought I had unfinished business in the Brecon Beacons, that's why I was desperate to go back, draw a line under it and move on. I hadn't failed. I just didn't feel I had succeeded to the level of expectation I had set myself. It was the same feeling I had about that first trip to Scotland with big Paul, where I failed to summit Ben Nevis via the Carn Mor Dearg arête (CMD). It was about time I put that demon to bed as well. I didn't just want to tick off these previous failures, I wanted to smash them out of the atmosphere and into space. I was going back to the Brecon Beacons and I was going back Scotland. I was going back to take on the CMD arête. But I wasn't just going to amble up to the summit of Ben Nevis, on a mild autumn day as before. I had decided to go in the depths winter, in the snow! I was of course, as per usual, keeping this all to myself.

The climb up to Corn Du

The Finish Line

Chapter 17

"I can dream big, I may not always achieve those dreams, but a lot of the time I get close."

As the summer approached things started to get busy. Emma and I managed to get away, spending the weekend at a friend's static caravan on the south coast. The weekend was blistering hot. We sunned ourselves on the beach, swam in the sea, ate fish and chips and woke early to see the sunrise. I had to keep pinching myself to make sure I wasn't dreaming. I was happy and I was enjoying life again, but I was also worried that at any moment it could all come crashing down. It was difficult to push these thoughts out of my mind, but I tried. I didn't want my inner negativity destroying the life that both Emma and I were building together. For some reason, whenever my life is going great, I sabotage it by doing something stupid, which of course I later regret. I was adamant that this was not going to happen again.

As the schools broke up for the summer, Emma jetted off to Egypt with the boys on holiday. I just carried on training, although not at the same intensity as before. Whilst I didn't have any events coming up, I still wanted to stay in some form of shape. I didn't see any point in getting myself reasonably fit, then returning to being a couch potato. While Emma was away, I just tried to stay busy and took this time to organise my return to Scotland, more specifically Ben Nevis the following winter. Turtle as always was up for it. I sold it to him as a winter adventure. We would set up camp by the north face of the Ben, I would do some solo walking around the hills, while he did some photography. The real plan of summiting Ben Nevis via the CMD arête was still top secret. I wasn't sure how or even when I should announce this plan. It felt good to get something in the diary, something that would motivate me to keep training. I booked tickets on the train for the following

February, just a few days after my forty-ninth birthday. I was now in the business of slaying my demons.

Emma returned, tanned from her week in Egypt and the following weekend we travelled up to Derbyshire. Mike and his wife Hannah had travelled from Canada to the UK for work. It was a great opportunity for them both to visit family, but they had generously made time in their busy schedule to spend a day with Emma and myself. This had been a weekend I had been looking forward to for a long time. It had been fifteen years since I had last seen Mike, who's life had changed considerably after his climbing accident, so he understood what it was like to lose a part of yourself.

It was a glorious day, I stared out the passenger window and watched the world pass by. It had been some time since I had been to Derbyshire. The days of travelling to the Peak District early in the morning with my mate Stuart to meet Mike and our other climbing friends at a crag somewhere, didn't feel all that long ago. It certainly didn't feel like fifteen years! A lot had changed for both Mike and I since we last climbed together. Mike as always, took on his own personal challenges, head-on, didn't quit and accomplished amazing things. What have I done? A bit of running and sat an exam. It was like our climbing. I was maybe an above-average climber at best, but Mike wasn't just in a different league, he was in a different division. Everything he did was done to the absolute best of his ability. Why they have not written books or made films about this guy I have no idea. When looking for an inspirational role model, you need to look no further than Mad Mike. It's hard not to put the guy up on a pedestal, where he deserves to be.

We rolled up outside Mike's parents' house. The last time I had seen or spoken to his parents was at the spinal hospital after Mike had been flown back to the UK from Norway. We walked up the driveway and knocked on the door.

Mike's wife Hannah opened the door and we were led through the house and into the rear conservatory, where Mike was sitting in his electric wheelchair. It was great to finally see him again. He didn't look any older than when I had last seen him, frustratingly. It was quite an emotional moment, but I hid that from everyone. We don't do emotions. We were climbers, our world was full of testosterone and crude banter. Even when Mike was in the hospital, seriously ill, we just resorted to taking the piss out of him. That's how we showed him we cared. He spun his electric wheelchair around like Professor X from The X-men and I introduced him to Emma. The next couple of hours were taken up with drinking tea and catching up.

Professor Michael Garton PhD.   *Snowdon 2005*

We bored the girls with tales of our climbing exploits and stories of conquering the mixed grill at the Little John pub in Hathersage. We had a great day, followed by a fantastic evening at a local restaurant, before heading back to our hotel. Visiting Mike was a reality check, the universe's way of showing me what the human mind was capable of. I was enthused with energy and enthusiasm after our visit with Mike and Hannah, just like I feel after our regular FaceTime calls. Mike has a way of making me feel that everything was going to be okay, a level head of sensibility which is still filled with adventure and risk.

Not long after our return from Derbyshire, I had an appointment with David the epilepsy nurse. This would be the first appointment that Emma would attend with me. I find these appointments tedious and frustrating. Don't get me wrong, David is very knowledgeable and helpful and can't do enough to help me, but the problem isn't David. Over the last few years, I had been cycled through so many different medications, it was hard to keep track. Modern medicine had reduced my seizures considerably but hadn't cured me of them. I was still having maybe one to two seizures a week, on average over a four-week period. I was also suffering from regular absent seizures. This is where I would just stare into space, daydreaming. The process of trying all these different medications and combinations of drugs was slow and very drawn out. I would be weaned off one, then slowly put on another, with the dosage being gradually raised. The problem with anti-seizure medication like all medications, is they all have side effects. I am left feeling very tired, headachy and nauseous after taking them. This doesn't seem to have got any better in the years that I have been on them. I was at the stage where I had accepted that this was probably as good as my epilepsy was ever going to get, for the foreseeable future anyway. I wasn't giving up, I wasn't quitting on myself, I was just letting go of something that I couldn't control.

We both sat in the small consultation room, going over the same old information. We recapped what was said at the last appointment and then talked about my seizures. How many was I having? Are they getting any worse? Am I still suffering the side effects from the medication? It was Groundhog Day. Emma was great. She took some of the burden off me, answering those mundane questions and being much more detailed than I would ever be. After recapping the last four months the conversation turned to moving forward, which usually meant increasing a medication or changing one. It was during this conversation that David mentioned a treatment called VNS (Vagus Nerve Stimulation). David went on to explain that in difficult cases this can be an option. A small wire is wrapped around your vagus nerve in the neck. It is then connected to a small power pack that is inserted into your chest cavity, the power pack then sends a small electrical current through the wire, stimulating the vagus nerve at regular intervals throughout the day. This treatment has in some cases reduced the number of seizures that some sufferers have, but in some cases, it didn't work at all. It was all a bit much to take in. I was lucky Emma was there to retain all of this information. It was then decided that David would put my case in front of the epilepsy council for further consultation. The council is made up of several neurologists who meet monthly to discuss difficult cases. Would my next appointment be in London, being measured up for an internal power pack and coil? But the big question was, would this make me look like Iron Man? If so I'm in. We left the hospital and as always, I felt nothing had changed. Emma was more positive and seemed very keen for me to consider the VNS surgery, but in my head, I wasn't sure I wanted to undergo such an invasive procedure.

The next couple of weeks saw Emma jetting off on holiday to Costa Rica with her sisters. At the same time, I headed off to North Wales to do my mountain leader training. I was lucky enough to catch a lift with another course attendee. Chris was a consultant in the construction industry by day and a volunteer for React, a disaster response charity that operates all over the world. Lucky for me, Chris lived on the south coast and would be driving past my home town on his way to North Wales. He kindly collected me and all my kit from a service station just off the M23 motorway. It was a warm and sunny day and Chris was suitably dressed, wearing a vest, shorts and wrap-around shades. He sported a short-cropped beard, with his long fair hair tied back in a ponytail. I wasn't sure if we were heading into the mountains, or down to the coast surfing. We threw all the kit onto the backseat of his Mercedes coupe. As we drove out of the services, I thought to myself, this guy is certainly living the dream!

It had been a long time since I had ventured into the hills and mountains of North Wales, so long that I couldn't even remember when it was. It could have possibly been when I was part of the team that pushed, pulled and dragged Mike up to the summit of Snowdon in his wheelchair. What an epic day that was!

As the sun began to dip behind the mountains, we rolled into the small village of Bethesda. After a few wrong turns, we pulled up outside our hostel. There was a bit of faff getting in, as the building was unmanned in the evenings. After a couple of phone calls, Chris and I were soon dozing on our bunks. Our quarters for the next few days were basic but more than adequate. The large room with an en suite shower and toilet was filled with two sets of bunk beds and one single bed, which I was sprawled out on. There were five people on Keith's course this year, me and Chris, future army officer Tom and two young ladies Ellie and Olivia (who had their own room). They both worked at an outward-bound centre in the North of England. Tom, our third roommate, appeared to be running late and arrived after dark, as did the girls. Keith our leader, would be joining us the next day.

The following morning, we gathered in the common room which was doubling up as a classroom. Keith, our instructor for the week arrived and started to brief us on the schedule. The next few days were going to be busy. I was going to learn the fundamentals of what it was to be a mountain leader or M.L. as it's known in the industry. It was like going back to school. We spent a lot of time out in the mountains, navigating our way through the hills and scrambling up cliff faces. All the while we were learning important rudiments, like map reading, taking bearings, handrailing features so as to not get lost, how to manage a group and what to do when it all goes wrong. We spent time in the classroom learning about weather and about the law, just in case something unfortunate happened while leading a group and we were taken to court. The week culminated in an overnight wild camp in the hills.

We hiked into the mountains and after several exercises, we were led to an idyllic camp location. A flat piece of ground that nestled between the mountains. After we had pitched up and eaten, we waited for dark. It was then that we put all of the navigation skills we had learnt in the week to the test, with a night nav exercise. Keith had relinquished the overnight expedition part of the course to a colleague named Dewi, a slightly dishevelled Welshman of the most affable personality. Dewi wasn't always a legend in the mountains, he was, before being a Mountain Leader trainer, the tour manager for the awesome Super Furry Animals. After completing the night nav exercise, we headed back to camp. On the return, I received an email with my English GCSE results attached. I couldn't wait to find out the result! But there was a problem, I couldn't get a clear enough signal to be able to download the file. Eventually, after scaling a small hill in the dark, the file downloaded. I scored a six. Which equated to a B in old money. I had passed comfortably but was still a little disappointed. I thought I had done better. This was becoming a reoccurring thought. Every time I achieved something, I was always left a little disappointed, like I felt I could have done better. I now realise that this is what keeps me striving forward, never content with what I have done, always feeling there is room for improvement. Later on, I found out that my daughter Grace had scored an eight, an A! She had smashed it, scoring very highly in all of her exams. I am so proud of all that she has achieved in her life so far. She worked so hard and the results proved it. What a proud Dad moment that was. I went back to the group, a little deflated about my result and carried on with the overnight exercise. I enjoyed this part of the course, crossing the mountains in the dark, navigating by compass and time and really honing those skills we had learnt in the week. The following morning, we packed up, did some more navigation exercises and practised different ways to cross a river. After which, we trudged back to the hostel dripping wet. Upon returning to the hostel, I set about showering and packing away my kit in preparation for the journey home.

I had met a great bunch of like-minded people. All of which had a love of the great outdoors and wanted to show others how epic it actually is. I had learnt a lot in the last five days, much more than I anticipated. I couldn't think of a better way of improving myself, gaining knowledge and learning. All done whilst in the shadows of the beautiful Welsh mountains. It was evident though that a career in the outdoors would be virtually impossible for me to attain, or should I say being employed in the outdoor industry. Keith was very open and honest, saying that he thought it would be tough for me to use the qualification to get a job, because of my epilepsy. I kind of knew that this would be the case. It's something that is repeated to me over and over again.

I returned from Wales, Emma returned from Costa Rica and we saw out the rest of the school summer holidays. It wasn't long before the golden sun started to melt behind the horizon incrementally earlier. The days getting shorter and shorter, as we crept into autumn. I love the colder seasons. Training seems a little easier, as you're not battling with the heat. The forest and woods of my local area take on a different hue, crisp browns and unsaturated greens as the vibrance of summer is drained from the pallet. The tendency is to slow down. A self-imposed hibernation, fill your bellies with fare and stay warm in front of wood-burning stove fires. I, however, shy away from this. I prefer the shorter days. I feel more creative and more disciplined to get out into the outdoors.

I was continuing to shoot videos for YouTube during the autumn, favouring the permission woodland I could use at a local farm. This allowed me to sleep in the open, next to an open fire. The woods take on a personality all of their own when lit by natural flame. The flicker of red illuminating the inner canopy of trees, broken only by the odd crackle of fire which would shoot glowing sparks into the air. It's an inner peace that has withstood millennia. The end of the day where the only task is to stay warm. Within the tranquillity of these moments is usually where my brain conjures up new ideas and new thoughts. Where I reminisce about lost loved ones or think about my two daughters, who although I see reasonably regularly, I miss terribly. It was one of those nights, where I lay quietly, listening to the sounds of the outdoors and feeling the warm glow of the fire, when I had an idea. A crazy idea, an idea that sounded so far out that nobody would believe it was achievable.

I had proved to myself that with careful planning and preparation, I could achieve a good level of physical endurance. But even though I was nowhere near the realms of an elite endurance athlete, I had, in a way performed remarkably well, for a middle-aged man, who suffered from anxiety and of course epilepsy. I wanted to show people that I could achieve amazing things. Prove to myself that I could prepare, plan and execute a mission from conception to conclusion. How was I going to show the world this new found confidence and optimism? I was going to run the London Marathon…in military kit, including boots and carrying a forty-pound bergen. As the receptors in my brain fired with enthusiasm, I could already hear the sighs of nervous apprehension in the voices of my loved ones! I'd already taken on and completed the Fan Dance, this was the next step, the evolution. I giggled to myself. Nobody is going to be prepared for this. I lay in my sleeping bag, planning the entire strategy in my head. It was

October. The Marathon was in April, there wasn't much time to prepare. I had to hustle.

The first hurdle was that I didn't actually have a place in the marathon. London is probably the most famous marathon in the world, so places are hard to come by. I had two options. I could enter the ballot and try and get a place by pure luck, which was a long shot, as there are over four hundred thousand applicants and only seventeen thousand places. Alternatively, I could try and get a charity place. This came with the added pressure of having to raise a predetermined amount of money for the charity you are running for. I decided to do both. After returning home from my overnight camp, I entered the ballot and applied to the Epilepsy Society for a charity place. All I had to do now was just wait. And so, once again, the training regime started.

Everything was slotting into place. I was staying as healthy as I could. I was training, I was coping with the seizures (which were still one or two a week) and I was comfortable in a relationship. After everything that I had been through, I had no cause for complaint. I had reached a level of acceptance and I was still continually focused on being a better human being. But in the darkest corners of my mind, something still wasn't quite right. I wasn't sure why, but very occasionally, when I was on my own at home, when the world couldn't see me, I would suddenly have outbursts of uncontrolled emotion. I would sit and sob. I would feel like my life was over, even though things were going great. This would also be accompanied by a massive wave of anxiety. This would make me angry, as I had worked hard to banish that particular demon. I would lock myself away and make excuses for not answering the phone, or replying to messages. In those moments I would have very dark thoughts, thoughts that had not entered my mind for a long time. I wasn't sure what to do. Maybe I needed to talk to someone about it. But being a typical man, I dismissed these outbursts as just a one-off, an isolated instance of feeling low. We all have those, right? Moments when we forget ourselves. Moments when the world just catches up to us for a moment. As usual, I was deluding myself that everything was and will be okay. I didn't have time to feel sorry for myself. I had a marathon to potentially prepare for, a winter trip to Scotland to prepare for, a YouTube channel to keep going and other commitments such as a book to write. I was settling into a routine, a routine of training, writing, being a boyfriend and looking after Emma's boys when she had to work late. I was papering over the cracks to get through the weeks, as per usual.

Then on October the twenty-fourth, the ballot results for the London Marathon were announced and as predicted I did not secure a place. I was disappointed. I kind of thought in my head that I would get one. I didn't deserve one any more than anybody else. It was a lottery. I just thought in my mind that I would get lucky. I should have guessed really. Luck was not part of my genetic makeup. I was not a lucky person, or should I say I did not feel lucky. Luck seemed to have alluded me over the last few years. Maybe all those years risking my neck rock climbing, had used all my luck up. Maybe I was just lucky to be alive? Then later on in the afternoon, I received an email from the Epilepsy Society, "Welcome to team purple for the 2023 TCS London Marathon". I got a place! Bloody hell, it was really going to happen, I was going to run the London Marathon the following April…. Shit!

It was a fun day letting my family know that I, Gareth de la Torre was going to take part in one of the biggest sporting events in the country. My Mum looked excited, proud and concerned all at the same time. Until I then elaborated that I would be running in military kit, carrying a forty-pound bergen. The excitement drained from her face. She looked at me as if I had lost my mind. It took a while for the receptors in her brain to process this new bit of information and then form a response. I was bloody mad…. apparently. I had (over some time) slowly drip-fed some information to Emma, regarding running the marathon. After announcing the full plan, on receipt of my place in the Epilepsy Society team, she was not amused, but she hid it well. I could start to see that look of frustration and worry on her face. She knew what was now going to happen. She'd been here before. The lead-up to the Fan Dance saw me training hard, but worst of all (for her) would be my non-stop rhetoric regarding the event, which would go on until completion. She wouldn't complain and she would be totally supportive. It's possible that these events were just as strenuous on her mentally, as they were for me physically. Once again, I had something big and tangible to sink my teeth into; a marathon, in military kit and forty-pound bergen, I was on a mission. I still had something to prove, or at least I thought I did.

There were some conditions accepting one of these charity places, one of which was a target of two grand to raise for the charity. I had some experience in raising money for charity, as I had raised over eight hundred pounds for the Epilepsy Society when competing in the Fan Dance back in June. It was tough, not the actual event (well that was also tough) but raising money for charity. The country was in the grips of a cost-of-living crisis and nobody had much spare cash. I wasn't sure what was going to be harder; training and completing the marathon or raising the required amount of money to justify my place. I took to social media straight away, thinking that I needed to be on this fundraising kick every week, right up till the race. I recorded a short reel on Instagram and posted it. An old mate Mick Penny was the first out the gate dropping in a donation. I hadn't seen Mick in years, but he has followed my exploits via social media over the last few years, always drops a 'like' on my posts and had donated when I was fundraising for the Fan Dance. Next was big Paul. Again, he always donates without hesitation. This is what real mates do, they support you. They buy merch and they donate when you're raising money. I don't need people to sit with me and hold my hand. I don't want people feeling sorry for me and I certainly don't want sympathy. If you want to show your support, buy a t-shirt, watch and 'like' the videos, 'like' the social media posts and drop a text every now and again checking in. Just like these guys.

It was time to get serious again. Time to start clocking up the miles and to make sure that when I stand on the start line, I'm prepared. I had a responsibility to make sure that I was healthy and fit and that I wasn't going to hurt myself. I'm in my late forties. My body hurts from years of exertion, I have high blood pressure, and my mental state balances on a knife edge most of the time, but I have learnt how to control this. I had become disciplined. Not Jocko Willink (ex-Navy Seal, whose no-nonsense approach to fitness and life has gained him millions of followers all over the world) disciplined, but disciplined enough to get the job done. That's how I saw it. A job I had tasked myself to do that needed doing. I had little to no idea how to train for a marathon. It was different to the Fan Dance as it was mostly flat, whereas the Fan Dance was there and back over a mountain. I decided to swap the undulating training runs in the forest, for more flat routes on paved or shingle paths.

I was now slipping between training, writing, recording and editing YouTube videos and more training. I enjoyed the challenge of getting the miles in. The Rocky Balboa moment of waking early, preparing and eating breakfast, throwing on my pack and rucking. I truly felt like this was what I was supposed to do, making use of my time and being proactive. I was still having regular seizures, I'd come around sprawled out on the floor, with no recollection of what had happened, feeling like I'd been hit by a car. Sometimes (if I had been wearing it) my fall-alert band would trigger an emergency response from my mother, who would be there, usually with my brother Phillip, to help get me into bed, or onto the sofa. This would then see me laid up for at least twenty-four hours. It was frustrating but I'm sure those rest days helped me recover. The universe pulling the plug, ensured that my body got the amount of rest it needed. Worryingly, whilst my seizures were not getting any better or worse, I felt that my absent seizures were on the increase. I often felt like I would lose up to ten minutes of time, like I was zoning in and out. This was more noticeable when I was watching television, I'd miss blocks of a film and feel like I didn't know what was going on. I'd also drift away in conversations. This was awkward. I'd find myself suddenly staring at Emma, who was staring back, complaining that I wasn't listening, so I'd make an excuse that I didn't hear her. I was of course hiding all this, or trying to. I wasn't sure if this was to protect myself or to protect those who cared about me. I hated people worrying about me.

The nights grew darker. The wind got colder. The chimneys of the market town where I lived were now starting to shed the white smoke, as log burners were lit to warm their brick houses. It was soon to be Christmas, mine and Emma's second Christmas together. Emma's boys were spending Christmas with their dad that year, which meant for the first time in a while, I wasn't going to wake up Christmas morning on my own. I was due to have my girls on Christmas day. This would be spent at my parents' home with my family, exchanging gifts and sitting down to a huge Christmas dinner. Then, in the evening, after my daughters had gone home, I would head back to Emma's and enjoy the rest of the day's festivities with her family.

A few days before Christmas I received a text from my youngest daughter. They were just going to pop in for a few hours on Christmas day. They wanted to spend the day with their mother's family. To say I was devastated was an understatement, I felt like my heart had been ripped out of my chest. I had an arrangement with the girls' mother that we'd alternate Christmas, but I was told that their mum now feels they are old enough to decide where they spend their time. I guess our arrangement no longer stands. How could I ever rebuild a strong relationship with my children, when

I'm left to feel that I'm not that important in their lives? It was hard not to feel that I was still being punished for mistakes that I had made. All I want to be, is a good Dad.

It was soon Christmas Eve and Emma and I sat in front of the log burner in fluffy socks, drinking snowballs (a Christmas drink made from advocaat and lemonade) and watching Raymond Briggs' "The Snowman" on television. I often think how much better Christmas was when I was a child, growing up in a small three-bed council house, with little to no money. We didn't have much, but we always had a real tree and Mum always managed to procure a reasonable gift for us all. We spent time with family, grandparents, aunties and uncles and played with our new toys with our cousins, before sitting down to watch the evening Christmas movie. It was easy back then to find happiness in the little things and to appreciate the little we had. Most of all to appreciate the family that surrounded us. As we move into adulthood things change. Grandparents pass on. We have families of our own and we lose touch with relatives that we were close to as children. Before splitting from my first wife, I had enjoyed many a Christmas with my children. I hang onto those memories, being there when they excitedly came down the stairs, to be confronted with a stack of carefully wrapped gifts propping up the Christmas tree in our lounge. They are older now and I don't get to spend nearly the amount of time I would like with them, so all I have now are memories. After hearing that the girls were not staying for Christmas dinner I was on a bit of a downer. But sitting on the sofa with Emma, watching a children's animated film on television (like I would have done as a nine-year-old) made it feel a little bit better. I felt a bit like Scrooge, reminiscing about Christmas past. It was a warm and happy moment, which encapsulated the entire Christmas holiday.

The amazing "Emma"

Chapter 18

It was again time to haul the bags into the car, then onto a train to London and onto Scotland, where then, we had to drag ourselves up to the foot of a mountain. It had arrived without warning. The last few months had been taken up with marathon training, long rucks in the woods, long rucks on the roads and weighted speed work on the dreadmill. The only thing on my mind had been the marathon. The only thing I spoke about was the marathon. It was all I was concentrating on. Even though the trip to Scotland had been booked way back, it was a shock when the departure date suddenly loomed over us. It was almost an inconvenience.

Turtle and I arrived at Fort William station just after ten a.m. Like on previous trips we had taken the Caledonian Sleeper from London the night before. We struggled off the platform with all the bags and headed to the area where the luggage lockers were situated. Turtle's pack looked shambolic. I'm not sure how he had packed it, but it looked like he had set his pack up at one end of a room, then thrown his kit in from the other. It was all lopsided on his back, the weight was not evenly distributed and the pack looked huge! I decided to empty all of his kit onto the floor of the luggage area and repack it. This took around fifteen minutes, but once completed, it looked much better. Straps all done up and tight, no empty spaces, everything compressed, much tidier. We loaded the overnight bags into a large storage locker (which we would collect upon our return), threw on our packs and headed out of the station, into the winter wall of weather that is Scotland. The hike up to the north face of Ben Nevis was not that long, just a steady incline all the way up on good paths. It was the same route Paul and I had taken on that first trip a few years ago, so I knew the way. Turtle waddled out of the station and down a short path. He ambled past a big Morrisons supermarket, crossed the road and straight into

McDonald's. We'd been on the road for approximately forty seconds.

We sat munching our way through a large breakfast and several coffees. Turtle cannot function in the morning, not until he's had a smoke and a coffee, and who was I to deprive him of his daily routine? You can convince Turtle to do pretty much anything, he's that kind of guy. If I was going to rob a bank at gunpoint, I'm sure he'd be in, no questions asked. He'd purchase the ski masks off Amazon, maybe even source the imitation firearms. But he wouldn't pass a Costa Coffee without going in and ordering a latte, no matter where he was off to; even a bank job.

We'd almost finished breakfast and Turtle was pretty much done telling me how shit the coffee was in McDonald's, which he does every time we eat in one. I rang a taxi, which would then take us to the north face carpark. Turtle dumped his trash, then went outside for a smoke. As he took the long last drag of his cigarette, the taxi arrived.

The large north face carpark looked quite busy as the taxi rolled up. The driver manoeuvred the car right up close to the start of the trail and came to a stop. We decamped into the cold misty morning of the highlands. The driver popped the boot open; we dragged our packs out of the car and onto the ground. I closed the boot shut and the taxi disappeared up the shingle track road. We stood, just checking our kit, making sure we were ready for the next part of the journey, the slog up to the north face. I helped Turtle shoulder his oversized pack, before hoisting on my own. I pulled down on the straps, locking them down tight and fastening the hip belt, making sure it was comfortable for the hike ahead. Turtle lit up another cigarette and we departed.

It was a grey day, the kind of day where you feel like it's raining, but isn't. It was mid-February and it was cold, although I didn't feel cold. This was either due to having the correct clothing or because I was slightly exerting myself hiking in, either way, I was comfortable. Turtle on the other hand was sweating profusely, gasping for air and struggling. We were maybe ten minutes in and a quarter mile up the road. He was carrying a lot of kit. Not only did he have his now repacked rucksack on, but he was carrying a holdall containing all of his camera kit. No wonder he was struggling! We stopped to rest. I got him to take off one of the many layers he was wearing and take on some fluid. He took several blasts of his asthma inhaler and we pressed on. We heading upwards along a wide trail. This was flanked on either side by thick Scots pine forests, funnelling us along an inclined path. The dense congestion of trees was blocking out what light was strong enough to pierce the grey skies. Now and again, we would have to take a break. Turtle would try and catch his breath by sucking in the O_2, sucking on his inhaler and sucking on a cigarette. After which we would then carry on. It was slow progress, but we had the whole day to get to where we intended to camp. The bleak highland weather made the world look grey, as we meandered slowly up the path. Eventually, we moved out of the forest and caught our first glimpse of the mighty Ben Nevis. Rolling clouds filtered steadily past its summit, which from where we stood was just out of sight. Small patches of snow clung sporadically to the steep north walls, although not as much as I would have thought for the time of year.

An extremely large wooden stile crossed over a large fence, which now separated us from the next part of our hike. It was made up of several high steps, which then lead onto a flat platform, followed by several steep steps back down. I negotiated myself over the stile and down the other side. Turtle was having difficulty. His short stature and even shorter legs were making hard work of the steep steps and he was not amused. Letting loose with all the profanity the world had to offer as he ascended the steep wooden stairs. He had nothing but contempt for the carpenter who built this small engineering wonder and he made no effort to hide it. Eventually, he descended, slowly and carefully back down to ground level, slightly worn out from his little ascent. We now had breathtaking views of the Nevis range. The steep climb onto the Carn Mor Deag ridge lay to the east, although the ridge was out of sight and hidden by a false summit. To the south of our position, the huge walls of the north face. These towered above, forcing our eyes to scan the jagged horizon. Somewhere up there was a small cairn which marked the United Kingdom's highest peak. A small track now led the way. This ran alongside the river Allt a' Mhuilinn, which is fed from the river Lochy and would take us further into the range.

The wind was starting to pick up and I could feel the temperature starting to drop. It was early afternoon and it wouldn't be long before the light started to fade. We needed to find a flat spot to camp. I pulled left off the track and started to head east across the marshy glen, up towards the potential start of my route. It was tough going through the soft marsh. Every time I thought I had found a flat spot to camp, I found it was just too sodden, so I had to continue up, hoping that some elevation would see me onto dryer ground. I had left Turtle trailing behind as I pressed on. Eventually, a potential site presented itself. I relieved myself of my pack and got busy putting up the tent. As I had just finished erecting my tent, Turtle arrived, a bit dishevelled and windswept. He had plodded on at his own speed and was now ready to chuck it in for the day. I helped him off with his pack, unclipped his tent and went about helping him put it up. No sooner were the tents up and the kit stored away, the wind picked up and the rain started. We lay, hunkered inside our tents, zipped up in our sleeping bags, hoping that the wind didn't gust so hard that it pulled the tent pegs out of the soft ground.

Before leaving we had purchased some snow stakes, just in case we found ourselves having to erect tents in the snow. The extra-long tent stakes were driven deep into the damp soft marsh, helping to secure our tents in the high winds. I even pegged out the loop attached to my tent door (a weak spot) with my ice axe, driving it in, all the way up to the head.

Darkness descended and the wind and rain continued to batter the tents. All we could do was lie there and hope it didn't get any worse. I assembled my cook kit and went about boiling some water for a hot drink and dehydrated meal. I always feel better about any situation, if I'm suitably fed and watered. I drank the most amazing army ration hot chocolate, along with smashing my way through an Expedition Foods mac and cheese, finishing with an Expedition Foods hot chocolate pudding. I was absolutely stuffed. I hunkered back down into my sleeping bag, listening to the rain and the wind trying to dislodge me and my tent from the mountain.

At some point sleep must have crept up on me, as I was woken by the sound of gusting winds, battering against the thin walls of my flimsy tent. The tent rattled within the weather vortex, as if trying to frighten me, testing my nerve. It was the early hours of the morning. I lay and just listened to the hypnotic world of mother nature, as she vented her slight annoyance down upon the mountains.

The plan was to pick the best day for my ascent to the summit of Ben Nevis. It was clear to me that this day would not be it. I had kept quiet about my plan to conquer the Ben via the CMD arête. Turtle was told a couple of months before departure and was sworn to secrecy. I then floated the idea in idle conversation with my family, trying to implant it into their minds without them realising. It was quite easy with everything else that was going on. All the talk at that time was about tabbing the London Marathon. I had succeeded in slipping this little adventure past those who would be concerned for my welfare, stuffing it inside a trojan horse that was the London Marathon, then disembarking the plan a couple of days before leaving. It worked a treat. In the week leading up to departure, the national press had picked up a story about a hiker being lost in the mountains. He had been missing for a while and was now sadly presumed dead. This had all happened in the same region and on the same mountain where Turtle and myself found ourselves, so I understood their concern.

The day rolled on, occasionally I would poke my head out into the weather and summon Turtle from his cave, (which was his Snugpak Scorpion tent). A head of unkept hair would poke out and we'd have a quick conversation, before retreating into the safety and warmth of our tents. Then, around mid-afternoon, the rain stopped, as did the wind. We emerged from our self-imposed incarceration and breathed the fresh air of the Scottish Highlands. It was still grey and overcast. Chunks of clouds raced passed the jagged skyline as if huddled together, like a team that was planning the next play of wind and rain. We took a short walk down to the river and refilled our water bottles, before returning to the tents. The wind had dropped significantly so I decided to get the drone out. It was great to get some awesome footage of the valley for YouTube. My previous trip to summit the Ben had ended in disaster, so I scrapped all the footage. I was determined to make sure this trip was captured for prosperity. I wanted to capture the amazing landscape on film, with the best cinematography my equipment could deliver. As dusk started to descend, we once again retreated into our temporary dwellings, hoping that the morning would bring the weather we needed. I spent the evening checking my gear and testing the two-way radios, which would enable communication between myself and Turtle. This was a failsafe should the worst happen and I needed rescuing. I also had my satellite tracker and my Garmin watch, which would also track me. If I missed a comms window and was considered missing, I could be easily found. I ate, I packed, I rechecked my kit and then got an early night. Tomorrow was a big day, a long day, another day of reckoning.

I drifted gently out of sleep. It took a while to become fully cognitive and turn the alarm off on my phone. It was five a.m. and still the world was jet black. The wind, which had been a constant reminder that we were not in Kansas anymore, eerily was not present. If this was going to happen, then today would be the day. I began the prep, getting into my kit, loading my pack and checking and double-checking I had all my equipment. I opened the inner tent door and retrieved my boots. Hunched up in the porch of my tent, I slid my feet into the boots and loosely tied them. I unzipped the outer door and stepped out into the cold. It was colder than it had been. I could just see through the darkness the silhouetted peaks of the Nevis range, which had received a blanket of snow during the night. I made a brew and just stood, watching the light slowly radiate across the range. It was difficult to find the discipline to get going, such was the beauty of the sunrise. A moment can last forever, but this moment needed to be cut short. I needed to get on my way. I dragged my pack outside, pulled my ice axe from the ground (which had been keeping my tent door from flapping in the wind) and strapped it to the outside of my pack. I packed light with only the essentials and nothing more. I retied my boots, pulled my ThruDark strike trousers over the tops, and strapped on my gaiters. I had a steep climb up onto the ridge, so opted to stick my outer jacket into the top of my pack and just start in a ThruDark merino wool base layer. I was ready to go, but not before cramming in some breakfast. It was going to be a long day and I needed to fuel up as much as I could. It had just gone six thirty a.m. There was a light orange glow mixed with blues and browns drifting in the atmosphere. It was time.

I wasn't used to the lightness of the pack. Hiking in I was carrying around twenty-five-kilos. All of my training runs for the marathon had been with around sixteen-kilos, I was now strapping on about eight. I grabbed the radio, switched it on and clipped it to the side of my pack. The radio had an earpiece which I teased into my ear, clipping the push-to-talk button to the left shoulder strap of my pack. This meant I could communicate with Turtle much more easily. "Radio check, one two, one two......talk to me Goose," I squawked over the radio.

"Yes, I can hear you", replied Turtle. He sounded like he was half asleep, smoking a cigarette, getting dressed and making a brew, all at the same time. I turned on the satellite tracker, started my Garmin watch, grabbed my hiking poles which were sticking up out of the ground and took the first step.

The first section was a steep hike up onto the ridge. This was maybe two miles in distance, but the steepness of the ground made it a hard slog. I paced myself, moving at a comfortable speed. Although a small track had been worn into the mountain from years of ascents, it was not always obvious. I picked my way past the larger stones and continued upwards. I could feel the incline starting to niggle at my body. I was breathing slightly heavily and the calves were starting to burn, but I remained consistent. Slowly but surely, I continued to gain elevation.

Although it was slightly overcast when I set off, the morning sun had now burnt away most of the greyness. As I climbed higher, the rocky track began to get partially hidden by clumps of frozen snow. The higher I climbed the more snow lay on the ground, until eventually I reached the snow line. The sun had now lifted itself over the jagged skyline, bleaching the snow to an impenetrable white. It was as if the ground had suddenly been lit up from within the earth. I pulled my snow goggles down from the top of my head and gently placed them over my eyes. The polarizing lens wiped the brightness from the world, replacing it with a rainbow halo which stretched over the ridge, completely invisible to the naked eye. My walking poles were now coming into their own, making sure every step had a firm footing and ensuring I was balanced. Driving them into the snow, they acted as a second pair of legs. I made steady progress towards the top, moving closer to the ridgeline that looped around in an arc to the summit.

The route upwards was littered with false summits. Just as you thought you were almost at the ridge; the flat ground ahead would shift upwards again. I was starting to wonder whether I would ever meet the ridge line. Then, in the distance the snow flattened out before me, laying smooth and crisp. I moved on carefully, until I stood, perched upon a knife-edge ridge. I was careful not to move too close to the edge. In winter conditions the snow can form cornices over the edge like a false floor. Get too close and the cornice could collapse, sending you hurtling down the mountain, probably to your death. I had amazing views. To the north were the other Munros which littered the Nevis range, to the east was the ridge line, which undulated around, before shifting southeast and up onto the summit plateau. I was frozen to the spot, entranced by the winter beauty. I stood, perched on the ridge, silhouetted against the amber glow of the morning sun.

I took off my pack and sat on it, pulled my water bottle from the side pocket and took a large gulp. My breath was starting to return to normal. I munched my way through a protein bar, staring across at the steep north walls on the other side of the valley. I could have been the only person on the planet in that moment. A slight wind was all that was present and brought with it a gentle peace, making my frozen world a winter paradise, of which I was the only beneficiary. I was a lone man, sitting high upon a mountain. As the sun reflected off my snow goggles, I felt the warmth of its rays bathe the small amount of exposed skin on my face, (which was mostly covered.) I could have lost hours in that moment, but I was a slave to time and weather, which seemed to be moving in from the east, as clouds started to form on the distant horizon. I put away my water bottle, stuffed the wrapper of the protein bar into a pocket and pulled out my crampons (spikes mounted to a metal frame that strap onto the bottom of your boots) from the top of my pack. The ridge was covered in frozen snow, trying to work my way along it in just boots would be foolhardy and downright dangerous. After securing the crampons to both boots, ensuring they were strapped on tight, I reached back into my pack and pulled out my climbing helmet. Securing it firmly onto my head, I teased the radio earpiece through the strap and back into my ear, before clicking up the chin strap. I unstrapped my ice axe from the back of my pack and replaced it with my walking poles, which would be useless on this section of the ridge. I dug the ice axe into the snow, leaving only half the shank and head visible. Rising to my feet, I stood, taking a short moment drinking in the amazing snow-covered landscape, before shouldering my pack. Then, bending down, I grabbed the shaft of the axe and pulled it from the snow like Excalibur. I was now ready to negotiate the knife-edge ridge, all the way around to the cairn of the Carn Mor Dearg arête.

Just as I was about to move, the radio crackled into life "Boo Boo to Yogi Bear, are you receiving…over." Turtle giggled slightly, as he tried to come off all pro on the radio.

"This is Yogi Bear, good copy…over" I replied. I gave Turtle a brief update on my progress, which he was then going to relay to Emma via text. After a brief conversation about timings and weather he signed out

"Boo Boo over and out" and I giggled slightly.

My crampons gripped the snow as I set off. The familiar sound of crunching snow emanated from the bottom of my boots. The way ahead was flat, so I moved more quickly, precariously perched upon a knife-edge ridge, with long drops on either side. This added to the exposure of my surrounding. Now and again, I would have to use the bottom point of my axe to stabilize myself, as I worked my way past small outcrops of rock. Large rocks cascaded out from the ridge, breaking through the snow like the dorsal fin of a Great White Shark. The outcrops got bigger the further on I went. Eventually I was having to move off the ridge and around them, skirting past on the steep south wall, exposed over a drop which disappeared down towards a small climber's hut way down in the valley. The scrambling over and around rocks went on for a couple of hours, sapping my energy. The weather was starting to close in. The wind had picked up and was starting to blow the loose snow off the top of the ridge line. I now had to be super careful. One slip and it would be curtains! Progress was painfully slow, as I battled both the ridgeline and the weather. Visibility was getting poorer. The sunny views of the Nevis range now seemed like a distant memory. I moved along past a large outcrop, traversing around the side, protecting myself from the wind. This didn't feel like scrambling anymore, more like actual rock climbing. I used the front points of my crampons to gain purchase on tiny ledges, anchoring my axe into cracks or in between the rocks for additional support, as I slowly crept along the rock wall. The traversing eventually started to get easier. As I got to the far end of the rock wall, I could see a large flat plain of snow, which then led to a large cairn. This marked the end of the arête. I can honestly say that I was very happy to now be sitting behind the cairn, out of the wind, taking a well-deserved break. I can imagine that doing this route in the summer is a mere stiff day's hiking, with a little bit of scrambling. However, in winter, it was (as I would have said, back in my climbing days) sketchy as fuck!

All that lay before me now was a steep incline of ice, that went all the way to the summit of Ben Nevis. I kicked the left front point of my crampon into the ice, then dug the point of my axe in a little higher, before then kicking in the right foot. It was a slow, but methodical way of tackling this steep slope of snow and ice. I anticipated that it would take around an hour to reach the summit, if I could maintain a consistent pace. I was slow, but continually moving. Left foot in, axe in, right foot in and repeat. Climbing forever upward, surrounded by the wind which whipped up the fine powder snow around me. Left foot in, axe in, right foot in, left foot in…Then all of a sudden, my left slipped and I slipped. I plunged my axe into the snow hard to prevent a fall. After my heart rate had returned to a reasonable level, I decided to move on. I kicked my left foot into the snow but couldn't get any purchase. My foot just kept slipping. I looked down to discover, to my horror, I had lost a crampon. A slight panic started to ripple through my body. What was I going to do now? I looked down to see if I could see the offending piece of ironware. After a couple of minutes of eyeballing where I had climbed, I spotted the crampon sticking out of the snow, around fifteen metres below. I now had to descend carefully to retrieve it, strap it back on, then climb back up. It felt heartbreaking and, for a split second, the thought crossed my mind about leaving it and carrying on. I moved back down the slope, descending sideways, using my right foot which still had the crampon attached as the downward foot. I reached the crampon and spent a significant amount of time strapping it back on, ensuring it would not come off again. After taking on some fluids and a couple of energy gels, I proceeded, upward, retracing my steps. I was now pretty much in a whiteout. The wind was so strong, it was whipping up the snow and throwing it about the air, making visibility approximately five metres. I could see the edge of the mountain on the right and made sure that I didn't stray too close in the poor visibly. Gradually the incline lessened and got shallower until eventually, I crested onto the summit plateau. In the distance, through the snow that was blasting into my face, I could just make out the emergency stone shelter which sat next to the summit cairn. I trudged on through the wind, being sandblasted with snow, until I reached the stone building. I walked past the shelter, climbed up a small step and onto the cairn tapping it with my axe. I was now standing on the highest piece of real estate in the United Kingdom.

I had made a big thing about returning to Scotland and slaying those dragons of previous failures. You would have thought that this would be an emotional moment. A moment of closure. I felt nothing. No sense of achievement. No closure…nothing. There I stood, at the highest point in the United Kingdom, in the howling wind, emotionless. I wanted to feel something, anything, but I just stood, on my own. I pushed the button on the radio "Maverick to Goose, do you copy, over"

"This is Goose, over" squawked Turtle, who sounded like he was half asleep.

"I'm on top of the world, over" I replied.

"Well done, see you in a bit, over" was all I got back from him.

I stepped down off the cairn, took a bearing to follow for the descent and left. The summit of Ben Nevis is very close to the north face. In a whiteout you could easily step off the edge. It has been known to happen. I followed the bearing meticulously, until I reached another stone cairn. From there, in the distance I could see another. These were markers for hikers to follow in the event of bad weather. I moved from marker to marker, slowly descending. Coming down was much easier than going up, although now and again I would meet descending sheets of frozen snow. These had to be negotiated with extreme care, carefully descending the ice using the sides of my crampons and axe as support. I was mesmerised by the vastness of space. Clouds of spindrift blew across sheets of frozen snow, like a tumbleweed blowing across an arid desert, but the polar opposite. I was a stranger in a strange world, all alone with my thoughts as I worked my way back down the mountain. Most accidents that happen in the mountains, happen upon descent. I was making sure I was not a part of that statistic, so moved with caution and confidence. Eventually, the snow started to thin out enough that I could remove my crampons, put away the axe and switch to my hiking poles. The sun was low now, casting radiant reds across the sparse patches of snow which clung onto patches of heather, refusing to melt in a defiant salute to the impending warm weather.

As I approached the right-hand turn off the main track, which would take me past a small loch called Lochan Meall An T-suidhe, the sun fell behind the Munros of Nevis. I would soon be plunged into darkness. I was tired but felt surprisingly fresh considering the day's events. I soldiered on across the heather, past the loch, until I was stood at the top of the valley looking down towards the river. It was now almost dark. The last light of the day was being aggressively pushed out by the night. I needed a marker to head for. I reached for the radio.

"This is Bravo Golf Oscar to base camp, are you receiving.... over?" No reply. "Bravo Golf Oscar to base camp, are you receiving.... over?" Still no reply. Then, after a minute or so, the sound of a radio sparked into life as if someone was having difficulty orientating the radio to talk into it.

"Base camp receiving, over" eventually came the reply. Turtle sounded out of breath, I pushed down on the talk button,

"What took you so long?"

"I was taking a piss", I laughed, Turtle had probably been waiting for ages for a radio update, then chose that exact time to take a slash. I imagined him frantically zipping himself up, then trying to cross the soggy marsh at speed, before diving into his tent to retrieve the radio, probably throwing his back out in the process.

"Can you light the beacons of Gondor...over" I waited, scanning the area on the other side of the river, adjacent to where I was standing. Then, in the far distance, I saw a faint light, which gradually got brighter and brighter as Turtle turned on every torch and light that he had. I could see our camp. I now had a clear direction of travel, but I had one crucial decision to make.

From the walk-in we had seen that the river was running fast, too fast to cross on foot. There were, at some of the narrow points on the river, large boulders which acted like makeshift bridges, which could possibly allow you to cross. This seemed very sketchy to me. The other option was to bear left and head to where the river runs through a set of weirs. Just passed the weirs was a bridge. This would add another couple of miles to the trek back to base camp. It was a no-brainer. I wasn't going to cross a fast-flowing, deep river in the dark, by skipping over wet boulders. I was going to take the long way. I let Turtle know the plan and then started to descend diagonally southwest, towards the weirs. It was a slog walking in the dark, with just the light from my head torch illuminating the way. As I got closer to the river, I could hear the sound of raging waters gradually getting louder. I stepped onto the path that handrailed the raging torrent of water and headed west to the weirs. I drifted away with my thoughts, just thinking about the day, thinking about home and then ultimately thinking about my dinner that night. I was starving. I crossed the bridge at the weirs and picked up the track heading east. I was constantly scanning for Turtle's beacon of lights, hoping they would show me the way. However, I was now in the lowest part of the valley. I needed to get to some higher ground. Moving off the path, I clambered up a steep bank. Scanning the area, I soon found the tents illuminated in the distance, piercing through the darkness. Various flashing lights were strobing in the blackness. Bloody hell I thought. How many torches and lights did he bring? You could have landed a Chinook helicopter with the amount of illumination Turtle had splayed out. I headed in the direction of the Pink Floyd light show, moving ever closer to hot food and a warm sleeping bag.

It took me eleven hours and forty-one minutes to cover seven point-eight miles. That was the total distance from our wild campsite to the summit of Ben Nevis, down the tourist path and back to the tents. I started the process of shedding all my kit, dropping the pack, losing the poles, removing my helmet (which I was still wearing for some strange reason) and taking off my jacket. I slumped in the doorway of my tent, totally exhausted. Turtle stood over me, cigarette hanging out the corner of his mouth.

"Here you go mate" he said, handing me two full one-litre bottles of water. I looked up at him. He just stood there. I thought he was going to offer some words of congratulations or even just a "well done". But no! Not Turtle! He just looked down at the wreck of a man I was. Silhouetted against a clear night sky peppered with stars, he took a long pull on his cigarette, exhaled for what seemed like an eternity and in his gravelly voice said "Filtered that for you mate," turned on his heels and went back to his tent. Legend.

That evening, I ate and slept with a feeling of contentment. The same kind of feeling you get after completing a hard day's work. I had succeeded in my quest, mission accomplished. I didn't feel like it was a spectacular achievement. I felt I had conceived and then executed the plan as intended. Maybe, feeling an overwhelming sense of accomplishment would eradicate the motivation to carry on with these kinds of endeavours. Maybe the lack of feeling is what drives me on further. Chasing the dragon, always looking for the next hit.

We left the mountainside the following morning and started the long journey home. I was eight weeks out from the start of the London Marathon.

Winter summit "Ben Nevis"

Chapter 19

After returning from Scotland, the only thing on my mind, the only thing I was focused on, was the London Marathon. Although I had been training and training hard, I was sure that to execute the mission, I would be relying more on my mental fortitude than my physical stamina. I'd worked hard to get myself into physical shape, enough to be able to drag myself around the twenty-six-point-two miles of the course anyway. I'd also worked extremely hard raising money for the Epilepsy Society, but I was still short of the required target to justify my place. A team WhatsApp group had been set up, with all those running for the Epilepsy Society swapping training stories, talking about their insecurities and generally supporting each other. I didn't go in for these types of groups usually, but I occasionally found myself contributing now and again. Nobody in the group however was running in military kit, boots and bergen. Had I over-committed myself? Was I setting myself up for failure? Was it too much?

I continued the training, I continued fundraising and I continued to push myself relentlessly. I was scared, scared of failing, scared of letting people down, scared of having a seizure whilst training, scared of having a seizure on the course and scared of actually dropping dead. At night, in those alone times, at home, when nobody could see me, I sobbed. I couldn't work out why. It would just happen. I wasn't feeling depressed or lonely. I had no reason to be upset. I'd just wipe away the tears, give myself a good talking to and get on with something. I was ignoring the issue, but I didn't know what the issue was, so how could I fix it? I'm not an emotional person, or a crier. I'm a tough-it-out, fall-over stand-up and repeat guy, not a whiner baby. I needed to sort myself out, train harder and be tougher, that was the answer. It was back to the early morning runs, a reminder that it was those early morning jaunts into the forest that jump started my recovery.

I awoke to the sound of my Alexa alarm going off. The gentle hypnotic music pulled me into the dark reality of the morning, it was six a.m. I didn't want to get out of bed. I knew today was just going to be nothing but pain and misery. It was the last long run in my training programme before the marathon. Twenty miles along the Downs Link, from my home town to the coastal town of Shoreham. I sat up sluggishly, motivation at zero, but it is not motivation that gets you out of bed, into your kit and out the door…it's discipline. Over the last few years, I had built up a level of discipline sufficient enough to override the voices that tell me to go back to bed. I started the familiar process, get up, throw on some scruffs, let Lemmy out, feed Lemmy, coffee, breakfast, prep nutrition, prep feet, prep kit, get into my combats, boots on, weigh and then put on the pack, set Garmin, start satellite tracker, step out the door and go. None of this happens with motivation. It's all discipline. If I was relying on motivation, I would still be fast asleep in bed.

I had hiked this route several times, so was more than familiar with the distance and terrain. This time though I was taking it on in anger and with a forty-pound bergen. I had a plan. I was going to run two miles, then walk one and repeat this all the way to the seaside. The first couple of miles went through town and passed by with relative ease. Then we hit the trail. The gravelly track made me work slightly harder but the next few miles sailed by. The weather conditions were perfect, it was slightly overcast, with a little drizzle now and then and a very light constant breeze. I was managing to stick to my pre-planned pace, twelve-minute miles for the run and fifteen for the walk. The Sussex countryside wafted past as I cruised down the disused railway line, passing by the derelict station of West Grinstead and its abandoned rolling stock. I hit the halfway point and was surprised at how good I was feeling. It was tough, but I was managing to maintain the pace and I felt comfortable being uncomfortable. Eventually, the trail opened out into rural farmland which sat close to the South Downs. The terrain became more undulating, and the further I went, the more the wheels slowly started to fall off. I tried to take my mind off the persistent pain in my thighs, by trying to enjoy the beautiful Sussex landscape, but it didn't work. I was feeling it now, in every muscle. By mile seventeen I was digging deep into the darkest corners to carry on the forward momentum. One boot in front of the other, working hard for the next hundred yards, then the next and the next, breaking the distance down into manageable chunks. I moved out of the secluded trail, flanked on one side by the river Adur and some industrial units on the other. I followed the track which went underneath the Shoreham bypass and pushed hard up a slight rise towards a metal sculpture. A memorial dedicated to the victims of the twenty fifteen Shoreham air disaster, when a Hawker Hunter aircraft performing at the air show, crashed into the road killing eleven people and injuring sixteen others.

As I approached the memorial my Garmin beeped, informing me that I had done twenty miles. It had taken me four hours thirty-six minutes and sixteen seconds, averaging thirteen minutes and forty-nine seconds per mile. I was broken, I dropped my pack and sat down on one of the benches adjacent to the memorial. I had my sleeping bag in my pack. I could have easily dragged it out, laid it out on the ground and fallen asleep, but I still had a one-mile walk to the train station. Once I had recovered enough to tackle the journey, I began the walk to catch my train. This was difficult. I was experiencing sharp pain in my right foot where the heel meets the arch. I hadn't noticed it while I was running, but now it was impeding the way I walked. I had to limp, all the way.

Arriving at the station in what felt like critical condition, I limped up the short ramp to the ticket machine, selected my ticket and tapped my debit card against the payment pad. I moved onto the platform and slumped into a metal bench. I was so tired I couldn't even think. The only thing keeping me awake was the pain in my right foot. I must have looked terrible. My shirt was soaked in sweat, as were my combat trousers. The metal bench was far from comfortable, but I didn't have the energy to shift about to accommodate my sore muscles. I had twenty minutes until my train home was due, so I just sat, being uncomfortable, staring vacantly into space. Worrying whether I had some kind of stress fracture in my foot.

"Have you been on an adventure?" A voice suddenly snapped me out of my daymare. I looked up to see a man in a business suit.

"Errr, no", I replied, cutting the conversation short and closing it off.

"What's with the rucksack then?" asked the stranger on the platform, failing to take the hint that I was not in the mood to swap stories or pleasantries. I didn't want to be rude, so I thought I would engage with him briefly. Hopefully, once his curiosity had been satisfied, he'd Foxtrot Oscar.

"I've been on the Downs Link" I replied, with as much of a smile as I could muster.

"How far you come?" He wasn't going away.

"From Horsham." I thought by keeping my answers short and to the point he'd move on quickly, but no.

"What you do? Take a couple of days?"

"No actually, came down this morning." I knew this was now going to spark his curiosity even more.

"Wait, what, you came from Horsham this morning?" he looked at his watch, "but it's only just the afternoon now?" He sounded confused. I just decided to put him out of his misery. It was draining having this conversation.

"I ran".

"You ran from Horsham, with that pack?" He wasn't going to let me off. I was going to have to spill the beans.

"Yes, I'm training for the London Marathon, trying to raise some money for charity, so I'll be running in military kit and carrying a forty-pound bergen". The stranger looked shocked.

"Which charity?"

"The Epilepsy Society" I replied. The stranger then pulled out his wallet, removed a twenty-pound note, and handed it to me.

"Here, take this, and good luck. I'll look out for you on the tele." With that, he looked up at the board to see when his train was due and said, "My train's not due for another half an hour. I'm going to have a pint in the pub across the road." With that he walked off, leaving me gobsmacked, holding a twenty-pound note. What a nice gesture that was, surreal, but nice. Not long after my strange encounter, my train arrived and I was on my way home. I arrived at my home town station around an hour later. Emma picked me up outside with her youngest son Bertie, who greeted me with the middle finger and a smile (a sign of endearment), he then told me how much I stank! He was right. I went home to shower and nurse my foot.

By the following morning, the pain had got worse. I was having trouble walking and just wearing shoes was painful. There were now eight weeks to the marathon, this was not good. Over the next few days things didn't get any better. I was hobbling about, putting a brave face on everything, but inside I was shitting myself. I wasn't going to pull out of the marathon, no way. So I knew I was going to have to come to terms with twenty-six point-two miles of sheer agony. I deep-dived into the internet to try and diagnose the problem, rapidly becoming a foot expert. The pain didn't respond to any kind of pressure exerted onto where it hurt, so I ruled out a fracture. This meant it was probably ligament damage or muscular. In the end, I took a blanket approach and drafted a rehabilitation programme. Starting with the basics, rest, ice, compression and elevation. I iced my foot for fifteen minutes twice a day, every day and did daily exercises to strengthen the muscles around the ankle, along with stretching out my calves. Day by day the foot felt better. After a week I had no pain when walking. I carried on with the programme and after another week, I felt no pain at all. I started walking on the dreadmill, after a few days I was running on the dreadmill, until I was doing longer loaded runs. The training was back on track and disaster was averted. It was another lesson, a lesson in perseverance, commitment and consistency. There is always a way, you just have to be able to focus on the issue, formulate a plan and execute it.

I was in full-on marathon mode, training and fundraising, hounding my social media followers for sponsorship. It was a full-time job. In the background, I was being supported one hundred per cent by my family. Nobody in my family had ever taken part in the London Marathon before. So, with all the support and potentially being the first member to do so, I felt under an inordinate amount of pressure, which I was piling on myself. Looking back now, if I hadn't felt the pressure, then I wouldn't have pushed myself and I probably wouldn't have trained so hard. I then wouldn't have been in good enough shape to stand on the start line. It was all starting to come together, but inevitably now and again the whole plan would get derailed by a seizure. I quite often forget I have epilepsy. I'll be going about my normal day, completely oblivious that at any moment my soul will leave my body and crumple to the ground wherever it was standing. It was frustrating, recovering in bed or crashing on the sofa, unable to do anything other than feel terrible and tired. This had an impact on training and it was always hard to pick it back up again. I had built myself up to be the tough guy, the guy that can tackle anything. Strong, committed and able to push himself past what people thought he was capable of. There are days when I am not that person and I fall very short of the high standards I have set for myself. Days filled with confusion, headaches and hopelessness. It can be rough, not just for me but for everyone around me. There lies the opportunity, the opportunity to get up and not be beaten. To show the world you won't lay down and become a victim. The reality I have found, is I have no choice but to get back up after every knockdown. What would be the alternative?

I was one week out and final preparations for the big day were underway. I had booked an apartment close to the start line. Neil the Tash and myself would travel up the day before and stay in London overnight, making sure that I was fresh and ready to go marathon morning. Emma was travelling up on the day with Bertie and her sister Sarah (who had friends running). My Mum would be escorted up to London by Turtle, where they would then meet my brother Michael and his husband David. I'm not sure what was more difficult. The six months of preparing for the marathon or the logistics of getting everyone there.

On the Thursday before the start, my mother and I travelled to London to pick up my race pack from the Marathon exhibition show. It was good to spend some time with her. I couldn't remember the last time we had spent some quality time together, just us. We negotiated the train and the underground, just like we used to do when I was a kid. When we would travel back to Horsham from our home in north London to visit my grandparents. We arrived at the exhibition centre, to find a long line of cubicles which traversed one wall of the marathon show. This is where I was to collect my race pack. I strolled up and showed the lady the QR code on my phone, which she scanned. She then grabbed a clear bag, printed off my number and placed it carefully into the bag. This bag was marked with my race number and could be used to store any kit that I wanted at the finish line. Before starting the marathon, I had to hand it to a truck with the corresponding number. This truck would then be waiting at the finish, ready for me to collect it. I was number six two one two one. It was now real. It was happening.

We spent the rest of the morning walking around the show, checking out the exhibitor stalls which showcased the latest kit, from running shoes to energy bars. My mother was desperate to buy me a memento, a t-shirt or a hoodie that was emblazoned with the TCS London Marathon logo. I didn't want anything, I thought it might put a jinx on me. I thought it presumptuous as I hadn't run the marathon yet. We left the show and had a nice lunch near London Bridge, before catching the train home. It was nice to spend that day with my Mum. Normally, the only time we spend together on our own is when I've had a seizure. She would then sit at my home, reading on her iPad until she thought I was well enough to be left on my own again, which could be hours or even the following day. I wouldn't be able to live or survive without her. I owe her so much, and I try really hard not to take it all for granted.

Friday rolled in along with Neil the Tash. The day was spent preparing everything I would need for the next few days. Once all the packing was done, checked, then double-checked, we sat down to work out the logistics of the nutrition plan. The idea was to have four strategic points along the route where we would meet. I would be given two energy gels and a five-hundred-millilitre bottle of water, which would be pre-mixed with electrolytes and carbohydrates. With the route map opened out on the coffee table (the inanimate object which changed my life) we worked out the stops, potential time of arrival and closest underground stations to those locations. We were primed and ready to go.

The weekend also happened to be Neil the Tash's birthday! He'd given up his birthday weekend to support me. If someone looked up the word friends in the dictionary, instead of pictures of Jennifer Aniston and David Schwimmer, there should be pictures of Turtle and Neil the Tash. I couldn't let Neil's birthday go without some form of celebration, so I booked a table at my and Emma's favourite curry restaurant, The Akash (owned by one of the friends we went to school with). After our meal, Emma went back home and Neil and I walked back through Horsham Park, slipping into my local Cricket Club, (which happened to be Turtle's bar of choice and local drinking hole) on the way. It was around nine in the evening so I knew Turtle would be well-oiled by then. I was not left disappointed. Neil stood beside him at the bar, which Turtle was leaning against. Turtle turned and looked up at Neil, gave a slight nod and returned to his pint. Slowly Turtle's intoxicated brain cells started to fire. The cogs upstairs started to grind away, until eventually, an electrical connection in his brain let the rest of him know that he did in fact know the person standing next to him. It took a while and I'm sure he couldn't quite believe it in his drunken state. We got some drinks in, forcing another pint of lager into Turtle, who had already drunk way too much. Turtle staggered about bouncing off several patrons in the bar. Then, through slurred speech gave me a lecture about how I shouldn't be drinking so close to running the marathon. I had one pint of Guinness, (compared to Turtle who was probably on his tenth pint of lager.) Neil and I left him staggering about and headed home. Tomorrow was going to be a busy day.

On Saturday the twenty-second of June, twenty twenty-three, Neil and I took a slow drive up to London. The apartment we had rented for the night was situated in Woolwich, approximately one mile from the marathon start line. This meant we had great access via the rail network the following morning, ensuring that neither one of us would be under any pressure to get to where we needed to be. The ground-floor apartment was basic but functional. If the truth be known I was astounded at how cheap it was, seeing that all local hotels were booked and the ones that weren't were extortionately priced. We set about making it home for the night, I sank into an armchair while Neil crashed onto the sofa. We ordered food from Frankie and Benny's and immersed ourselves in a movie. I was stuffing my face with as many complex carbs as I could, which that night was Mac and Cheese. While Neil smashed his way through a ginormous burger! It was a relaxed evening, just two mates hanging out, shooting the breeze and watching television. There was no tension or pre-race nerves. I felt relaxed and confident. We had a strategy and we had a plan. We also had a contingency if we had to deviate from the original. It was all worked out. Nothing had been left to chance. I retired to bed around ten o'clock. Closing my eyes, I ran through the following day's events in my head, before naturally falling asleep.

As morning forced its way through a small crack in the curtains, I drifted out of sleep and gradually immersed myself into the day. It was six a.m. and the procedure was the same. I had run through this morning run routine a hundred times, but it was marathon day. It felt different. I tackled breakfast first which was more Mac and Cheese and some coffee. This was difficult to get down, but I slowly worked my way through it, eventually managing to finish it all. I was also hydrating with just water, trying to prepare my body for the day ahead. Fuelling up and making sure the tank was full. There seemed to be a nervous energy in the air like we were both a little anxious maybe. Neil was planning his route from checkpoint to checkpoint, whilst I had a hundred different things running through my head. All my kit was laid out on the bed, meticulously arranged in order of how I would dress. This is a little quirk of mine, I do this even at home, laying my clothes out neatly on the bed before dressing. I think Emma finds it a bit weird. I showered, then took my time taping up my feet. I gradually got dressed into my kit. Underwear, Dri-fit t-shirt, calf compression sleeves, toe socks, merino wool socks, combat trousers and finally my Epilepsy Society running vest which was emblazoned with the name 'Grizzly'. It was time to make our way to the start line, just a short walk up the road to the station, then a two-stop train journey to Blackheath Common.

It was a big day, but it didn't feel like it. Maybe I wasn't fully aware of the enormity of the challenge ahead. The sky was overcast and now and again we'd feel a few spots of drizzle. Ideal marathon running weather I thought. I'd much prefer this weather than it to be blisteringly hot. Neil and I stood on the platform under a shelter waiting for our train, chatting as if it was just another day. As we waited other runners started to turn up, milling about, anxiously moving on the spot. Everyone was in their own little worlds, having conversations of encouragement with themselves. I looked different to the other runners, who were decked out in flash running shoes and the latest windproof jackets. I on the other hand, with my big pack and military gear stood out from the crowd, attracting a smattering of curiosity from the other runners.

The train arrived and quietly we all filed on. There was a disconcerting silence on the train, occasionally a hushed voice could be heard over the sound of the rolling stock but it was barely audible. Everything felt so surreal, like it wasn't really happening, as if everybody was pretending that they were somewhere else, not just about to enter a world of pain and suffering. Pulling up at Blackheath Station the crowd disembarked onto an extremely busy platform and queued patiently to enter the stairwell. We climbed up a short flight of stairs and then swarmed onto the street. It was then that I started to appreciate the whole magnitude of the event. There were masses of people in the street. A mixture of runners and supporters parading towards the start line. It felt like a carnival atmosphere as we surged through the streets and towards the Heath. It was crazy, like we'd somehow found ourselves caught up in some kind of march or protest, swept through the streets along with the masses.

More light rain floated out of a grey sky as we got to Blackheath, the official start line. We sheltered under a tree at the edge of the common and checked all the kit. We went over the plan one last time, checked the kit again, then Neil wished me good luck, gave me a hearty slap on the back and headed off to the first checkpoint. I was left on my own. I sauntered up to the entrance of the marathon village, had my pack checked by security and was let in through a makeshift entrance. What do I do now? The rain had got a little heavier and people were standing up tight against the barriers to shelter from the worst of it. A long line of trucks was parked at the far end. These were the trucks that collected our clear marathon bags and then ferried them to the finish line. Music played over the loudspeakers, while big screens showed runners being interviewed before departing. A thousand temporary toilets stretched into infinity, playing host to those with last-minute calls of nature. Everything was highly organised, but at the same time, nobody knew what was going on. With fifty thousand people taking part in the marathon, the starts had to be staggered. I was due to start at eleven fifteen. With some time to kill I decided to pay one last visit to the toilet and joined the queue. I stood in the rain for around fifteen minutes, eventually, I was ushered into an available cubicle where I spent ten minutes evacuating myself. I couldn't believe how many people were there and yet I felt very alone and isolated. My mood started to reflect the weather, dull and damp. I wanted to take it all in, feel the atmosphere, pat myself on the back for being here and in the moment. But it felt like just another day, standing in the rain. I thought the splendour and majesty of the day would somehow miraculously fill me with inspiration, carry me around the course like it was effortless. Had the last few years of pain, hurt, disappointment and abandonment turned me into a person who simply cannot process these kinds of emotions? I was standing at the end of six hard months of preparation. I'd sweated through miles of uncomfortable pain, pushed myself to the limit and then past that limit every week. This was my time. My moment of triumph. I should be feeling waves of adrenaline surging through my body, chomping at the bit to get going, but to me, I was just standing in a soggy field in the rain. The elation of being part of the surging crowds moving towards the start line earlier that morning had fluttered away, only to be replaced with the inconvenience of waiting to start. It may as well have been the local park run.

After what felt like hours, the announcement came over the loudspeakers for my start. I took off my damp waterproof jacket, stuffed it into the top of my pack, clipping the lid back down. I tightened every compression strap before hoisting it onto my back, pulling the shoulder straps tight and clipping the waist and sternum straps up. I moved into the mass of runners slowly edging towards the official start, until we found ourselves crammed into a narrow pen. We all carried on filtering through, like lambs being loaded into a truck, ready for slaughter. The large gantry that spanned the road indicated the start line and was now only five metres away. This was it. We all shuffled forward, getting ever closer. I pushed the button on my Garmin watch, which loaded the correct screen in preparation for hitting the start button. The rain had stopped for now, but it had left a damp chill in the air. A typical day that encapsulates British weather. Whilst others jumped about trying to keep warm, I just slowly shuffled forward, in my own world, not really caring where I was or what I was doing. Maybe the grandeur of the event was lost on me. It could be possible that I felt it was a bit of an anti-climax. Maybe it wasn't living up to expectations? The London Marathon was supposed to be the pinnacle of five years of struggle. My life building to a crescendo right up to this very point, but for some reason, it wasn't, I felt disappointed. I thought about my loved ones who were waiting patiently on the course. I thought about Neil the Tash who was working his way on the crowded underground, trying to get to the first checkpoint. But mostly I thought about the endless miles I had run to get here. It had been nearly five years since my accident, four and a half years since I lost my job and nearly three years since my second marriage broke down. I had been hospitalized more times than I can remember. I had been visited by so many paramedics that some now knew me by name. I'd spent a night in a psychiatric hospital and it had been around three years since I tried to take my own life. Yet here I was, standing on the start line of the London Marathon.

I was snapped out of my lucid daydream as I moved onto a large mat which covered the road. The gantry was now overhead and I just caught a glimpse of the digital timer as I passed underneath it. I hit the start button on my Garmin and the world instantly came alive. The vibrant colours drained back into brightly coloured running vests and the luminous running shoes of those around me. The noise was no longer muffled but loud and crisp. It was like the world suddenly went ultra-high definition in both sound and vision. I started running, moving into my own space so as to not hold up the faster runners. The realisation that I was now running the London Marathon in military kit, carrying a near on forty-pound bergen, suddenly flooded my body with adrenaline. All those emotions that I wanted to feel leading up to the start, now swarmed into every cell inside me. It was hard not to get carried away. I needed to keep to the pace that I had trained to, not go out all guns blazing.

I cruised by the first mile, soaking it all in, the noise, and the crowds lining the streets. People were shouting out my name which was emblazoned across my running vest, offering kind words of encouragement. I guess I was an oddity compared to the masses of conventional runners, plodding along in all my kit. Now and again a kid would scream "COME ON GRIZZLY" and hold their hand out over the railing, where I would then move across and bump fists with them. I arrived at the first water station. It was carnage, with plastic bottles strewn everywhere. I didn't need to rehydrate at any of these stations, as Neil was taking care of that. I also had my water bladder in my pack, which had been pre-mixed with carbs and electrolytes before we left that morning. Then out of nowhere, I heard somebody shouting my name "Gareth!" I turned to see who it was! It was my cousin, Claire. She was volunteering at the water station, which I had no idea she was doing. I gave a wave and a quick "Hi!" and pushed on. The course suddenly dropped downhill and I found it hard to not let my legs run away with me, always conscious that I had a long way to go. I assumed that at some points on the course, the lines of people would thin out, but I was yet to see any breaks in the crowds behind the barriers. Spectators sat outside pubs, enjoying a pint, enjoying the atmosphere and cheering on the runners. It felt more like a carnival.

I was comfortable with my pace. I had run through all those little niggles that plagued me at the start, as my body got to grips with the workload. The five-mile marker was approaching and this was the first checkpoint with Neil. To make sure I could find him in the crowds he had been issued with a giant Jolly Roger pirate flag, which I should be able to see from a distance. I ran past the marker and kept my eyes peeled on the left-hand side of the road. All this had been meticulously planned, even down to which side of the road he would be on. In the distance, fluttering in the wind, there she flew! The Jolly Roger and the first checkpoint. It was good to see Neil and it felt good to know the plan was working. Neil had already prepared everything I needed, my bottle of pre-mixed drink and two energy gels. I tore off the tab on the energy gel and squeezed its contents into my mouth, all in one go. Neil was asking how I was, whether I needed anything and generally looking out for my welfare. I took a quick slug out of the water bottle, exchanged a few words with Neil and I was away. It had been like a Formula One pitstop, no messing, all business, the next checkpoint was mile eleven. I carried on down the road, periodically taking swigs out of the plastic water bottle until it was empty, which I then discarded by the side of the road in a designated bottle drop area. I was glad we had prepared these little pitstops. In my head I was working out my pace, then calculating the time I should arrive at the next one. I was essentially moving from checkpoint to checkpoint, this made the distance a lot easier in my head to overcome.

Crowds of people amazingly still lined the streets. People continued to cheer. Kids were giving out Jelly Babies and of course, the hand slaps and fist bumps were still required. We had now looped around on ourselves and were heading out of Greenwich and towards Deptford. This was an iconic part of the marathon. As I came to the end of Greenwich Park, I took a sharp right and passed the famous tea trading ship, 'The Cutty Sark'. I remember looking up at the tall masts and rigging, dwarfed by their size as I ran past. This section of the marathon is always on television. It felt good to be ticking off these iconic moments. I was seven miles in and still feeling comfortable. I was cruising, sticking religiously to my pace. I was in no pain and I was enjoying every minute, being carried along on a wave of enthusiasm and excitement.

At mile nine I would pass the first of two Epilepsy Society checkpoints. This is where I had told my family to wait. I was excited about seeing them, but I was probably more excited about them seeing me if I was being honest! I wanted my Mum to see her son, strong and athletic, taking part in one of the biggest events in the world, fulfilling his goals. Breaking down stereotypes and showing the world that he won't be beaten, or go quietly into the dark to die. Instead of how she sometimes sees me, lying on the floor, contorting, making strange noises and urinating himself. A slave tied down to his disability.

As mile nine approached the streets narrowed and the crowd got louder. It felt like there had been a sudden influx or a surge of people flooding the streets of London. The atmosphere was electric. Then through the mass of runners, I saw the purple flags of the Epilepsy Society and their makeshift stand. Then, amongst the crowds, I caught sight of my family. My mother was shouting and waving, next to her was my brother Michael and his husband David both waving and shouting, and next to them Turtle, smoking a cigarette and taking pictures. I moved over towards the barrier, high-fived Michael and carried on. I didn't stop. I didn't want to break the rhythm and ruin the pace. I would have liked to have hung about for a few minutes, but I needed to keep going. Seeing my family gave me a boost, an emotional power-up to keep moving. Having two younger brothers who are fourteen months apart, meant that Mum was never able to come and watch me play football as a kid, or watch the rugby matches I played as a teenager. I think this must have been the first time she'd seen me do anything athletic. It had only taken forty years.

Reinvigorated I kept pushing. My run plan was working well, two miles running and one mile walking. I was now working towards the next checkpoint at mile eleven. Unbeknown to me at the time, Neil was trying to negotiate the London Underground, which was rammed with marathon supporters. Some of the trains were so full, they would pull into the station and nobody could get on! The distance between checkpoints was not that great and on any other day, it would have taken around twenty minutes max, but not today. Whilst I was executing my mission, Neil was on a mission of his own.

I was starting to feel the soreness creep into my legs. My thighs and calves were starting to ache, as were my shoulders. It was not as bad as I would have thought, but I was now starting to feel a slight uncomfortableness. I just concentrated on my breathing, trusting the process. My experience of tabbing twenty miles had taught me that pretty soon, things were going to get tough. Between miles ten and eleven the inner voice kicked in.

"Yo! This is starting to get tough" it whispered. I focused on the checkpoint. At least I'd get a thirty-second rest, which would maybe take the edge off everything. I came down a slight hill and onto a roundabout, I could see Neil on the side of the road. It felt strange to stop, like my body wasn't used to being stationary any more. Neil went right to work, he handed me a bottle and held out the energy gels in the palm of his hand. I was still in good shape and I was still sticking to the pace. I grabbed the gels, stuffed one in a pocket and necked the other. I adjusted my pack slightly, fist-bumped Neil and I was away. The next checkpoint was mile seventeen. Heading off I finished my electrolyte drink and slung the empty bottle into a pile of other empty bottles at the side of the road. I pulled the energy gel out of my pocket, ripped off the tab and squeezed the gooey liquid into my mouth. I hated the consistency of these gels, but after trying several different brands throughout training, this particular one tasted better than most, even if it did feel like you were swallowing apple-flavoured frog spawn. With nutritional needs now taken care of, I picked up the pace and headed towards one of London's most famous landmarks.

The River Thames runs from Kemble in the Cotswolds and then enters out to sea through the Thames Estuary at Southend-on-Sea, carving London in two in the process. I'd worked my way west along the south side and now it was time to cross the river, over the magnificent Tower Bridge. Built in eighteen eighty-six Tower Bridge is one of the most recognisable landmarks of the marathon. I turned the corner and started up the short approach to the bridge, which acted like a choke point, funnelling people off the road and onto the bridge. The cheering crowds got louder and louder, until almost deafening. The tall tower on the south side blocked out the grey sky as I started to make my way across the bridge's eight hundred feet. Then, over the noise I could hear someone shouting my name. I looked around to see who it was, but the crowd was so big and the bridge was jammed up with runners, it was hard to see. I frantically looked about in the direction of the shouting. Then, on the right-hand side of Tower Bridge, I spotted Emma. She was pushed up against the barrier shouting frantically, as was Bertie. I made my way across, high-fived Bertie, gave Emma a hug and a quick kiss, then carried on. I have no idea how long she had been waiting there with Bertie and her sister Sarah, but they all looked suitably damp from the sporadic rain that had plagued us so for that day. I carried on across Tower Bridge, trying to soak up all the excitement and emotion around me. I wanted to make sure that I didn't forget this moment. The pain was starting to creep into my muscles now, but it was okay. I was being carried across the Thames by a wave of enthusiastic cheering and waving from a sea of supporters, which for a moment numbed all the aches and pains. As Tower Bridge disappeared into the rear-view, the pain reappeared, nothing too serious, but I realised then that the honeymoon was over.

After the bridge, a sharp right took the course east and back along the river. Runners were now heading in both directions. Those that were faster were now passing on the opposite side of the road. I was heading towards the half marathon mark, whilst those on the opposite side were nearly at mile twenty-three. I couldn't think that far ahead. Mile twenty-three may as well have been mile fifty. I was focused on hitting the half-marathon point, then the next checkpoint at mile seventeen.

It was still grey and occasionally you'd feel the cooling effects of the light rain, which would drop delicately from the sky like a light haze being thrown across the world. I didn't notice the weather. It didn't even register. I had bigger things to worry about than a little light rain. I hit the half-marathon point and took stock of how I was feeling. My body was now starting to slowly break down. I didn't have any serious pain, but I was uncomfortable to the point where I was trying to make adjustments to ease the discomfort. I was struggling now to maintain the two-mile run one-mile walk pace. It was difficult to get going again after walking a mile. I hung in through gritted teeth and despatched the next few miles. I was now looping around the financial district of Canary Wharf with its high-rise office buildings. Mile seventeen was looming and I was eagerly looking out for Neil amongst the crowds. I needed this stop, I was hurting. I'd almost run past Neil before he managed to grab my attention. I slowed and walked over to the kerb. The wheels were now starting to fall off. I was feeling every step and my shoulders were now weary of carrying the forty-pound bergen. We set about the routine, rehydrating and then taking onboard a couple of gels. The pit stop was slick, but I wasn't in such a rush to get off. I was reaching my physical limits. It was going to be a head game now, all the way to the finish. I adjusted a couple of straps on the bergen, straightened myself out, finished off the second gel and went on my way, slowly building back up to speed.

The pace was now slower. I wasn't fixated on how long a mile was taking, I was just thankful to get another mile under my belt. The noise coming from the crowds didn't seem so loud anymore. Was it because I was now desensitised to it, or maybe the novelty was starting to wear off for some? I mean, how long can you stand in the drizzle watching an endless procession of runners? I'd still get the odd kid holding out his hand for a high-five, but not as often. I hit mile twenty, or rather mile twenty hit me. I was suffering badly, as were those around me. All I could do was keep making the next one hundred yards, then the next. I was sure my feet were trashed. I think I was still standing upright through sheer willpower alone. It was grim.

Then, in the distance, I could hear music. I thought I had started hearing things. I had heard that ultra-marathon runners can sometimes hallucinate during races. Was this now happening to me? Was I starting to hear music and if so when will the voices start? The music got louder. Where was it coming from? The road narrowed ahead just before a bend; this made the area look more congested than it actually was. As I rounded a gentle curve in the road, the source of loud music was revealed. At mile twenty-one the LGBTQ (lesbian, gay, bisexual, transgender) community had a stage set up. Rainbow banners were strewn across the street. The area was swamped with people. It was like running through a nightclub. It was amazing! The music was pumping, people were drinking, dancing and having an amazing time. Snacks and jelly babies were being handed out to runners as they went by. Nothing encapsulated the spirit and pageantry of the London Marathon more than the LGBTQ stage at mile twenty-one. It was just the pick-me-up I needed. I was feeling low and sorry for myself. I was hurting and I was starting to wonder why on earth I had chosen to do this. But for a few minutes, some loud music and some happy faces made it seem a little less arduous.

It was a straight road now, all the way to Westminster and St James's Park. Someone from the crowd shouted, "You got this Grizzly. Just five more miles." Five more miles felt like a world away. My head couldn't process five more miles. My head was too busy putting one foot in front of the other. My body was screaming to stop, trying to override my brain which wanted to bring the whole show to an abrupt end. I was tabbing more and running less, but I was still in it. I was five miles away from the achievement of a lifetime. Time was now moving very slowly and mile markers seemed to take forever to come around. I was now on the return leg; Tower Bridge now on my left. Every step was an immense effort. Every thought was wrapped around blocking out the pain and every shout of encouragement now fell on deaf ears.

I reached mile twenty-three and the final checkpoint with Neil. I went through the motions of rehydrating, but it was an effort. Even standing still was now painful. I think Neil could see this. At the previous checkpoints he'd been chatty and animated, we'd bat some banter back and forth before I ran off. Now, he was more sombre, reassuring, supportive and encouraging. I prepared for the last three miles, finished my drink and stood up straight. Neil put his arm on my shoulder and said "I'll see you at the finish brother," I then slowly ran off.

The streets were now rammed again with spectators. Shouts and screams of encouragement filled the air to the point I could hear nothing else. I was heading into Westminster along the

Embankment. The London Eye gazed down from across the water as I passed mile twenty-five. As the pain in my body got more intense, so did the crowds. The noise and mayhem hit fever pitch as I rounded Westminster Bridge and headed towards St James's Park. Everything intensified, crowds, noise, chaos, pain. Everything. I just had to keep myself in check and keep one foot in front of the other. I forced my body to run. It rebelled by making me feel every ache, every pain, hoping that I would stop, but I didn't. I don't quit. As I reached Buckingham Palace everything was just chaos. I could hear over the loudspeakers in the distance runners being congratulated as they crossed the finish line. I ran past the famous Queen Victoria Memorial which stands proud outside Buckingham Palace, then turned onto the Mall. I was on the home straight. Suddenly, from out of nowhere, I heard my name being called. I looked right to see my mother and Turtle leaning over some railings cheering me on. I had waited all my life for that moment. It still felt like a long way to the finish line, but it was only around one hundred metres. I ran up the Mall with people cheering my name from the grandstand, the archway of the finish line getting closer and closer. I heard a "C'MON GRIZZLY", from the front of the stand, I pointed in their general direction to acknowledge the final word of encouragement and support. I kicked hard, I wanted to finish strong. Every cell in my body fired pain into the central nervous system trying to bring me to the ground, but it failed and I succeeded. I crossed the finishing line in six hours thirty and some change. Mission accomplished.

A young lady wandered over, congratulated me and placed a finishers' medal over my head, letting it hang around my neck ready to have my picture taken by the official photographer. I walked up to the trucks and collected my bag. There was no big finish, nobody running up to hug me and no motion picture ending. Just me on my own. I stood right there on The Mall amongst a melee of people, tired and sweaty and I just laughed, a quiet laugh, a laugh that whispered to the world "Fuck you". I staggered through the crowds of people and into St James's Park, found a big 'ole' tree, took off my pack and slumped to the floor.

I couldn't quite believe what had just happened, it was hard to comprehend the enormity of it all. I looked out, watching runners meet their families, receiving hugs of congratulations from their loved ones. I felt a tear roll down my face. I didn't want to cry. I didn't want my family and friends to find me sobbing by a tree, but it was difficult. I didn't feel like I had just run twenty-six point three miles. I felt that I had been running for the last five years, and now I could finally stop.

It still feels like yesterday that my life was dramatically altered, where I spiralled into a dark and lonely pit of misery, which ultimately saw me hanging by the neck of a door handle. I shouldn't have been there, sitting in St James's Park after just completing one of the most physically and mentally demanding events in the world. I should've been a memory. A thought that crosses people's minds when they see or hear something that reminds them of me. A pile of ash in a box on someone's mantelpiece, or a brass plaque in a memorial garden somewhere. I should be dead. But, for some reason, I wasn't. For some reason, the universe seems to feel that I should stay around a little longer, and I am truly grateful that it does.

Epilogue

If I look back to May of twenty-eighteen and the person I was then, I feel like I'm almost unrecognisable to myself now. So much has happened in a relatively short space of time that it's sometimes hard to comprehend. My life now is not what I would have planned or chosen for myself, but it is ever-evolving and I feel very positive about my future, whatever that may be. The last five years have been an amazing journey. I have experienced extreme happiness and contentment, some loss and of course some hurt, pain and sadness. But I'm still here, the world hasn't drifted off its axis and started to hurtle towards the sun, burst into flames and then died. The world continues to turn and people will continue to go about their daily lives, regardless of what my situation is, although at times it doesn't always feel that way.

There are days that I feel very proud of myself, days when I look back at all my achievements, the framed medals and race numbers hanging on the wall. It's then that I thank the part of my personality that continues to push me, both mentally and physically. The part of me that never gives up. I wonder where I would be today without it.

The seizures? Well, I still have them, but it's a part of my life that I have come to terms with. Every day new treatments evolve as we move closer to eradicating this debilitating illness. My medications are constantly being changed to try and find that magic cocktail to reduce the seizures and side effects. But for now, I will have to live with epilepsy, possibly for the rest of my life. But I don't let it define who I am, as I have since learnt, I am much more than that.

Yes, there has been some bad luck, misfortune and errors of judgment on my part, which has forced me to walk a path I would not have chosen to take if I had the choice. This could possibly have been my salvation, as it led to a rediscovered love of the outdoors, which fuelled the fire of perseverance and determination within me. I truly believe that this has been the best medicine. I still have to rely on neurologists and doctors for the physical side of my illness, as for my mental wellbeing, well I try and take care of that myself. Those long rucks running with a heavy pack is where I learnt who I was again. Where I freed myself from the shackles of a hatred toward myself and an overwhelming feeling of failure, self-doubt and worthlessness. I ran till my body screamed to stop and then I ran some more. It was in those moments, amongst the pain and sweat where I purged myself of all the hate, anger and resentment that had consumed me. The strength needed to run twenty miles, carrying sixteen kilos is nothing compared to the weight of carrying all that negative emotional baggage. In the end, it wasn't about forgiving myself for my failures. It was about learning how to live with them and then moving on.

The Dalai Lama said, "Our prime purpose in life is to help others, and if you can't help them, at least don't hurt them". I have learnt through my own experiences to be more patient and empathetic than I may have been in the past, that happiness is not wrapped around wads of fifty-pound notes. Happiness is found in a "love you" text from your kids, watching the sunrise over the beach with your girlfriend and spending time with your family. Happiness I have found is not a given, it's a conscious state of mind that has to be continually worked on, and only you can do that. I don't rely on others around me to make me happy, that's not their job, it's my responsibility to ensure the continuous growth of my own happiness. If I were to stand still and not move forward with my life, I would be reliving the past over and over again. There has to be a statute of limitation, live it, feel it, then cut it loose, because nobody needs any form of negativity in their lives.

I often think that my accident and the 'aftermath' that succeeded was a form of penance for the life I was living. It was also very easy to portray myself in those situations as the victim. As your world starts to crumble around you, you clamber for supporters and allies. In that moment you present yourself as vulnerable and beaten, looking outwards for any kind of sympathy or empathy. You spend your time searching for a quick fix, someone who will wave a magic wand and make it all go away. A saviour that will not only pull you from the quicksand but also demonise those who threw you in. The reality however is, there is no quick fix, no superhero is coming to save you. The hero has to be you, and to get there you have to take responsibility for your actions past and present. You're not going to get away with blaming other people forever for your misfortune. Life is very much like a mirror, the way you conduct yourself towards others will always be reflected back. I've watched as people (some of those I thought of as friends) turned their backs and walked away when I desperately needed them, it's been a hard lesson to learn. It's only when there is nothing and nobody left, when everyone else has run away and left you standing in the cold all alone, do you truly understand that your destiny relies solely on your strength to survive.

If you want to be somewhere else in your life or be somebody different, then do it. There are no excuses. It's been hard and sometimes overwhelming, but I continually try to improve myself, but it's a constant work in progress. I have not been idle with my time. I have done some amazing things that I thought I would never be able to do. Things that were achievable, but only because I truly desired change and I put in the hard work and dedication. It can feel daunting to stand up to the world. You will fall often but you have to get back up. There will be many hurdles to jump and mountains to climb. I'm no superhero and I don't possess any form of talent; my mental fortitude often lets me down because well…I'm human. But a wiser man than me once said, "No matter how slow you go, you're still lapping everyone on the couch".

Now I look at every new day as an opportunity. On the good days, I load up my pack and head out the door and I run, looking at the trees and the amazing Sussex countryside. Or I drag Turtle and Neil the Tash out on a mini adventure, which is always eventful and full of laughter. If I'm lucky, Emma will drive me down to the coast. Then, in the evening sun we will wade into the sea, where I will stand shoulder-deep in the cold water and just listen, letting my body and mind free themselves from the constraints of an illness and the life I now have to lead. I now cherish each day, because one day (hopefully not too soon) it will be my last and I don't want to waste any of it.

Through hard work, self-motivation, discipline and perseverance I have achieved many things in the last five years. I worked through some tough mental challenges and of course some physical ones too. These however are not my greatest achievements. My greatest achievements sit with me at Sunday dinner and call me Dad. My beautiful daughters Grace and Daisy are and will always be, my greatest achievement and the motivation to continually strive to improve myself as a person. I feel extremely blessed to be able to watch them grow up and I will keep working hard, to be a better son, brother, boyfriend and of course a better father.

This is not the end; the story doesn't finish just because the final page is turned.

London Marathon 2023 Finish Line

Acknowledgements

It would be unfair of me to pretend that this book was entirely of my own making. There are people in my life that deserve my appreciation and eternal thanks.

My mother, who is my greatest supporter, without whom I would have truly perished.

Michael and Phillip. Who knew growing up would be so hard, even as adults.

Emma, who has inspired me to be the best I can be, who has loved me unconditionally, faults and all.

Turtle and Neil the Tash. True friends, the ones who stayed.

Libby and Frank, for painstakingly correcting my grammar and spelling.

And finally, Lemmy. My best mate and companion. You were my comfort when the world decided to plunge me into darkness. Every day I miss you. Sleep well my Puppy

Cover Design Nord Creative – WWW.NORDCREATIVE.CO.UK

Printed in Great Britain
by Amazon

37005699R00175